MW01627216

John Bard's

HISTORY *of the* OLD BUCKTAILS

(INCLUDING CYRUS B. LOWER'S ACCOUNT OF HIS ESCAPE FROM A REBEL PRISON TRAIN)

Written by

JOHN BARD

Edited by

DENNIS SHAFFNER

With images from Ronn Palm's Museum of Civil War Images, Gettysburg, Pa.

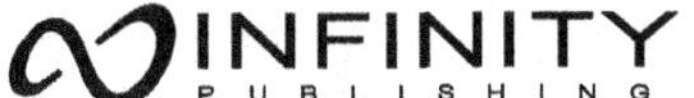

ISBN 978-0-7414-8369-0 Paperback
ISBN 978-0-7414-8370-6 Hardcover
ISBN 978-0-7414-8371-3 eBook
Library of Congress Control Number: 2013904255

Printed in the United States of America

Published October 2013

INFINITY PUBLISHING
1094 New DeHaven Street, Suite 100
West Conshohocken, PA 19428-2713
Toll-free (877) BUY BOOK
Local Phone (610) 941-9999
Fax (610) 941-9959
Info@buybooksontheweb.com
www.buybooksontheweb.com

This transcript is of a series of newspaper articles written by John P. Bard, (copyrighted 1895 by J. P. Bard). Mr. Bard was the editor of a newspaper in Curwensville, Pennsylvania, called the *Curwensville Herald*. These newspaper articles were cut and pasted in a scrapbook and acquired by the Clearfield County Historical Society in 1966. The scrapbook was donated in memory of John P. Bard, father of Fred T. Bard from Ardmore, Pennsylvania (acq. # M.66.66). To our knowledge, it may be the only existing copy of the articles. The Society refers to this acquisition as "Bard's Scrapbook" and we are offering it during this 150th anniversary period to honor the veterans of the American Civil War. Bard heavily reflects upon the activities of the Pennsylvania Reserve Corp. Therefore it is a good read for those looking for a source of information on the general history of the Reserves.

The Bucktail Regimental history, published by William H. Rauch who served as the secretary of the regimental association through 1905, gives credit in the preface to Captain John P. Bard of Co. K for being one of two newspaper histories useful in assembling the regimental story of the Bucktails. In fact the Bucktail Regimental history leans heavily on Bard's account. This transcript attempts to be largely faithful to the original text as it was printed. Misspelled words and punctuation errors have not been corrected. Bard occasionally printed "notes" at the end of an article to correct a fact which had been misrepresented in a prior number. Those corrections have been made in the text and are not included as addendums.

The Society is extremely grateful to Ronn Palm, owner of Ronn Palm's Museum of Civil War Images, in Gettysburg, Pennsylvania. Ronn provided many of the images which are added to this narrative. He seeks to honor the memory and service of the veterans, many who gave their full measure to the cause of keeping our country united. Ronn made himself available for consultation and enthusiastically encouraged this project.

Clearfield County is proud of its veterans from the War of the Rebellion. They are buried in cemeteries across our country and the nation. Those regimental members from the first muster of the Bucktail Regiment were particular about their status as "original" and they made that distinction through out their service and on into the reunion years of the regiment, and so this transcript begins simply with the title given it by Captain Bard. The Clearfield County Historical Society is happy to provide this historical narrative during this special time in our nation's history.

Denny Shaffner,
President CCHS, editor

No. 1

It is almost a quarter of a century since the Southern leaders in their wild rage hurled the thunder bolts of their wrath against the foundations of the Government, and kindled the fires of rebellion upon every hill top, from the Potomac to the Rio Grande. When the shot was fired which tore the Nation's Standard from the walls of Sumpter, and startled the world, the call for help was heard, clear and startling, from the Capital of the Nation, sounding from hill to valley across the continent, from the Atlantic to the Pacific, and from the Lake of the Woods to the Gulf of Mexico. It floated through the South, warning Rebellion's leaders that the Union should be maintained at any cost; and it penetrated every nook and cranny of the North, arousing it to a sense of this new danger to the Republic.

The loyal North caught the spirit of its leader, Abraham Lincoln, and prepared for the defense of the Constitution and the law. But what a preparation. The National Government stood paralyzed in the presence of a robbed treasury, empty arsenals, and an army of disciplined Rebels. The leaders of the great revolt had for years been in possession of the Government, and had long looked forward to, and prepared for that time. But the South mistook the spirit of the Northern Mudsill.

In a short time the fires were kindled in the furnaces, and inventive genius was at work utilizing the old cast off machinery of war: the old smoothbore flintlock became the deadly rifle, and the wooden ship the iron-clad man-of-war. The empty treasury was again filled with the offerings of a generous people. Yet after all these preparations none could realize the magnitude of the storm that was to deluge the land with blood, the issues involved, or the vast changes to be wrought. Old men and boys with sticks instead of guns, were drilled in the manual of arms in halls, and on the hillsides, with no thought of war beyond a mere skirmish, and an early settlement by mutual concessions. But it did come—grand and terrible. From 1861 to 1865 will ever be memorable in the history of our country. Not alone is the history of that war written and hidden within the archives of the Government, but it is indelibly stamped upon the minds and hearts of millions, North and South, East and West, in letters of living light. The long rows of wooden head-boards that streak the National Cemeteries of Andersonville, Salisbury, Gettysburg, and others, some with the name of the dead soldier, and many a blank, tell its history. White-haired men and tottering women, who slowly tread the white bordered walks, and closely scan the glaring records for an unforgotten name, know its history by heart. Yet there are thousands throughout the land who have for years exercised the rights of freemen, to whom the history of that war is an unfamiliar page. Men of intelligence are living at the age of twenty-five who know nothing of its cause, events, or results. To them it is too far away to be remembered, and too near to be studied.

Our object is not to write a history of the war, but to tell the story of a regiment, the name of which is recognized wherever it is spoken. To give a complete history of the regiment would be to write one of the Army of the Potomac, so closely were their fortunes interwoven.

It followed the fortunes of McClellan, Pope, Burnside, Hooker, Meade, and Grant through victory and defeat from Dranesville to Coal Harbor, where many of them laid down their lives after the expiration of their terms of service.

When the snows of '61 had melted and come down from the hills to swell the rivers, many of the men from the head-waters of the Allegheny River, and the North and West branches of the Susquehanna, were away from their homes, either on the waters or at the lumber markets below. When they heard the call for seventy-five thousand volunteers to put down a Rebellion in the South, they hurried to their homes, formed themselves in companies, returned to Harrisburg and offered their services to the Government. Thomas L. Kane, of McKean county, a brother of Elisha Kent Kane, the noted Arctic explorer, arrived at Harrisburg with a battalion of rafts, each having a bucktail in his hat. It is of a regiment formed by these backwoodsmen, with Kane's battalion of "Bucktails" as a nucleus, that we would write. Its organization was coincident with organized Rebellion; therefore, no time could be more fitting for a historical record of its deeds, than that marked by the restoration to power of its old enemies. The men who composed the Bucktail regiment, enlisted for the three months service but on arriving at Harrisburg, the call for seventy-five thousand three months men was full. Thad. Stevens, Simon Cameron, Gov. Curtin, and other prominent Republican leaders of Pennsylvania believed that the war would assume far greater proportions than was generally believed; and this admirable forethought took form in the organization of fifteen regiments, consisting of thirteen of infantry, one of cavalry, and one of artillery; to be called the "Pennsylvania Reserve Volunteer Corps," and to be held in readiness for any emergency.

The "Bucktail" regiment, which afterward formed part of this corps as the 13th P.R.V.C., was formed of companies that had come down from the counties of Tioga, Cameron, Warren, Elk, McKean, Clearfield, and Chester, Carbon, and Perry. The idea of organizing a rifle regiment, originated with Thos. L. Kane, as we have before stated, and resulted in the formation of the following companies:

"Anderson Life Guards," Co. A, of Tioga Co, commanded by Captain Philip Holland; the "Morgan Rifles," Co. B, of Perry Co. Capt. Langhorn Wistar; the "Cameron County Rifles," Co. C, of Cameron Co. Capt. John A. Eldred; the "Raftsmen Guards," Co. D, of Warren Co. Capt. Roy Stone; the "Tioga Rifles," Co. E, of Tioga Co. Capt. Alanson E. Niles; the "Irish Infantry," Co. F, of Carbon Co. Capt. D. McGee; the "Elk Rifles" Co. G, of Elk Co. Capt. Hugh McDonald; the "Wayne Independent Rifles," Co. H, of Chester Co. Capt. Charles F. Taylor the "McKean Rifles," Co. I. of McKean Co. Capt. William T. Blanchard; the "Raftsmen Rangers," Co. K, of Clearfield Co. Capt. Edward A. Irvin. The Penn'a Res. Vol. Corps was organized under an act passed May 15, 1861 which gave the corps the privilege of electing its own officers. The following is the section of the act relating thereto:

SECTION, 24. That the several regiments and companies composing the said volunteer corps shall be entitled to elect, and the governor shall commission officers similar in number and rank to those allowed like troops in the Army of the United States: *Provided*, that the governor shall have power to appoint and commission chaplains for said corps, and to designate their rank.

Thos. L. Kane was entitled to the Colonelcy, but knowing that the organization and discipline of the regiment required a man at its head, of a military knowledge and experience which he did not possess, withdrew in favor of Charles J. Biddle, of Philadelphia, a captain in the Mexican war, and a disciplinarian of the strictest type.

Biddle was elected Colonel; Kane Lieutenant Colonel; Roy Stone, of Warren County, Major. John T.A. Jewett of Warren County was appointed Adjutant; Lieutenant H. D. Patton, of Clearfield Co., Quartermaster; S.D. Freeman, Surgeon; W.T. Humphrey, Assistant Surgeon; and Rev. W.H.D. Hatton, Chaplain.

The organization was perfected on the 12th day of June 1861, and on the 13th, Col. Biddle superceded Col. G.A.C. Seyler as commandant of Camp Curtin. Common sense was thereafter the guiding principle in the government of the camp. Under Biddle it assumed the appearance of a military station, rather than that of a convict camp. Under Seyler, the guard in point of strength, resembled a skirmish line. Ten men were on guard at the gate, with crossed bayonets; this force was reduced to a single guard, and in the same proportion around the camp.

The camp drill was of the most primitive type; every company drill master having a system of tactics of his own, drawn from memory of old militia days; but Biddle's appearance on the drill ground united all these incongruous elements into one harmonious whole.

One serious trouble in the ranks of the new soldiers, was the inability or disinclination of Gov. Curtin to supply them with the Minnie rifle and sword bayonet which he had promised them. When the general government made a requisition on the State for more aid, and the "Bucktails," with others were to be sent across the border, they were armed with the old Harper's Ferry musket, a gun that would shoot in a very indefinite manner. The distribution of these guns almost created a mutiny in the regiment, but through the pacific influence of Col. Biddle, and the promise of better arms soon, the trouble was allayed.

On the 21st of June Col. Biddle, with the "Bucktails," the Fifth Reserves, commanded by Col. Simmons, and Battery A, the First Pennsylvania Artillery, commanded by Col. Chas. T. Campbell was ordered to Cumberland, Md. to the relief of Col. Lew Wallace, commanding the Eleventh Indiana regiment.

No. 2

The soldiers of the Fifth, Battery A., and the Bucktails, hailed with delight the order to move. After laying weeks in camp Curtin, idle, ragged, and only half fed, any change was desirable. The old camp was to be to them a thing of the past, the realities of war, of which they had long been dreaming, were now to be an experience. Arms were to be supplied, that had deadly and death dealing properties. The old Flintlock loaded with mud was to be seen and handled no more. Men were to rise from the semi-condition of prisoners, to the full stature of patriot soldiers, the object of their enlistment was about to be realized. The hardy, loyal backwoodsmen, miners and mechanics forming this brigade were no holiday soldiers; they enlisted not because they preferred the life of a soldier, but in response to the call of their country in danger. And these men were now to be given an opportunity to render some service to that government for whose success they had prayed, and for the preservation of which, they had freely given up home and all it holds most dear.

After the busy preparations were all made, arms, ammunition, accoutrements, clothing, and rations had been drawn and distributed, and letters written home to tell the dear ones that we were "going to the front," we bade good bye to camp Curtin, and were loaded on box cars on the Pennsylvania Railroad and taken to Huntingdon, from there by the Broadtop road to Hopewell.

At Huntingdon the citizens gave the troops refreshments, we might well say that they opened their houses, stores, and saloons, and invited them to freely help themselves. All along the route to Hopewell, at every station were crowds of citizens with baskets filled with everything the market afforded.

The brigade arrived at Hopewell early in the evening, and here was the first field camp, a new experience for many, particularly those who had never attempted to do their own cooking. The novelty of the situation however covered up the inconvenience, and it was with cheerful hearts the troops for the first time slept in the field. Early next morning the Reveille was sounded, breakfast hurriedly prepared, when the order to march was given. On the 28th of June, 1861, a hot summer day, with the roads covered with from one to two inches of dust, the first march was made, and a distance of twenty-three miles traveled. This was as severe and perhaps the most trying march ever made by this body of troops. Unused to the Cartridge box, Gun, Haversack, Canteen and other equipments that make up the load to be carried by the soldier in the field, the terrible dust, with the unfitness for exercise of any kind, caused by a life of inactivity at camp Curtin, made it so much harder to bear. The same troops, in after years would have made the march in less time, and not have been the least wearied.

At Bloody Run (now called Everett) the citizens had prepared an elegant dinner spread in the yard, under shade trees and in their houses. The preparation of a meal for 1,500 men is a labor of no small account, Bloody Run being then a small village the citizens deserved, and received the highest praise for their goodness of heart. This was to be the last "picnic" enjoyed by these men for years, and will never fade from their memory.

After dinner the march was resumed and before dark the brigade went into camp near Bedford Springs where they remained until the 27th of June. At Bedford was established, in the courthouse, the first "field hospital," many who were completely worn out by the march, and many others who were really unfit to march, and should have been left at Harrisburg, were here treated by our surgeons Freeman and Humphrey, while the citizens of Bedford did all they could to relieve their suffering. The ladies supplying them with every delicacy which could tempt the appetite. We will not undertake to say whether or not the presence of Bedford's beautiful ladies had anything to do with the rapidly increasing "Sick List."

On the morning of the 27th day of June we again took up our line of march to the state line, Col. Biddle having received orders to march to a point near that line and on the route to Cumberland, where he would be in readiness to assist Col. Lew Wallace, then camped at Cumberland, in case an attack was made on him. On the evening of the 28th the Brigade arrived at what was named Camp Mason & Dixon, but better known to the soldiers as Camp "Misery and Death," so named on account of the sickness which prevailed, and scarcity of rations. Here we first celebrated, as soldiers, the anniversary of the Declaration of Independence. Not by Feasting and display of fireworks. Instead of the usual demonstrations of joy which were wont to hail this glorious day, a feeling of gloom spread over the camp. We had been on very limited rations for several days and the fourth of July found the brigade entirely destitute of provisions, we observed the day by fasting. A few months later, the men would have supplied themselves, but this was a lesson yet to be learned. In those early days of the war when all was confusion, great allowance had to be made for officials, yet we cannot forbear to severely censure our state authorities, for neglecting to supply this brigade with plain rations, they could have been provided by the country surrounding us, our officers only lacked the authority to procure them.

Here also began the enforcement of that rigid discipline which was to tell in after years, in the conflicts in which these troops were to bear a conspicuous part, Col. Simmons, of the Fifth, Col. Campbell, of the Artillery, and our own Col. Biddle deserve the highest praise for the early training given the men under their command. And we wish to here state, that everything we write of our regiment in this campaign, will, apply to, and is part of the history of the other troops forming this brigade.

Here we had our first regimental drill, and who of the survivors will ever forget it. On a rough stony hillside, the ignorance of the line officers to give the command by which a movement was to be executed, and the utter inability of the men through ignorance, to execute it when the command was given, the crowding, the impossibility to affect an alignment approaching to anything like a straight line, the "double quick" &c, were indelibly stamped upon the memory of those who participated in that first drill. But before we left that camp the men, and officers had learned that the persevering patience of their colonel would not be exhausted until they were perfect in regimental drill. Company commanders were required to devote 2 or 3 hours each day to company drill, and all the accompanying duties were strictly enforced, such as guard mounting, policing the camp, attending sick call, &c. so that there was but little time to spend in idleness, all this under the untiring and never resting eye of Col. Biddle, whose experience in the Mexican war, had taught him the necessity of educating these citizen soldiers in the duties and discipline, necessary to fit them for a conflict of arms.

On the 7th day of July Col. Biddle gave orders to break camp, and in the evening we were again on the march, some time during the night we arrived in Cumberland Md., and the following morning occupied the camp vacated by Col Lew Wallace and his Indiana Zouaves.

As reports had been continually coming to us at camp Mason and Dixon, that a large force of the enemy were threatening an attack on Cumberland, the troops were disappointed at finding the city quiet and peaceful. While in camp here we had out first target practice, in fact the men were for the first time permitted to test the arms with which they had been provided and a rather amusing scene occurred. Our guns were old Harpers Ferry Flintlocks altered to percussion, the bore being deeper than the tube, or nipple, made quite a chamber behind the point where the powder was ignited, and consequently produced a "back action" neither pleasant or profitable. After the first discharge, those who were fortunate enough to remain on their feet, could laugh at their less fortunate comrades who were "hor du combat." Yankee ingenuity, however, soon overcome this difficulty, by forcing down one or two silver dimes the chamber was filled up, and the "three bucks and a ball" could be "sped on their death dealing course," without any further danger in the rear.

Lieut. Col. Kane not being willing to wait for the enemy to come to us proposed to go in search of him. He proposed to Col. Biddle to organize a company of scouts to make reconnoisances through the country, the scouts to be selected by him (Kane), Col. Biddle approved this plan, and authorized the organization of "Kane's Scouts." This body of men was composed of 60 enlisted men and 3 commissioned officers. Lieut., Col. Kane; Capt. E. A. Irvin; First Lieutenant, W.R. Hartshorn were the officers, the men were selected from the various companies in the regiment. On the 12th of July this scouting party started out for the first time. They went by rail through the Cumberland mining region, up over the "switch back" on through the tunnel under the town of Frostburg Md. And halted the first night at an old stone grist mill on a small stream, a few miles from Piedmont. When we arrived at the mill the rain was coming down in one unceasing pour. It was one of those nights when nature seems to have opened up all her flood gates, and was determined to again deluge the world. Darkness had settled down before all our pickets were posted; along both sides of the stream was a thick growth of low bushes, which made it difficult to find a picket after he had been posted. Every man supposed he was in the heart of the enemy's country, and Col. Kane kept the "corporal of the guard" busy all night looking after the men on post. Before daylight next morning we were on the move, Col. Kane had divided his command in two parties, one lead by himself, the other by Capt. Irvin, they were to march on parallel roads in the direction of Piedmont. The party under Capt. Irvin had not proceeded very far when they discovered, through the trees and thick fog which had settled down upon the little valley, what they supposed were the white tents of the enemy's camp, the writer was at once dispatched to Col. Kane to acquaint him with the situation, and suggest to him that he move up from the other side, attack simultaneously, and capture the whole force. But before the messenger reached Col. Kane the two roads had come together, and the supposed camp turned out to be a white house and several white-washed out buildings. This was a great disappointment, and was soon the cause of much merriment and chaffing. Early in the morning we crossed the Potomac river at Piedmont V. where the rebel cavalry command of Col. McDonald had been the day before. Guards were at once stationed at the various approaches to the town, Col. Kane with the greater part proceeded to reconnoiter the country, he soon found traces of the enemy on the road to New Creek. After traveling some distance in that direction he became satisfied that quite a considerable force was camped on New Creek a short distance from the mouth, at New Creek Station on the Baltimore and Ohio Railroad. A horse was pressed into service upon which John Kratzer was mounted and sent back to Piedmont with a written order from Col. Kane to the Serg't in charge of the Round House, the order read as follows:

> Serg't- - - You will move with the men under your command
> at once down the road to New Creek, time double quick, if
> attacked take cover on the right.
>
> THOS. L. Kane
> Lieut. Col. Comd'g.

This implied danger of an attack, hence we must move with caution, but then we were ordered to move on "double quick" time, and to come at once, this implies the urgent need of our assistance, hence not knowing any better the Serg't and his 10 men started on the trot in the hot sun and kept it up for a mile or so, when going through a thick woods, the road running along the base of a high hill on our right, we saw something that looked strangely like a rude barricade, just then the woods on our left gave place to a broad flat meadow, lying between our road and the river, close by the roadside was a house, lately deserted, while down in the meadow sat a woman with a group of little children gathered around her, the Serg't gave the command to halt, sent two flankers ahead along the hillside and proceeded cautiously until the woods on the right was passed, then taking up the double quick he kept it up until he overtook Kane's party near New Creek, where they soon arrived. 10 men in charge of Serg't J. E. Kratzer were left back at Piedmont, Kane's party numbering but 50 men, these he soon quartered in a brick house known as the Armstrong House of which he had taken possession. Here we captured a Presbyterian Preacher, a redheaded, redmouthed rebel. Col. Kane, after assuring him our force only numbered 50 men with no troops in supporting distance, swore him to "carry the news" to Col. McDonald and invite him to call on us, Col. McDonald paid his respects to us the next morning at day light.

No. 3

Soon after we had sent off our preacher, guards were stationed so that we might not be caught unawares, after making ourselves comfortable we lay down to rest, "tired nature" was soon soothed by "balmy sleep." Just a little before daybreak the picket gave the alarm, when in a very short time every man was at his post, soon we heard that peculiar roaring noise made by a body of horsemen riding at a canter on a hard road. Reader this was to be our first time to meet an armed foe, we were to receive our baptism of fire, was there a man in that little party who fully realized the situation, we had been looking for this, almost hoping for it, and now we were to experience that "strange sensation" we had so often read of. Looking out we saw more than double our number ride down the road toward the station, on past the lane which leads to and along in front of the house which we occupy. Yes they go on past, what do they mean, what is their object, quick as thought Col. Kane remembers that our faithful guide is at the station, fears for his safety are awakened, Capt. Irvin is ordered to take a file of men go out across the lane and fire into the party and draw them to an attack, but too late, our guide lies sleeping soundly on the station porch, the rebels in cold blood cut his throat Capt. Irvin's fire then caused them to turn their attention in another direction. Now we hear something, that in coming years was to have a far greater significance to us, a sound that would thrill through every nerve, and cause a tighter grasp of the rifle, it was the rebel yell as they rushed upon us, Capt. Irvin and his party had a close run to get to the house, one of the men seeing he could not make it threw himself down in the tall grass and lay concealed. Col. Kane now cautioned the men not to fire until he gave the command, and had his orders been obeyed we no doubt would have made terrible slaughter in their ranks, every man had his piece ready. The house stood back from the road or lane some seventy-five feet. The enemy came up the lane led by Lieutenant Booton of the 3rd Virginia Cavalry, they commenced firing when they got within two hundred yards of the house, it was with the greatest difficulty that Col. Kane could restrain his men, and just as the head of the column reached a point opposite the centre of the house, an insubordinate soldier tired of being fired at without returning the compliment, let go his piece and killed the gallant Lieut. Booton, at once every man fired his gun; with a yell the rebels wheeled their horses and hurried away at still greater speed than they had come. Our pieces were now empty, but the boys with more "courage than conduct' rushed out of the house and after the retreating enemy, following them at least one fourth of a mile, by that time they were out of sight far enough. Had the rebel leader turned upon us after we got away from the house he would have been able to have captured the whole party, they were better armed for close work, having double-barreled shot-guns and sabers ground to a sharp edge. The man who had hid in the grass rose up as they passed him and got a parting shot at them. When we returned to the field of battle we found Lieut. Booton and two private soldiers lying dead. Lieut. Booton, was armed with a double-barreled shot gun the same as his men, his piece was not discharged, and we found it loaded with slugs and buck-shot. The scouts had all escaped without a scratch, our only loss was that of our faithful guide, and when our men learned that he had been killed while sleeping, the sorrow they would naturally feel for the first men they had seen slain, gave way to a wicked feeling of revenge. By Col. Kane's orders we at once proceeded to bury the dead. That afternoon we learned from a Union citizen who lived some distance up the creek, that the enemy's loss in that little skirmish was nineteen in killed and wounded.

As we look back upon that skirmish, we blush at the ignorance of both parties, two years later, you would not find a Virginia Cavalryman reckless, or fool hardy enough to charge mounted upon an enemy located in a brick house, the cavalry should have been dismounted and charged us in front and rear, there was over one hundred of them and fifty-one of us. On our side two years later not a man of that party would have dared to follow that retreating party. It was simply a game of chance, we were the lucky party. To the victor in the first fight the result is of inestimable value, our little party would have been willing to charge a much greater number, just after their little victory. The loss of the brave Booton, who seemed to be the life of the attacking party, caused consternation among them, I have been thus minute in detailing the occurrences here, at this skirmish, my object in doing so is to impress upon my readers the importance of success in the first engagement, this we all learned in after years. A new regiment that was badly whipped in their first fight, required several victories to make them as efficient as they would have been had they been victorious in the first fight.

Col. Kane took the precaution to at once station pickets at several points where they could have a view of the surrounding country. We had learned ere this, that there was a considerable force of the enemy not far away, and we waited thinking the party that had paid us the visit that morning might get re-enforcements and return to the attack, but as we heard nothing further from them we returned to Piedmont that evening, where we remained for several days, during this time we made several trips to New Creek, the distance between New Creek and Piedmont was about seven miles. The Baltimore and Ohio Railroad Company placed at our disposal a locomotive and a train of freight cars, these box cars we lined with thick oak plank, concealed our men in them and backed the train down to New Creek, but never come across any of the several parties that were continually prowling around the country. One night while we are at this place the rebels came in on us, our pickets commenced firing just after dark and we had gotten up quite an interesting skirmish, with a prospect of a general engagement of our little party when a train arrived loaded with a brigade of Ohio troops that had been sent out by Rosencrans to go up New Creek and try to cut off the retreat of the rebels from Cheat Mountain, the arrival of this body of troops soon put an end to the little entertainment we had on hand, the rebels hastily retreating and the darkness was too great and the woods too thick for us to follow, this may have been lucky for us, who knows?

Col. Kane volunteered to go with these troops, and his offer being accepted we at once got ready and moved with them. After finding that there was no hopes of intercepting the force we were after, Kane and his party returned, the Ohio troops kept on until they reached their command.

Col. Biddle learning of our skirmish brought up the Brigade and went into camp at New Creek, Cols. Simmons, Campbell, and Kane taking quarters in the Hotel, Col. Biddle occupied the Armstrong House. While we lay here Col. Kane with his scouts made several excursions through the country, the most important was out in the direction of Romney. We left camp one day and marched rapidly over the country, which is very much broken up, a succession of hills with little fertile valleys between, we passed some fine farms. Near midway between our camp at New Creek, and Romney was the little village of Ridgeville, situated as its name indicates, on a high hill, just as we reached the top of a hill separated from that on which the village is situated by a deep hollow, and perhaps 1,000 yards distant, we came in sight of the village, the land lying between being cleared, soon we saw a group of horsemen ride out in front of the houses, and then several little puffs of white smoke, and then the vicious *ping* of the rifle ball was heard sharply followed by the report of the rifle, we halted and formed in line but the horsemen disappeared, and after traveling a short distance in line we resumed the march by the flank, preceeded by a few skirmishers, but we were not favored with another sight of the enemy. We passed on through Ridgeville and continued our march until about sundown when we halted only a few miles from Romney, where we took possession of a stone house, against the vigorous protest of the owner. Col. Kane had us tear down a hewn log building, and with the timber barricaded the windows and doors, he then drew from his saddle bags a small United States flag, which we mounted on the top of the house, fired a salute over it, gave it three cheers, posted our pickets and laid down to rest, it being then well on in the night. Soon all the men, except those on duty, were asleep, except also Col. Kane, who was very anxious that the enemy should attack us, and no doubt expected them as every citizen we met was a rebel and the news would certainly be carried to Romney just as soon as a messenger could travel the short distance. When we were fired upon at Ridgeville, Kane sent a scout back to report the situation to Col. Biddle. We were now near 20 miles from New Creek, perhaps 25, and not more that 4 or 5 miles from Romney, (some comrades put it at 3), some time in the night our pickets who were posted on the road in the direction of Ridgeville commenced firing, the writer was stationed on a hill some distance from the road, and plainly heard the moving of troops, with artillery, this put an entirely new face on the whole situation, against infantry we felt secure in our stone fort, but against artillery the walls would not be of much account. Hark! What do we hear? A command rings out clear and sharp on the night air, "Battalion halt, company A into line from centre deploy as skirmishers, march." All danger is passed, it is the well known voice of Col. Biddle who is bringing up his brigade, Col. Kane who had his men in position at the first alarm on the picket line, and was now repeating the caution not to fire until he gave the command, recognized the voice of Biddle, and we greeted the boys with three cheers, Col. Biddle, realizing the critical situation we were in turned around and marched back. Charley Campbell said he would like to try his guns on that stone house and was indeed disappointed because he was not to get a chance to show his skill in handling them. We got back without meeting with any occurrence worthy of note. On one of our scouts we camped all night close by a large Virginia plantation we did not arrive at the place until the Planter and his family had retired, and our movements were so quiet that they knew nothing of our presence until just at day break Col. Kane had a Sergeant knock at the door, getting no response he told the Sergeant to kick the door, which he did vigorously, Col. Kane then told him to break it in, very soon the Planter made his appearance, when Kane informed him that a more prompt response in the future would save him some trouble, he then said to him: "We have had the pleasure of camping on your premises over night and merely called to say good morning. Good morning Sir."

All the time we were camped here the severest discipline was enforced, and the troops of the Brigade were constantly drilling, and what wonderful progress they had made. The effect of this could be seen in the carriage of the men even when off duty, how many lessons had to be learned, and it was of the greatest importance that these first lessons be well learned, Biddle, Simmons, and Campbell were admirable drill-masters, and paid strictest attention to the smallest details of drill and everything pertaining to our preparation for active and efficient service. An attachment was formed between the Fifth, Battery A., and the Buckails that lasted all through the war, and indeed still lasts, this is true also of the entire division but in perhaps a more marked degree between those named. After remaining at New Creek some 10 or 12 days, after the brigade came up, we were taken to Cumberland by rail, before leaving we heard of the Bull Run disaster and knew our destination was Washington, from Cumberland we marched back as we had come to Hopewell, there we took the cars to Harrisburg where we went into camp, not in camp Curtin, Col. Biddle preferring a camp of his own, camped in a field down near the river, here we remained for several days drilling, getting clothing, &c., &c. A great many of the boys who had been engaged in the skirmish were the lions of the day. By request Col. Biddle marched his regiment into Camp Curtin and held Dress Parade one evening, and as this had been announced the evening before at Dress Parade, the Camp was crowded with visitors from Harrisburg. The boys got themselves up in their very best style, and every man was on his good behavior, the Colonel seemed to know that his regiment would acquit themselves with credit. The parade ground was in perfect order, smooth, clean, and hard, and when the companies wheeled into line, the movement was executed with the uniformity and precision of machinery, and when the Colonel put them through the manual of arms, their execution was as near perfect as it is possible to get it, at the command "order arms," the blows of the butts of the gun on the hard ground was more like the report of a six pounder than eight hundred rifles, and called forth cheers from the soldiers and citizens present. Never at any future time were we able to excel the manner in which we executed the manual of arms on that Dress Parade, the smile that lit up the face of our Colonel and Lieutenant Colonel was sufficient notice to the men that they were well pleased. All old soldiers will pardon the pride with which the forgoing description is written.

We at last received the orders to draw three days rations, this meant to march. Again we are loaded in the cars, this time we do not know our destination. We crossed the river at Harrisburg, and go down the Cumberland Valley to Baltimore.

No. 4

The disaster at Bull Run had opened the eyes of both North and South. Neither section of the country had until that battle given up all hopes of an amicable settlement of the trouble. The South jubilant over their victory looked forward to the capture of Washington as an event easy to accomplish, and the idea which was general throughout the Southern states, that the people of the North were no match for them on the field of battle, seemed to be confirmed by the result at Bull Run. The South saw the success of their Confederacy in the near future; to them everything indicted an easy victory. Does it not appear that their leaders, having a contempt, for what they termed a lack of martial spirit in the North, expected, after Bull Run an offer of compromise, or cessation of hostilities from the government. How else will we account for their not reaping the fruits of their victory at Bull Run by capturing the city of Washington. Had they closely followed up their victory and pushed the routed, disorganized, and completely demoralized Union army to the banks of the Potomac, would not the Capitol have been taken. Had Grant been in command of their army, the capture of Washington would most assuredly have followed the defeat at Bull Run. If they had captured the city, their occupation would have been of short duration, but the moral effect, at that time, would have been immensely to their benefit. A delay of twelve hours saved the Capitol, and they never after had an opportunity to take it.

The result at Bull Run instead of producing a panic in the North only inspired them to more determined effort. They were awakened to the reality that there was a war on their hands, and they responded to the demands of the Government with a promptness and determination that must have surprised the rebel leaders. The soldiers who had enlisted and those now to enlist, realized that the holiday affair they had supposed the war to be, was instead to be a real war, "Greek was to meet Greek." The rebel leaders were terribly in earnest, and the government must be maintained at all hazards. All ideas of compromise must be set aside, there must be no peace until they who fired upon the flag should ground the arms of rebellion, It was with this determination that the Northern soldier now donned the blue and shouldered his rifle.

On the evening of the 8th of August our regiment boarded the cars, and the next morning we arrived in Baltimore. Col. Biddle fearing some outbreak gave orders that our pieces should not be loaded, but many of the men, remembering the attack on the Massachusetts troops as they marched through the city secretly loaded their guns. We marched through however without any disturbance and arrived at Sandy Hook, Md., one and a half miles from Harpers Ferry the same day, where we remained for 6 or 7 days. While camped here many of the men visited Harpers Ferry and got a sight of John Brown's Fort, which is a low brick house built up against the hill. I will not attempt a description of the wonderfully impressive natural scenery here. It has been painted time and again by competent writers. These vivid pictures should not be marred by the *daub* of an unpracticed hand.

We had now been separated from the Fifth, and Campbell's Artillery, and assigned to Col. Thomas' (afterward General George H. Thomas) brigade, in Gen. Banks Division. Capt. Wm. McMichaels, of Phil'a who had been acting Adj't General for Col. Biddle while commanding the brigade in West Virginia had left us. Here at Sandy Hook we first saw an army. I cannot forget the splendid regiment of Col. John W. Geary, dressed in a neat fitting grey suit with black trimming. While camped here we witnessed daily some fine artillery practice, under direction of Major Doubleday (afterward General) of the regular army.

From Sandy Hook we marched to Hyattstown, a distance of near fifty miles, marching only eight to ten miles each day. At Hyattsville we remained some time, and while camped there we took charge of the 23rd Regiment of New York Volunteers, who had refused to do duty. Our regiment was ordered out, we were not allowed to load our pieces but with fixed bayonets we marched to the camp of the 23rd, they were in line with their arms, Col. Biddle commanded them to stack arms, which they promptly did, we then opened ranks and marched the length of the regiment having them beside, two files of our regiment being in front and rear they received the command, right face, which they obeyed, when we marched them near to the camp of our regiment were we established a very extensive guard house. The men composing the 23rd New York were a good body of men, and really good fellows. There was some difficulty in regard to their enlistment and great dissatisfaction with some of their field officers, the Bucktails all thought that they were not fairly treated. Quite a number of prominent gentlemen from New York visited them and tried to urge them to return. Gen. Banks came there one day, and made a most touching appeal to them, and to which they gave respectful attention, when he closed, their spokesman told him that they were honest in the position they had taken, and none of the appeals made to them had provided a riddance of the grievances, which had caused them to assume the position of insubordination, but while they would not return to the old organization of their regiment, they were willing to serve their country, and as an earnest of this, they would not to a man join the Bucktails, and serve until the time of that regiment expired, this offer was hailed with joy by our boys. The number at this time under guard was perhaps near two hundred, every day a few would declare their willingness to return when they would be released. General Banks could not establish so dangerous a precedent and their offer was not accepted, their number continued growing smaller until at last only about seventy-five or one hundred remained, these by general orders were assigned to the Dry Tortugas, and were sent under guard of (I think) Co. A., of our regiment. When they got to Baltimore, Gen. Wool then in command there, came out to see them, he tried to persuade them to reconsider and return to their command, they told him, they would join any other regiment but the 23rd New York. Gen. Wool being convinced of their sincerity interested himself in their behalf and they were transferred to other commands, and I have no doubt they rendered valiant service to their country. This little history has been given in detail to correct an erroneous account the author saw published some time ago, by whom and when he cannot now recall, and gladly distributes this testimony in favor of a body of men with whom the whole regiment had been on intimate relations, and for whom the Bucktails entertained a high regard.

From Hyattstown we marched to Darnestown Md. Where we arrived about the first of September and remained there about one month. Colonel Geo. H. Thomas was appointed a Brigadier General, and ordered West, Col. Biddle succeeded him in command of the Brigade, he however, still retained command of his regiment and continued to drill them as before, the Regimental Headquarters now became the headquarters of the Brigade. We had a pleasant camp here at Darnestown. On the 26th of Sept. the 46th Pa. Volunteers joined the army, while marching in that day one man whose name was Langly shot their Major and killed him. Langly was behaving badly when Col. Knipe ordered the Major to tie him behind one of the wagons, which he did, first disarming him. One of Langly's comrades came along shortly, cut him loose gave him a gun and ammunition, at the first sight he got of the Major he shot him dead, was court martialed the next day, and hung the following day, and the man who gave him the gun was sentenced to a term of three years in penitentiary.

Alex Irvin, Sr., came to our regiment while we lay here remained with Lieut. Patton, our Quarter Master, and who was now acting Brigade Quarter Master. The teams of this Brigade train were all four-horse teams, and were brought from New Mexico and Texas with the Regulars that had been stationed there, and were the finest lot of horses the writer ever saw, perfect in form, good spirit and in excellent condition.

During the month passed in the camp near Darnstown, Col. Biddle continued to drill his regiment daily. Reveille called us to Roll Call, breakfast soon after, at 8 o'clock sick call, at nine Guard mounting, at ten o'clock battalion drill, which usually lasted until noon, from two until three company drill, four, battalion drill which generally lasted until night, and closed with Dress Parade. The men who were present and able to go through these daily drills were the healthy men of the regiment ever after. From Darnestown we marched to Tennallytown, only a short distance from Washington. We now joined Gen. McCall's Division of Penn'a Reserves, here we again met the Fifth and Battery A. Our camp being but a few miles from Washington, at Dress Parade in the evening great crowds of people from the surrounding country came in, and for one or two hours a continuous train of carriages. They, however, did not come out to see the Bucktails, they hurried past giving us a wide berth, our boys could not understand this. The Pie, Apple and Peanut venders also steered clear of us, we began to compare our personal appearance with that of the other regiments and concluded we were about as clean, and nearly as good looking as they were. After we had been there a few days, citizens became reckless and ventured into our camp from them we learned the reason we were shunned as lepers. The other regiments had prepared the way for us by representing the Bucktails as a body of outlaws who took by force everything they saw and wanted. We soon outlived the joke and had our full share of visitors. In the other regiments of the Division our boys found many friends and formed acquaintances which were to last through the war.

We had exchanged our Harper's Ferry muskets for the Springfield rifle, we had by this time gotten over the sore disappointment at not getting Minnie rifles with sabre bayonets. We had made a lucky escape. After remaining at Tennallytown some time we got marching orders, this time we were to cross the river into Virginia. We drew an extra quantity of ammunition, three days cooked rations and were put in light marching order. We had not seen a Confederate in arms since we left West Virginia, now we were to invade the enemy's country. Our preparations indicated that we would be engaged with them.

No. 5

On the Ninth day of October our Division crossed the Potomac river at the chain bridge and went into camp a short distance west of the village of Langley, and about two miles west from the chain bridge. A line of pickets was established, our left connecting on the right of General Smith's Division and our right resting on the Potomac. The next day our baggage, stores, and camp equipments were brought over, Camp Pierpont was here established, named in honor of the loyal Governor of West Virginia. The Bucktail Regiment now occupied the position of honor in the Army of the Potomac, that of the extreme right. Our Division, about the middle of September, was organized into three brigades as follows: The first composed of the First Cavalry, the Fifth, First, Second, and Eighth regiments. The Second brigade was composed of the Fourth, Third, Seventh, and Eleventh regiments. The Third Brigade was composed of the Tenth, Sixth, Ninth, and Twelfth regiments. The Bucktails being a Rifle regiment were not assigned to any brigade. The Division was to be known in the Army as McCall's Division. The First brigade was commanded by Gen. J. F. Reynolds, the Second by Gen. George G. Meade, and the Third by Gen. E.O.C. Ord. The Bucktails had been very fortunate in the selection of their officers, both field and line. No less fortunate was the Division, very few Divisions at this early period of the war had in command of their several brigades, men who were not only to wear the stars of a Major General but were to be numbered among the distinguished officers of the Army. On the 20th of October, Col. Kane got permission to take five companies of the regiment, A, G, H, I, and K, and make a reconnaissance in the direction of Hunter's Mills, where he got into a light skirmish. As we were marching along that day, a squad of rebel cavalry showed themselves on a hill opposite the one we were on. A strip of woods soon shut them from our view, one of their party, bolder than his comrades, rode out through the woods, and quietly examined us. No doubt he considered himself perfectly safe, as he was over one half mile away. Col. Kane called by name one of –I think—Company I, and told him to shoot that Cavalryman. The soldier stepped to the front and quietly raised his Springfield rifle, taking deliberate aim. We all looked upon this as a piece of foolishness, but when the Bucktail's gun cracked, the Cavalryman fell from his horse. His comrades rushed forward and carried him back, and we saw nothing more of them. The distance was estimated by Colonel Kane and others to be not less than one thousand yards. It, at that time, was thought to be only by chance that the bullet hit its mark. Many times after than we covered that distance with deadly effect. We gathered up a large amount of forage on these expeditions, but seldom came across the enemy. Col Bayard with the First Penn'a. Reserve Cavalry, which was camped near us, was out every few days and had quite a number of skirmishes during the winter.

The weather growing very cold, the men set about putting up comfortable quarters. They inquired of the commanding officers whether or not we were going into winter quarters. They told them they had no orders to do so. The men, however, concluded to make themselves comfortable, and soon everything was bustle, as the gently sloping hill, on which we were camped, was leveled down by each mess for a foundation for their tents. Quarter Master Patton sent his teams, and logs were hauled from the woods near by. In the course of two or three days, a town had sprung up. And what a variety of architecture was there, displayed. As we had not gone into winter quarters, by general orders, the men were permited to build according to their own ideas of what they needed. A careful observer could have determined the character of the Messes by the construction of their winter quarters. The prudent men had taken great care in providing for themselves comfortable and convenient quarters. While the careless and improvident had erected very temporary structures which they were constantly repairing. A large Virginia mansion, whose owner was an officer in the Confederate army, stood close by our camp. This house was turned into a Hospital, and during the winter was pretty well filled.

At the fall election Col. Biddle had been elected to Congress from Philadelphia. On the 12th of December he resigned his commission. Colonel Biddle left us without having led his regiment in a battle, this no doubt, was a sore disappointment to him as well as to the regiment. On several occasions when we were ordered out, and when we were almost certain that a battle was at hand, Col. Biddle's bearing convinced his command that under fire he would be as much at home as on drill.

During the six months he had been in command of the regiment he had won the respect, aye more, he had won the love of every good soldier in his command, and we parted with him as children part with their father. Two months later we firmly believe he would have decided to resign his commission to Congress and remain with us.

Lt. Col. Kane was at the time Biddle left us, almost the unanimous choice of the men for Colonel, and had he then ordered the election would have been his successor. But he said he would prefer that the men should first try him, and then they could determine whether he would suit them. This was very unfortunate for Kane. Nearly every man being fully competent to drill a company, and very many could have handled a battalion with skill. Col. Kane had not paid so much attention to drill, and when he attempted it, the contrast between Biddle and Kane was so great that the men began to doubt his ability. From the first day he undertook to drill the regiment, his popularity among the men began to wane. Some disagreement had occurred between Biddle and Kane. The later knowing that some very important change had taken place in the regard with which the men felt for him, blamed Biddle for it. The result of this was a challenge from Kane. Col. Biddle very wisely made no reply whatever. The line officers fearing that Kane would not be a fit successor to Biddle, and knowing his unpopularity with the men, began to look around for a suitable man to fill the position. Colonel Charles Campbell of the Artillery regiment of Penn'a Reserves, was about to lose his position, for the reason that the U.S. Government did not recognize regiments of Artillery. A committee waited upon Campbell, who was very much pleased with the prospect of becoming the Colonel of the Bucktails, and it it was arranged that he should run against Kane. For some reason the election was delayed. In the meantime information was received that Col. Campbell was very much dissipated, that he frequently became intoxicated, and entirely unfit for duty. This of course done the business for Col. Campbell. It is but just to him to say that the report we received was very much exaggerated, if not altogether false. Charles Campbell was afterward made the Colonel of the 57th regiment Penn'a Volunteers and did noble service, was several times wounded. He won the name of "Fighting Charley Campbell," and was certainly a brave and gallant hero. There was a very strong desire to have Biddle back. A letter was drawn up, signed by nearly all the line officers of the regiment, this letter was sent to him by the writer, who had a pass to Washington that day, and was charged to deliver the letter only to Col. Biddle. He was found at his hotel, and the letter was handed to him. After reading it carefully, he was very much affected. Then turning to the messenger he said: "The kind words of these officers, and their appeal to me to return and again take command of the regiment touches me very deeply. But I must decline the high honor they would confer upon me. It would not be just to my constituents, and certain relations now exist that would be unpleasant." When told that we were at sea, and could not find a successor to him, he quickly responded. "There are several Captains in that regiment, sir, fully competent to take command of it. If there were not, I would feel that I had not done my duty by it." Failing to induce Col. Biddle to come back the election was put off for some time longer.

Some time during the summer Capt. Jno. A. Eldred of Company C, resigned and L. W. Gifford was elected Captain in his place, first Lieut. W. R. Hartshorn of Company K, was transferred to the Signal Service. Our chaplain the Rev. W. H. D. Hatton joined us here, and was kept busy distributing "tracts." Many amusing incidents occurred, quite a volume indeed could be made from the happenings in and around camp. It was here that bold Kelly took supreme command of the Guard House, with his able Lieutenants Jimmy Ward and "Reddy."Samuel Huss of Company H while on guard one bright moonlight night, when the Grand Rounds made their appearance got himself into the Guard House. For the information of those who are not soldiers I will explain the Grand Rounds. In order to ascertain the efficiency of our sentinels Gen. McCall, two or three times, and sometimes oftener, during the week, had the Field Officer of the Day of each brigade make the round of the guard. The sentinel was supposed to be pacing his beat, and on the approach of any one would cry out, "Who goes there, Halt!" the approaching party, would reply, giving his rank and business. When it was the Grand Rounds, the Sergeant in charge of the escort, at the challenge of the sentinel would answer, Grand Rounds, the sentinel would then say Halt Grand Rounds, advance one and give the countersign. One would advance and give the countersign, and if correct, the sentinel would say, the countersign is correct Grand Rounds, pass on. On this occasion the fun loving Sam had procured a sutlers pie, one of those huge combinations of camp grease, flour and dried apples, about fourteen inches in diameter. Sam was seated comfortably on a stump, with his gun lying on the ground, waiting for the approach of the inspecting party. They shortly made their appearance, and were allowed to approach rather closer than usual, when Sam with his mouth full of pie sang out, Hello! Who's there? The Sergeant answered Grand Rounds. Sam taking another bite of the pie commanded, Grand Rounds "Mark time" till I eat my pie. This brought a roar of laughter from the escort, and was too much for the dignity of the Field Officer of the Day. He however, had Sam arrested, and sent in to the regiment under guard. The next morning he was brought before the Colonel and was released upon promising in the future to eat pie before going on duty. In the next number we will give our readers an account of the battle of Drainesville.

No. 6

One of the scouts of the First Cavalry, who had been out in the neighborhood of Dranesville, reported a body of the enemy's forces moving toward that place, their object being to secure the forage yet remaining among the farmers, and prevent its falling into our hands. In our several expeditions through that region of country we had gathered up a goodly supply. There yet remained a very considerable quantity, and, to secure it, General Stuart's brigade was ordered to move on the 19th of December, 1861. On the morning of the 20th, about five o'clock, we formed in line and soon joined the Third brigade composed of the Sixth, Ninth, Tenth and Twelfth regiments of Infantry, a part of the First Cavalry, under command of Lieutenant Colonel Higgins, and Battery A., of the First Artillery commanded by Captain Easton. Our regiment, which was for this occasion assigned to General Ord's brigade, was placed in advance. We moved out the Leesburg pike. On our approach to Difficult creek the command was halted and the men were ordered to load their pieces. Flankers were then thrown out. The Cavalry scouts were in the extreme front, followed by the other companies of Cavalry. Proceeding thus cautiously, for some distance, we arrived at a large farm house where we were halted. Colonel Kane here secured a native to act as guide and give information as to residents, one of the objects being to secure all the forage we could. Captain Hall, Division Quartermaster, with a large train accompanied the command for that purpose. After securing a guide we marched to a point near Dranesville when we were again halted. While we were resting at this place, a woman attempted to pass through our lines, going in the direction of Dranesville. Lieutenant Colonel Kane, after questioning her, determined that it would not be to our benefit to let her pass He suspected that her object was to carry information to the enemy, and, no doubt, that was her intention; he told her she could not pass, but that she had best go back to a house a short distance in our rear and remain there. She because very angry and turned back muttering something that did not sound like a blessing. We soon moved again and proceeded to a little hill close by the village of Dranesville. Lieutenant Colonel Kane ordered Sergeant D.C. Dale, of Co. K., and six men to go to a brick house, owned by a man named Thorton, near by, and arrest two men who were there. After they were arrested, the guide came up and satisfied Colonel Kane that they were released. Sergeant Dale and his squad, when at the house, saw about twenty Cavalrymen with blue overcoats, mounted, and on another road below the house, they supposed they were a part of the First Cavalry which were ahead, but learned afterwards that they were rebels. The Bucktails were again ordered forward and turned into a lane to the right of the pike. After marching near two miles in the direction of the Potomac river, we came to a white farmhouse and halted. Colonel Kane now inquired for a man who was accused of shooting our pickets. Two girls came out and told him the man was hidden in the house. A squad of soldiers went in found him and brought him out. He was turned over to the Pioneer Corps, and we saw nothing more of him.

We then started back the way we came and on the way we met one of General Ord's aids who delivered a message to Colonel Kane. After receiving the message Kane raised himself in his stirrups and gave the command, "Forward, Bucktails, there is fun ahead!" we re-started on a run and when we arrived at the end of the lane the rebels opened fire on us. When we got to the pike we turned to the left and ran down the road to within one hundred yards of the enemy, when we "filed right." and came into line, our line covering the brick house already mentioned.

Lieutenant Bruce Rice, of I company, with part of that Company occupied the house. The battle now opened all along the line. The rebel Artillery was directed upon the brick house, but their aim was not good, most all the shells passing over it. While the battle was raging Captain Easton came down the road with his Battery, the horses at a gallop, and in getting into position upset one of the pieces, the other three pieces were gotten into position in an incredibly short space of time. Among the first shots fired they struck and blew up a Caisson of the enemy's Battery which proved that they had gotten perfect range, and that their aim was true. The overturned piece was now righted and in a short time the rebel Battery was silenced. The right of our regiment was now moving forward through a piece of sapling timber to the edge of an old field, and within a short distance of the rebel line. We were here met by a heavy volley from them, but, dropping to the ground, it passed over us. The enemy occupied a woods on the opposite side of the old field which was between the two lines of battle. When our regiment made their appearance the rebels charged upon us, starting out in good form. Our fire was so sharp and well directed that they soon gave up the charge and fell back to the woods. The flag of the regiment in our front went down several times from the time they left the woods until they returned to it.

The Sixth regiment now came up on our right, shortly after the Ninth regiment came into line on the right of the Sixth. The rebel line now began to waver, and their fire slackened. Colonel Kane, in hope of capturing their Battery, and to secure all the results of what was now evident was a victory, ordered his regiment to charge, the men responded with a shout, but just as the line got well under way, Colonel Kane was shot in the face by a rifle ball. Springing to his feet he came forward and took direction of the movement. The rebels were soon in full retreat leaving their dead and some of their wounded on the field. One piece of Artillery also was left, the horses having been killed, the Bucktails saw this prize and determined at once to secure it. But, to their great disappointment, orders were received to fall back at once. Colonel Kane, with his officers and men, plead for a few minutes time, but the order was peremptory, and this trophy, already within our reach, had to be left.

The battle had lasted fully one hour and a half, and the troops engaged behaved like veterans. It was the first time the Bucktails were under the fire of Artillery. The peculiar tactics of our regiment, that of lying on our backs and loading, was wonderfully successful. The fearful punishment they inflicted on the enemy, with so small a loss, comparatively, can in part be accounted for in the perfection of their aim, the peculiar tactics above described, and their accurate estimate of distance. The regiment were regularly practiced in estimating distance. And each man's estimate was proven by actual measurement.

When the wounded rebels were gathered up and placed in houses, and our own wounded ready to move, it was almost dark. General McCall, who arrived on the field during the fight, deeming it unwise to camp on the field of battle, gave orders for the troops to return to camp. The march back in the night was a weary one, the men were tired, having been on the move since five o'clock in the morning, and did not arrive at camp until the next morning.

The total loss of the troops, on our side, is given by General McCall in his official report at seven killed and sixty-one wounded. Sypher in his history of the Pennsylvania Reserves gives it as follows. Sixth regiment, two killed and twelve wounded; Ninth regiment, two killed and twenty wounded; Twelfth regiment, one wounded; Bucktails, two killed and twenty-eight woundend; Artillery one wounded; total, six killed and sixty wounded. Bates, in his history of the Pennsylvania Volunteers gives the loss as follows: Bucktails, two killed and twenty-eight wounded; Sixth regiment, two killed; Ninth regiment, two killed and twenty wounded; Tenth regiment, no loss; Twelfth regiment, one wounded; First Cavalry and Battery A., no loss; total killed six, wounded forty-nine . There is evidently a mistake in report of Sixth regiment; they had a number wounded. Sypher's figures are more likely correct.

In his official report General McCall says the enemy left ninety killed on the field. By the usual proportion, of five wounded for every one killed, their loss would be over five-hundred. Bates does not give their loss. Sypher says, "the enemy reported the engagement as having been severe, and placed his loss at forty-three killed and one hundred and forty-three wounded and forty-four missing." This we know to be incorrect, a greater number of dead were left on the field. They had either four or five regiments of Infantry, one regiment of Cavalry and a Battery of six pieces engaged.

The history of James Glenn, of Company K., is rather peculiar, and as we will not find him with us after this fight, it will be proper to record it here.

On the 19th of November, at roll call in the evening, he arrived in camp a recruit. The next morning at daylight he was in line, bound for the grand review at Bailey's cross roads. About the 1st of December he helped erect winter quarters, on the 20th of December he lost a leg at Dranesville, taken off close to the body, and by one of the last shots fired at our regiment. Very few soldiers can show as much solid service in one brief month. Mr. Glenn is living at the present time and says he would not take his leg back, and give up the record he has.

The victory at Dranesville was hailed with joy throughout the North and Pennsylvania was justly proud of the conduct of the Reserves. The disposition of the troops engaged, at once marked General Ord as a leader who would make his mark. The precaution of General McCall in having the First and Second Brigades march out to Difficult creek to be ready in case they were needed, gave his command a confidence in him, which increased as they came to know more of him. The steadiness, under fire for the first time of the troops on our side, called forth the highest praise from McCall and Ord. The skill with which Captain Easton handled his battery, and the unusually close shooting done by them, placed him in the front rank as an Artillerist.

Reports of the battle had reached camp before the troops arrived. Camp guards, extra duty men and the sick were of course left in camp. Reader, can you imagine the anxiety of those left behind? Reports are always conflicting, and this case was no exception. Can you take in the situation? Your comrade, your messmate, perhaps your brother, has been engaged in battle. You hear that a victory has been won; a number have been killed and wounded; the report has been carried by an Aid, who has none of the details, perhaps cannot give the names of any that are killed, in fact, the number has not been determined, your near and dear friend may be among the killed, or, dangerously wounded. Oh, how you would like to annihilate time or borrow a piece of the coming night to bridge over the space of time, between hearing the report and the arrival of the victorious troops. Then imagine their marching into camp, tired with their twenty hours work; the wounded carried on litters, and in every sort of conveyance, which could be pressed into service, suffering intensely from the necessarily rough handling they have had on the long march, yet with rejoicing over their victory.

The battle of Dranesville was the subject of camp fire talk for a long time Could we reproduce the interesting details recounted around the camp fire, the incidents of personal bravery and experience, what an interesting chapter it would make. For many days our boys had the pleasure of entertaining hundreds of visitors with a recital of the fight. The newspapers were full of praise, and the men justly elated over their success.

Captain Hall had not been idle during the day, he had in his line been equally successful, having loaded all his wagons with forage. It was also in order for every soldier who had been in the battle to write an account home. The mail carriers found that it required double the usual capacity of their mail pouches to carry the letters addressed to the loved ones. The wounded received their full share of attention. The vast number of visitors helped to relieve the weary hours of suffering. The rebel wounded, that had been brought in, were quite a curiosity to many. They were good, genial fellows and made friends among the Union wounded who were in the hospital with them, and many a good story was told, to while away the time.

When every officer and man did their whole duty so nobly no especial mention can be made.

No. 7

As no attention was paid to chronology in the two numbers preceeding this, we must take our readers back one month. On Wednesday morning, November 20th, 1861, at about five o'clock, imagine yourself located in a balloon overlooking the country where were located the camps of the Army of the Potomac, you would have witnessed an unusual activity everywhere; men were forming and soon every regiment in that vast army was on the march, each column directed to one common centre, Balls or Bailey's Cross Roads. The ground here was well selected for the purpose for which the troops were assembling. This was the Grand Review of the Army of the Potomac by General McClellan and staff, President Lincoln, General Cameron, Secretary of War, and near 25,000 spectators. The weather was all that could be desired; everything, it appeared, was favorable to the success of this grand military display.

Now, from your elevated position, you see what looks like the greatest confusion as the lines march in from various directions; bands are playing, officers give their commands in loud clear voices; from this seeing confusion you, in a short time, see formed one compact, even line of men, broken here and there by Artillery and Cavalry. The men, after they get into line, are relieved to hear the command, "Parade Rest!" The line is formed and the last regiment is in position. Suddenly the earth is shaken by a discharge of Artillery, and, all along the vast line rings out the command, "Attention,--Shoulder Arms!" And soon the drums and bands sound the "cheer" and "present arms" runs down the line just in advance of the reviewing party lead by General McClellan and President Lincoln. They ride at a gallop the entire length of the line of over 75,000 men and near 20,000 horses. The reviewing party now take a position on the right of the line, on a spot slightly elevated above the vast plain stretching along the front; the army, in close column by division--that is two companies abreast—now march in review, saluting as they pass. Our regiment, being the extreme right of the army, passed first. Soon as we are well past we file off, form in line, and march by the flank back to camp. Now, for the first time, we get a view of that vast sea of glittering bayonets, and a sight never to be forgotten. The army marching, in quick time, were just three and one-half hours in passing. "Arms at will" comes as the most welcome sound we can hear. Come down now from your elevated position and march back to camp with us where you will arrive as completely tired out as you have been in a long time.

During the winter there was considerable sickness in the regiment; several deaths occurred from fever, and some were discharged for physical disability. Drs. Freeman and Humphrey had about all they could attend to. Our regiment, during the early part of the winter, had been filled up by recruits coming from the localities where the companies were raised.

The Bucktails, as an independent rifle regiment, were not required to do picket duty. After Biddle left us, Colonel Kane requested General McCall to have his regiment entered on the roster; from that time on we had to take our turn, being assigned to General Reynold's First Brigade. This was an unfortunate move for Lieutenant Colonel Kane for many of the men remembered it at the election soon to take place and voted against him.

As stated in a former number, Colonel Charles Campbell had been requested by several officers to become a candidate for Colonel of our regiment. For the reason given therein, he was dropped, and, after waiting micawber-like for something to turn up, Captain Hugh W. McNeil, of Company D., from Warren county, was settled upon as the candidate against Lieutenant Colonel Kane, and the election was ordered for the 22nd day of January, 1862. For many days preceding the election, it was the only thing talked of, everywhere you could see groups of two, three or more earnestly and seriously discussing this all important question. There was not a soldier in the regiment that did not entertain the kindest feeling toward Kane. They could not forget his noble conduct at Harrisburg in giving the Colonelcy to Biddle; they knew him to be without fear; they remembered that he raised the regiment and from him we got the name we were proud of, and at this time he was suffering from the wound received at Dranesville; all these things were in his favor, and demanded the support of the regiment. The entire regiment felt that it would look like ingratitude to elect any one over him. But we had learned the importance of having the right kind of a man at the head of the regiment. When Biddle was with us we felt perfectly safe. Kane's rashness was kept in check by the cool, clear head of Biddle. The objections to Kane were his want of knowledge of military tactics and his rashness. The latter, it was feared, would some day lead him to sacrifice many men when not called for. His object in getting the regiment assigned to picket duty was to get in a position to fight if there was anybody to fight. It was a wonderful change from the perfect discipline and drill to which we had attained under Biddle, to the want of order in camp and utter failure on the drill ground. Sitting here at home, with letters and papers relating to that important event, one must admire the heroism displayed by the men of the old regiment in sacrificing their personal feelings for the good of the cause.

For several days before the election Kane's defeat was a foregone conclusion. Had a pestilence entered camp and stricken down scores of comrades, with no prospect of checking the destroyer, no greater gloom would have been thrown over the regiment. This was the situation on the morning of the 22nd of January, when the election was opened and the men notified to "choose ye this day whom ye will serve." When the polls were closed, Captain Hugh W. McNeil having a majority of the votes, was declared elected. The majority was only a few votes, but one was enough. There was more at stake in that election than any other I have ever participated in.

It has always been a puzzle to the writer why Major Stone was not chosen instead of Captain McNeil, it was, perhaps, to break the force of the stroke with Kane.

Our new Colonel, as soon as his commission arrived, assumed command. McNeil was of Scotch parentage and he had all of the characteristics. He could like a man all over and could hate just as hard; vindictive to an unusual degree, he never forgave those who once done him what he conceived to be an injury; yet, if he wronged a man, would, in the most humble manner, acknowledge it and beg forgiveness. The regiment, under his government, was soon restored to its former high character. It, however, required some time for the new Colonel to be at home on the drill ground. There is quite a difference between the direction of a movement and the execution of an order.

Colonel Campbell had been requested to become a candidate by several officers of the regiment among them Captain McNeil. Without giving him any notice an election was held, no votes were cast for him and one of the men who had pressed him to be a candidate was elected. Colonel Campbell, justly indignant at such treatment, challenged Colonel McNeil, who insisted upon a prompt acceptance, declaring his willingness to fight. Several of his friends among the officers then gave Colonel Campbell to understand that they could not do other than take the challenge to mean them as well as McNeil, they being with him when the request was made, and all parties to it, they, therefore, felt it their duty, each in turn, to challenge Colonel Campbell should he survive the meeting with McNeil. The gallant Colonel was willing to fight any of them, but, when it came to fighting a whole company or regiment, one at a time, he concluded the odds against him were too great and he withdrew the challenge. The trouble was happily adjusted without bloodshed. This was the second and last challenge that passed in the regiment.

Our regiment had never been mustered into the service of the United States and when we made out our first Pay Rolls (this was before Colonel Biddle left us) we omitted or rather left blank that column on the rolls. The Paymaster, or Adjutant General, notified Colonel Biddle that his regiment was not in the service, but that a mustering officer would be sent to camp and muster us in. Colonel Biddle inquired if the muster would date back to the time we entered the service of the United States. He was informed that the muster would take the date the muster was made, that they could not antedate the muster of the regiment. Colonel Biddle promptly notified the authorities that we were not then in the United States service we never would be and that he would march his regiment back to Pennsylvania, there being no question about our muster there. Biddle's prompt and very decided answer brought an immediate settlement by a sort of compromise. The Secretary of War accepted us as in the service by an order. Our rolls were made out ever after in this way: "Mustered into service by order of the Secretary of War." And this was the only muster there ever was made of the old Bucktail regiment.

About the same time, the men from other regiments sent home and had their friends send the Bucktails. They would go out in the country, fasten these Bucktails in their caps, rob spring houses, hen roosts, and commit many other depredations; all these were charged to our regiment. To dispose of this trouble, which was giving us a notoriety we did not covet, Colonel Biddle got an order from the War Department authorizing our regiment to wear this badge. We also had the right to arrest any one found with a Bucktail on who did not belong to our regiment. This effectually put a stop to the plundering by Bucktails.

During the winter the good friends at home sent box after box, by express, to the boys. These boxes contained everything one could think of in the way of delicacies, and their arrival in camp were the occasion of much joy in the mess.

Hon. John Patton, then member of Congress from what was known as the "Wild Cat District," and from which five of the companies came, visited our camp and supplied a great many of the boys with envelopes franked by him, thus saving them many dollars in postage. During his term in Congress, Mr. Patton looked after the boys and took a deep interest in the welfare of the Bucktails and after every battle he was found on the battlefield or in the hospital, and many a poor wounded soldier had reason to bless him. His many deeds of kindness have outlived the score of years that have passed since then, and will be remembered after he is laid to rest. These are some of the gleams of sunshine that streaked the dark and dreary years of that war.

One morning we found about six inches of snow on the ground, just the kind that fills the heart of the schoolboy with gladness. Very soon after breakfast snowballs began flying; parties form and attack other parties, until finally the whole regiment took part, two sides were formed of about equal numbers; a stubborn fight ensued, and lasted until the men were completely done out.

One man captured, during the winter, a black fox and quite a number of interesting races were had with him. Notice would be given that the fox would be turned loose at a certain hour, when the time came the men would be on hand. They would form in a straight line, the fox would be taken out a few rods in advance of the center and let go when the chase would begin. Strange as it may seem the poor fox was always caught. He never got five hundred yards from where he was let loose.

No. 8

While laying at camp Pierpoint our men were learning a great many things, some of which were to be useful in the fierce battles in which they were to take a prominent part, and some things it were far better they had not learned. During the winter Frank Grunz, of Company D., or, as he was commonly called "French Frank," drilled the regiment in the bayonet exercise and the officers in the use of the light sword. "French Frank" was a character. He had been a soldier in the French army seventeen or eighteen years, and was wounded once or twice in Africa. Soldiering, as he truly said, was his business or trade, and he was a perfect master of it. He was perfect in the use of either sword or bayonet. Never, while he was with us, did he meet his match. I have seen him take a sword, give a soldier his rifle with bayonet fixed, and dare him to draw blood on him; he would even provoke the soldier with taunts, until, in good earnest, he would try his best to put the bayonet into Frank, but, with the greatest ease, he would parry every thrust and the soldier would leave the field with several bumps on his head, of which Phrenology gives no account, and several spots on his leg which needed repairs badly. Quite a number of the officers became very expert in the use of the sword, and, at that time, they were quite well able to take care of themselves should they have been engaged in a combat with sabers. Frank would get the regiment on the drill ground, in column by companies, then deploy the companies so that the men would be about eight or ten feet apart, in each direction. Imagine seven or eight hundred men, scattered over a level field at that distance apart, every man at the position of "guard," that is, the left foot advanced about two feet, the right foot turned so that the instep would be on line with the heel of the left foot, both knees bent slightly, the left knee fair over the toe, the butt of the gun fair in front of the right thigh, the body inclining forward, the gun on its side with the lock up; in this position of the body you could spring in any direction, the body could rise and sink on the knee joints, they bending equally. Frank now takes his position in the centre, and, in his broken English, gives the command. In an instant every man makes, what would seem to the unlearned, like a very queer movement; they would advance, retreat, vault to the right and left, "Lep on De rear," thrust, parry, Devil up" (develop), "guard on d rear," and perform several other movements, making to the looker-on the most laughable sight you could imagine. The boys called this "the grasshopper drill" and the name was a very appropriate one. The men looked more like a lot of overgrown grasshoppers, out on a frolic, than anything else. Frank, unfortunately, was apt to get drunk, and, when under the influence of liquor, was one of the most disagreeable men in camp. Had it not been for this bad habit he would have been promoted to Captain; he was several times made a Sergeant and as often reduced to the ranks; he was brave as a lion; an army of soldiers, all like him, would be invincible; a regiment of such men would have been able to destroy a Brigade or Division without firing a shot; but, as we will hear of Frank many times during the history, we will leave him for the present.

When McNeil took command of the regiment he found that a certain few had been holding almost uninterrupted possession of the guard house. Hoping, by moral suasion to accomplish what force had failed to do, he made a general guard house delivery, and then made a treaty of peace with the leaders, who were Martin Kelly or "Bold Kelly," Jimmy Ward, and one or two others. A short time after this, Jimmy Ward knocked at the Colonel's quarters, and was invited in. Colonel McNeil said:

"Well, Jimmy, what can I do for you?"
"I jist came in Colonel to git a pass down to Langly, sur."
"Well, Jimmy, what do you want to go to Langly for?"
"To git meself a pair of galluses sur, to kape me pants from dragging down around me fate. I want to look like a sojer sur."
"That's right, Jimmy, and I will give you a pass. But you won't get drunk will you?"
"Divil the bit of it sur. I want to do the fair thing by yees, Colonel."

The Colonel handed him a pass when Jimmy said:

"Could yees let me have a bit of a dollar, sur, to buy me galluses wid?"

The Colonel gave him the dollar, and, fearing he might spend it for whisky, made Jimmy agree to bring the galluses and show them to him on his return. In a reasonable time Jimmy surprised the Colonel by returning sober and coming into the tent, pulled out a very cheap pair of cotton suspenders which cost him about twenty cents, and said:

"Jist look at the galluses sur! Ain't they the beauties sur! Now I can kape me pants up and look nate as any sojer."
"Yes, Jimmy, they are all right and I am glad that you have come back sober."
"Och, indade sur, I am going to do the fair thing by yees, Colonel."

Then reaching down in the capacious pocket of his blouse, he drew forth a quart bottle of the cheapest and meanest kind of whiskey and, pulling out the cork, he presented it to the Colonel saying, "jist take a drap of the critter sur, it is the rale, pure stuff."

This winter was a good school to many of the men; some who could neither read or write, when they enlisted, learned both. The reading portion kept well posted on military matters and discussed quite freely the probably moves that would be made by the several armies in the Spring. We remember, very distinctly, one night during the winter, when quite a company had assembled and were discussing the war, and nearly all of the men were of the opinion that the end would come the coming summer and none would admit that it would last over one year, Lieutenant Dale had quietly listened to what had been said without expressing an opinion until called upon, when he said that when he left home he bade good-bye to his friends forever; that he never expected to live through the war; that he had been highly favored in being sent home to get recruits, but, since his return, did not ever again expect to get home alive; he said then, if we conquered the rebels in four or five years, we would do well. This statement cast a gloom over the assembly and I cannot give the argument as he made it that night, but have thought of it many times since. Lieutenant Dale never again saw his friends. But I am anticipating and must stop here.

Company D. presented Colonel McNeil with a very handsome sword and belt, and Chaplain Hatton was requested to make the presentation, but some of the fun-loving officers persuaded the Chaplain that the proper thing to do would be to preface the presentation by prayer and close by singing the long metre doxology. This rule cander compels us to say was not generally adopted in sword presentations.

About the middle of January we were presented, by the State, with a new regimental flag, on which was inscribed, "Dranesville," and, from this, was started the printing on the flags of the regiments the names of battles in which they were engaged. All over the North was heard the cry of "Why don't the army move?" The papers were continually urging a forward movement and most of the letters received from home contained the question: "When are you going to move?" and these of course, were taken as reflections upon the General commanding. McClellan, at that time, was almost worshipped by the Army of the Potomac. They would have exalted any one at that time just as they did "Little Mac" as they familiarly called him. We are said to be a nation of hero worshipers, and the wonderful hold McClellan had upon the army before he had done anything to justify the estimation they placed upon his ability to command an army, would seem to prove the statement to be true. The unearned fame ascribed to McClellan by the army is yet believed to be real and genuine by many soldiers who have not taken the pains to study well the history of his campaigns, and, he is to this day, looked upon by that class of soldiers as the greatest General of the war.

On Monday, the 10th day of March, 1862, we broke camp and bade goodbye to camp Pierpont; this was the grand forward movement of the grand army. We marched in the direction of Centreville and camped that night at Hunter's Mills. We laid here until Friday when we marched toward Alexandria. If anything was needed to prove that folly of our having spent so many months idle in camp, the retreat of the rebels on our approach should be sufficient. We found the nest, but the bird had flown.

No. 9

During the winter just closed, many important battles had been fought. The Western Army had been active and the armies and navy along the coast had been doing good work. All over the North there was manifested great impatience at the inactivity on the Potomac. The administration felt the pressure, and, no doubt, the President himself felt that ample time had elapsed since the army on the south side of the Potomac had been encamped there to fully prepare the soldiers for the field. The government, with an unsparing hand, had been contributing everything in her power to thoroughly equip and arm it, and the government and the country were not unreasonable in demanding that there should be some return for all the outlay. President Lincoln, on the 19th day of January, 1862, issued an order as Commander-in-chief of the army and navy, for a general movement of all the armies of the United States. General Halleck, who commanded the armies in the West, commenced the movement which resulted in the following victories to the Union arms: General Thomas defeated the Confederate General Crittenden in a hard fought battle, at Logan's Cross Roads, Kentucky, in which the Confederate General Zollicoffer was killed; Commodore Foote attacked and captured Fort Henry, on the Tennessee river; General Grant captured Fort Donelson, on the Cumberland river; General Curtis completely routed the combined rebel armies of VanDorn, Price and McCullough, at Pea Ridge, in Arkansas, General McCullough fell in this action mortally wounded. The most important engagements on the coast were the capture of Port Royal, Roanoke Island and Newbern, by General Burnside and Commodores Dupont and Goldsboro. Had the Army of the Potomac moved at the same time and actively engaged the Army of Virginia, there is no telling what the result would have been. Subsequent events proved the wisdom of the President, and demonstrated clearly the importance of an advance at that time.

General McClellan assumed command on the first of November, 1862, of all the armies, except the Department of Virginia, which comprised the country within sixty miles of Fortress Monroe. At the time the President issued the order McClellan had been in command of the army over two and one-half months. If other Divisions could be judged by McCalls, the army was in excellent condition, and amply provided with everything necessary for a forward movement. The conduct of these troops at Dranesville was enough to satisfy any one as to their efficiency.

General McClelan, in the *Century*, May number, 1885, says: "Upon assuming the general command, I found that the West was far behind the East in its state of preparation, and much of my time and large quantities of materials were consumed in pushing the organization of the Western armies." That this was the case will not admit of a doubt, as the Western armies were much farther from the centre of supplies, the government, and, the country at that time, were most deeply interested in the armies threatening and those that were to defend the seat of government.

These poorly prepared armies were able to do some hard fighting and won some very substantial victories before General McClellan was ready for active work with the army which had been all the while under his personal direction, Logan's Cross Roads January 19, Fort Henry February 6, Fort Donelson February 16, Pea Ridge March 8, and the armies that fought these battles and won these victories, had not as many facilities and were not as favorably situated for an active campaign, as the Army of the Potomac.

The order of January 19, not having the desired effect so far as the army in front of Washigton was concerned, President Lincoln, on the 31st day of January, 1862, issued the following order from the Executive Mansion:

> "Ordered. That all the disposable force of the Army of the Potomac after providing safely for the defense of Washington, be formed into an expedition for the immediate object of seizing and occupying a point upon the railroad southwestward of what is known as Manassas junction, all details to be in the discretion of the Commander-in-Chief, and the expedition to move before or on the 22nd day of February, next."

This order was signed by Abraham Lincoln.

General McCellan, not being ready to move against the enemy confronting him, submitted a plan to a council of war, composed of thirteen Generals; eight voted in favor of it and four against it, and one in favor on certain conditions.

The plan was to move the army, by way of Annapolis, thence down the Chesapeake Bay and up the Rappahonnock river to Urbana and across the country to Richmond.

Sypher, in his history of the Pennsylvania Reserves, says: "General McClellan hoped by this movement to elude the enemy, and arrive in front of Richmond before the forces at Manassas could be concentrated there for its defense." Could it be possible that General McClellan expected to accomplish a movement of such magnitude, by land and water, without the enemy finding it out?

On the 9th of March the Confederates began their backward movement; they abandoned their position at Manassas and fell back behind the Rapidan. In the article referred to in the *Century*, General McClellan says: "On the next day (March 9th) intelligence arrived that the enemy was abandoning his position. I crossed to the Virginia side to receive information more promptly and decide what should be done. During the night I determined to advance the whole army, to take advantage of any opportunity to strike the enemy, to break up the permanent camps, give the troops a little experience on the march and in bivouac, get rid of extra baggage, and test the workings of the staff departments." A sort of field parade, with no thought of the real work on hand. A little farther on, in the same article, he says: "When Manassas was abandoned and the enemy was behind the Rapidan, the Urbana movement lost much of its promise, as the enemy were now in position to reach Richmond before we could do so. The alternative remained of making Fortress Monroe and its vicinity the base of operations."

To one not versed in military science, only a humble volunteer, the fact that it never occurred to McClellan that the plan of President Lincoln, which was simply to go out after the enemy, overtake him if you could before he reached Richmond and engage him, was the easiest, least expensive and decidedly the most practical way of getting at him. If Sypher is correct in his premises, that McClellan "hoped to elude" the enemy, then, of course Mr. Lincoln's plan would not suite him.. Later on this subject will be more freely discussed; it has been introduced here because it will, to some extent, account for the marching and countermarching of the army.

After repeated interviews with the President and Secretary of War, McClellan adopted the plan making the Peninsula, or rather the York river, the base of operations. Accordingly, on the 17th of March, the troops began to embark at Alexandria. The President insisted on the Capitol being sufficiently protected, he therefore, directed that the First Corps, commanded by Major-General Irwin McDowell, should be left to operate in front of Washington. The Pennsylvania Reserves formed one of the Divisions of this Corps. The Bucktails were very much disappointed in not being permitted to join in the grand expedition. We went into camp at Fairfax Seminary, near Aleandria, where we remained four weeks.

On the morning of the 9th of April, just one month after we left camp Pierpont, we took up our line of march—during a storm of sleet and rain—for the depot at Alexandria. Here we were kept standing for several hours in the cold and wet waiting for the train, and, when it did arrive, the open cars, of which a great part of the train was composed, did not afford any better shelter from the storm which had now settled down to an old fashioned snow storm. The train arrived at Manassas Junction long after night, by this time there was five or six inches of snow on the ground. The night was very dark, and, when the men were told to go into camp, they had to hunt around, for something with which to start a fire and make themselves as comfortable as possible. This was one of the most miserable nights we ever passed. In a strange country after dark; in a snow storm without tents of any kind; on a deserted camp ground of the rebels, where very nearly everything that would burn had been consumed. The next morning the sun came out bright and we went into camp. We were now but a short distance from the Bull Run battle fields, and the men made frequent visits there, hunting relics of the battle.

The ground covered with debris of the deserted camps, remains of the huts occupied by the rebels as winter quarters, the earthworks, and the general devastation which is inevitable in a country occupied by an army, produced a picture of desolation that almost made one sick to behold. The country, at this place, before the war, was certainly beautiful in prospect; the natural scenery is grand; in the immediate vicinity of Manassas Junction, the country is only slightly rolling; the Bull Run mountains bordering on one side form a background to one of the finest views in Virginia. But war, desolating war, had left nothing but the background, that was pleasing to the eye. Poor Virginia, She was paying dearly for her treason, and this was only the beginning of her desolation.

While in camp at Manassas Junction several soldiers robbed the train one night, among the goods stolen was a box directed to the Medical Director of the Division which contained one dozen bottles of good whisky intended for use in the hospital. Pleased with this good fortune the same party made another raid on the train the next night, and finding a box very much like the first one, and bearing the same address, they carried it off and upon opening it found that it contained a number of bottles, it being very dark they could not see the labels, and, without waiting to make an investigation, three of the men drank from one of the bottles. Martin Kelly tasted the stuff and warned the others not to touch it declaring that it was "no bitters at all." It proved to be a preparation of laudanum and two of the men who drank it died the next morning. These were the only casualties that occurred in our regiment while we remained at Manassas Junction.

On the 16th of April we moved forward to Catlett's Station, repairing the railroad as we went. General McDowell was not satisfied, that his fine army, of forty thousand strong, should remain idle when active operations were going on all around him. By order of the President his

Corps was retained in the Department of the Rappahannock for the defense of Washington. While at work repairing the Orange and Alexandria railroad, General McDowell conceived the idea of pushing his Corps forward and capturing Fredericksburg. In his judgment this would not be endangering the Capitol and he accordingly submitted his plan of operations to the Secretary of War, who approved them and authorized the advance upon Fredericksburg. King's Division was the first to move from Catlett's Station, Colonel Bayard, with the First Pennsylvania Reserve Cavalry, and the "Ira Harris Light Cavalry" took the advance.

On the 18th of April they left camp in the morning at two o'clock the immediate object being to get possession of the bridge across the Rappahannock at Falmouth. The morning was dark and the Cavalry had to move with caution, as it was well known that a considerable force of the enemy were located this side of the river. Colonel Jones, of the First Pennsylvania, with a battalion of that regiment, was in advance, and after a two hours march they received a heavy fire from Infantry located behind barricades erected on each side of the road. A brisk engagement took place, the Cavalry behaved splendidly and were holding their ground against the rebel infantry when Colonel Bayard arrived with the Harris Light Cavalry. This fine body of troops, led by Colonel Bayard himself, charged at once upon the enemy and forced them to retreat. Several brisk skirmishes occurred before the bridge was reached. The rebels were at last driven across the river into Fredericksburg. King's Division followed closely and took possession of Falmouth. Our loss in these skirmishes was eight killed and eight wounded; Harris' Light Horse, five killed and nine wounded.

Falmouth is a very old town situate on the left bank of the Rappahannock river, opposite Fredericksburg. On the 29th of April our Division went into camp near Falmouth; the march from Catlett's Station was commenced on the 26th; we moved very slowly, and had a fine opportunity to see the country through which we marched. The inhabitants were nearly all outspoken in their hatred of the North, and the women were particularly hostile to the Yankees, many refusing to sell milk, butter or any article of produce. At Falmouth we got the idea that we were to remain sometime, and when we went into camp, every mess did their best in ornamenting the camp. Bowers of evergreens were erected in front of the tents on the Company streets with arched entrances all entwined with evergreen, at the end of the Company streets, facing the parade ground, immense evergreen arches were raised with the letter of the Company (in) evergreens suspended. The officers quarters were arranged with the same decorations. The camp of our regiment was really the most beautiful sight, and attracted visitors from quite a distance. Descriptions of it were written by correspondents of the press.

While we were in this camp a soldier of Company G, shot himself. His name was Daniel Nunn who had been in the General Hospital and had only returned a short time before. His mind had been very much affected, he was melancholy, and would not tent with any one. His tent was an oddity. He procured two logs about seven feet long and about fifteen inches in diameter, these were laid just far enough apart to admit his body. A stake was driven at the back end and two poles in the form of rafters at the front end, on these rested the ridge pole, over these was stretched his shelter tent, which was fastened to the logs on either side. One night while lying on his back in this tent he placed the muzzle of his gun under his chin and with his toe pushed the trigger so as to discharge the rifle. The ball went crashing through his skull killing him instantly and in its course the ball passed through the corner of the tent of two soldiers of Co. K. about eighteen inches above their heads, and, strange to say, neither of these soldiers heard the report and they knew nothing of the tragedy enacted so close to them until the next morning.

Colonel McNeil was taken down with fever soon after we arrived here, and at one time the surgeon thought he would not recover. He was taken to a private residence near camp where he received every attention. He left the regiment here and did not return until after the battle of Malvern Hill, when he joined the command again at Harrison's Landing. Lieutenant-Colonel Kane took command of the regiment; we were not required to more than drill a certain time each day; take our turn on picket and perform the usual routine of camp duty, this was indeed our holiday. The news from the armies in the West and the Army of the Potomac were eagerly sought, and the soldiers kept well posted on the military situation. Sometime after the election of Colonel McNeil, Lieutenant-Colonel Kane submitted to General McClellan a system of skirmish tactics and also requested that four Companies of the Bucktails be detailed and drilled as a separate command in these tactics. The system met the approval of the commanding General and it was returned endorsed as follows: "March 7, 1862. Respectfully referred to General McCall, with instructions to detail four Companies of the Kane Rifles to report to Colonel Kane, and until further orders to be drilled by Colonel Kane exclusively in the system of tactics devised by him so far as the same is not inconsistent with the official system."

On the 25th of May four Companies, C., G., H. and I., were detached, and, under command of Colonel Kane, were sent with Colonel Bayard's Brigade into the Shenandoah valley. These were the four Companies that gave Kane a majority of their votes for Colonel. Kane severed his connection with the regiment that day and never returned. As the four Companies remained detached until after the second Bull Run battle, this history, until that time, will only have references to the six Companies, A., B., D., E., F. and K. When we reach the time the detached Companies rejoin the regiment we will take up the . . . campaign of those . . . fell upon the regiment like a clap of thunder from a clear sky; some of the officers may have known of Kane's plans, but the men were entirely ignorant of them.

On the evening of the 24th, Colonel Kane held the dress parade. In putting the regiment through the manual of arms he gave a command which "was not in the book." Viz: "Left Shoulder Shift Arms!" Kane was a very small man but had a remarkable strong voice. This command was given in his loudest tone and provoked a burst of merriment from the men which the officers could not instantly suppress. The Colonel became very angry, sheathed his sword, and dismissed the parade. The next morning, very early, he left with the four Companies named.

The men of our regiment were always truly loyal to the organization and they appeared like one great family, and the separation was like dividing a family that had been bound together by the fondest ties of family affection. The memory of that day, although a quarter of a century has passed since the event occurred, is far too sad to dwell long upon. The four Companies were kept too busy to have time to think much over the sorrow they felt, but the six Companies that were left were hourly reminded by the vacant tents and the lifeless streets so lately occupied by their comrades.

It was a great relief when, on the morning of the 26th, they were ordered to break camp. We crossed the river, marched through Fredericksburg and camped in line of battle on the ridge behind the town. We remained here until the 31st when we recrossed the river and occupied the camp occupied by Berdan's sharpshooters before the movement across the river. After Colonel

Kane left Major Roy Stone took command. In the next number we will learn something about Fredericksburg and its people.

No. 10

Fredericksburg, a town of Spotsylvania county, Virginia, is beautifully situated on the right bank of the Rappahannock river at the head of tide water; it is sixty-five miles north from Richmond and one hundred and ten miles from Chesapeake bay; the population, in 1860, was a little over 5,000; Acquia Creek and Richmond railroad passes through the town; a canal extends forty miles above the town; the country surrounding Fredericksburg was a very rich farming region and some very wealthy Virginians lived in the town and some of the finest plantations of the State were located near here on the Rappahannock river. Some of these places have found a place in history; the Lacey house, occupied by Gen. McDowell as headquarters, opposite the town, was a fine specimen of English architecture, and is said to have been built of bricks brought over from England before the Revolutionary war. The house was situated on high ground, and afforded a view of natural scenery that has few equals in this or any other country. The course of the Rappahannock, below the city, can be seen for miles as it winds its way through the rich and beautiful plantations. Above the city your eye takes in the falls which furnish the motive power for the mills of Falmouth and Fredericksburg; immediately beneath you is the town of Falmouth, while you look down upon the little city at your feet on the opposite side of the river.

Many of the country residences have beautiful grounds laid out in walks and richly ornamented with flowers. Here the wealthy planter enjoyed his almost regal sway over the poorer class of whites and exercised absolute mastery over his slaves.

Frederickburg was the home of many of Virginia's statesmen, and here, the F.F. V's* flourished in all their boasted superiority. The inhabitants were what may fairly be Union. "Lincoln's hirelings," "Northern mudsills" and "despicable yankees" could be heard on all sides, and into this hot-bed of secession we were called as the defenders of the Government and the Union.

When we occupied the city, General Reynolds was placed in command in the city limits; he was a sort of a military governor. His headquarters were established in a building on the principal street in the centre of the city, and, to designate the place, a flag staff was run out of the second story window, the flag hanging over the pavement. It was soon noticed that the citizens would not walk under this flag, but they would cross over the street and go up and down the other side. The headquarters of one of the departments was then established immediately opposite General Reynold's headquarters, a flag was suspended over the pavement there also. The rebels then took the middle of the street until they had passed the offensive obstruction. The women were conspicuously offensive in their conduct, and, several instances are known, where they spat in the face of Union soldiers, and this without the least provocation. The writer remembers one instance where a Union soldier was quietly walking up the street, and, just ahead of him, was a well-dressed, middle aged woman. This woman ascended two or three steps to a small porch in front of a rather imposing residence when she turned around, just as the soldier

* Editors note: First Families of Virginia

came past, and without of a word, she coolly spit in his face, he, without one word, just as coolly spit in her face. One other instance: A woman and a soldier were traveling in opposite directions, and, when they met, the woman spit in the soldier's face, when the soldier in turn slapped her lightly in the face. These instances are given to show the extreme bitterness of feeling that existed among those who claimed to be the better class of Virginians. General Reynolds soon brought the city under subjection. The residents soon learned that they must submit to his authority for a time and they found him one who could not be trifled with. The women were taught that if they were to be treated as ladies they must show themselves worthy of such treatment by conducting themselves as ladies. We will have occasion to take the reader back to this beautiful little city in a future number, but, for the present, we will leave the inhabitants in the full possession of the joy they expressed at our departure.

After we recrossed the river and occupied the old camp of the Berdan sharpshooters, every hour brought a new rumor, one hour we were to go up the valley where our regiment would be reunited and serve as an independent regiment of scouts; the next hour we would be reported as ordered to join this or that army and do similar duty, then we would be taken to the Peninsula to join the Army of the Potomac. These rumors were constantly being circulated and would accumulate as they went. A very innocent and unassuming little report would soon expand into a very important movement. They were a sort of military necessity, and they kept the idle soldier out of mischief.

General McClellan, ever since his arrival on the Peninsula, had been urging the President to send him re-enforcements, Franklin's Division had already been sent, and now McCall's Division received orders to report to General McClellan.

On Sunday morning, the 8th of June, we received orders to cook three days rations; after dark we broke camp and marched to Gray's landing ten miles below Falmouth, reaching there about two o'clock in the morning.

Early Monday morning, June 9th, we began the work of embarkation. Soon after dinner the First and Second Brigades were all ready and steamed down the river. The Third Brigade had to wait at Gray's landing two days before transports arrived to carry them. The Bucktails were embarked on the South American, an old boat that really was not sea worthy. The trip down the Rappahannock was a delightful one; we passed many beautiful homes; the country, at that season of the year, was at its best; the river is a beautiful stream; at every landing there were crowds of slaves who were assembled to wave their good wishes, and, at some of the out of the way places, they would give vent to the most extravagant expressions of joy, and shout out to us their blessings, and prayers for our success. Had coming events cast their shadows thus early? Was it revealed to these unlearned and hidden from the wise, what in the Providence of God was to be the outcome of the war? These poor ignorant slaves, by some instinctive knowledge, saw from the start their freedom, and to them the year of jubilee had come. The cry of the oppressed, and the blood of the tortured had not appealed in vain to Him who had promised deliverance.

Tuesday afternoon we entered Chesapeake bay, and, taking a Southerly course we, before long, entered the mouth of York river.

On Wednesday morning we entered the Pamunkey river. The York river is formed by the Nattapony and Pamunkey. The latter is a very crooked stream, and, as we steamed up, we could see transports on all sides; the banks are very low, and, as we wound around through the flat, marshy country, we run all the points of the compass. The river was lined with government transports which gave one at least an idea of the requirements of a large army. We arrived at the White House, then the depot of supplies for the army, at about 9 o'clock in the evening of June 11th, and immediately debarked.

We camped that night a short distance from White House. The next morning we marched up the York river and Richmond railroad to Tunstall's Station.

On the morning of the 13th, we marched on up the railroad to Despatch Station, when we went into camp. We had just got comfortably settled when the word came that the enemy had come up in our rear and attacked the guard at Tunstall's Station, our last camping place. Our six Companies were ordered to arms and marched out to the railroad. We were then deployed as skirmishers and marched down the road, the other regiments following close behind. When we reached Tunstall's Station, a distance of eight miles, we found that the rebel General J.E. B. Stuart, with a large force of Cavalry, had been there. They had torn up a portion of the track and set fire to a train of cars, and then started toward the White House; the immense stores piled up there were in imminent peril, and there is no doubt were saved by what proved a very fortunate circumstance.

It has been stated that the Third Brigade, of our Division, were delayed by transports not arriving according to agreement, and to this delay, in their embarkation, the saving of these stores may be attributed. The Third Brigade had just arrived and were in the act of debarking when Stuart reached Tunstall's Station. The object of this raid was to destroy the railroad and depot of supplies at White House. The detachment sent to Tunstall's Station, knowing the train was about due, dismounted and awaited its arrival. When it approached they fired into it, killing one man and wounding several others. The engineer put on a full head of steam and saved his train. The near approach of our Brigade alarmed the rebels and they took to the swamps. We followed after them until satisfied that we could not overtake or cut them off, when we returned to our camp near Despatch Station.

On the 17th of June we were to be reviewed by General McClellan and were twice formed in line for that purpose but the General did not appear, and we were not reviewed. The same day we received orders forbidding the beating of drums, playing of bands or bugles, or making any noise that would enable the enemy to learn the location of the troops. There was firing all day by Artillery but not near enough to us to cause apprehension of an attack on our Division.

On the 18th we received orders to march and take our position on the extreme right of the army. On the evening of the 19th we camped near Mechanicsville. Our Brigade moved on the Walnut Grove Church road to Beaver Dam creek. The six Companies of Bucktails now occupied the extreme right of the army. The next day we formed our line and went into camp. The position was a strong one naturally. Beaver Dam creek ran in front of our camp; Beaver Dam was a sluggish stream, and we built a dam near where the road crossed it, the dam overflowed the narrow flats ordering each side of the stream to a point above where the right of the regiment rested, on our left was the Mechanicsville and Richmond road, on the opposite side of the road the Fifth regiment was camped. The road ran up a ravine, on either side the ground rose abruptly to an elevation of forty feet or more above the creek making a strong defensive position. General McCall at once went to work to strengthen the position by throwing up rifle pits and epaulments;

this work kept us busy for two or three days. Our camp was only six miles from Richmond, and we were about three miles below Meadow bridge.

The small village of Mechanicsville was just in our front. At the foot of the hill on which the village is situated, runs the Chicahominy river, a narrow sluggish stream, the water deep and of a very dark color. Our picket line was between Mechanicsville and the river, and the picket line of the enemy just across the river on the Richmond pike, at night was guarded at one end by Union pickets and at the other end by Confederate pickets; two deserters came into our lines when our regiment was on duty here. Our picket line was extended to Atley's Station, about two miles above Meadow bridge. There was no foolishness about the picket duty here, the greatest caution was observed, and each party watched the other with unceasing vigilance both day and night. The soldiers of both armies realized that a terrible struggle was soon to take place. General McClellan had assured the President that as soon as McCall's Division reached him he would be ready to attack the enemy. We arrived at White House on the 12th of June; two days were lost in our pursuit of General Stuart. On the 19th we went into camp at Mechanicsburg, by the evening of the 21st we had our rifle pits completed. The weather was all that could be desired and everything seemed favorable for an aggressive movement.

We were called out on several occasions expecting an engagement but returned to camp without meeting the enemy in force. The roar of the Artillery could be heard continually, and he pickets occasionally exchanged a few shots, all of which kept up a constant fever of excitement. A balloon station was established in sight of our camp, and ballon ascensions were of daily occurrence, and, when these balloons rose two or three hundred feet, they made a good mark for the Confederate Artillerists, and afforded them a fine opportunity to test their skill as marksmen, an opportunity which they never let pass. One day General McCall got into one of the smaller-sized balloons and when he had risen about one hundred feet a shell exploded very near the car. The range was dangerously correct and the signal to lower was given. There were three balloons at this station at one time, one very large and two smaller ones. It required an immense train to move them, and a considerable force of men to handle them. With McClellan the balloon disappeared from the army.

No. 11

Early on the morning of the 26th of June the six Companies of Bucktails and the Fifth regiment were ordered on picket, Companies A., E., and F. were put on post and Companies B., D. and K. were held in reserve. The advance of Jackson's Corps. Which was marching down between the Pamunkey and Chickahominy rivers, became engaged near Atley's Station with our advance Cavalry, the Eighth Illinois, and steadily pressed them back. When Jackson passed Atley's he uncovered the front of the rebel General Branch, who at once crossed on the Brooke turnpike, and marched down the river toward Mechanicsville. A little before noon the three Bucktail Companies in reserve were ordered forward in support of the Cavalry. They marched up near Atley's at the junction of three roads leading to Atley's Station. Crenshaws bridge, and Meadow bridge. Captain Jewett's Company, D., was thrown forward toward Atley's Station to support the Cavalry at that point. Captain Wistar with Company B was formed at the junction, and Captain Irvin with Company K. was thrown forward and to the left of the junction and deployed with his left resting near the swamp bordering the river. The Cavalry, near Atley's were offering a stubborn resistance, but could not check the steady advance of the superior numbers in their front. Captain Jewett deployed his Company, but before he had time to order an advance, he was vigorously attacked by the Infantry of the enemy but the brisk fire of Company D. caused them to halt and produced considerable confusion in their ranks. While these Companies were getting into position, the enemy crossed a Division of Infantry, accompanied by Artillery and Cavalry, over Meadow bridge and were in the rear of the Bucktails. Major Roy Stone, then in command, was, at this moment, informed of these facts and he immediately ordered Captain Jewett to fall back to warn Companies K. and B., but, before he reached the junction of the roads the enemy, by extending their left, had passed Captain Jewett and came in on the right flank of Captain Wistar who soon was hotly engaged. He, knowing that Captain Jewett was somewhere in his front and that Irvin was on the left and in front of him, determined to hold his position if possible until these Companies joined him.

While he was thus engaged Lieutenant H. D. Patton, our Quartermaster, rode up and told Captain Wistar of the crossing of a large force of the enemy in his rear. Wistar, knowing that if he remained in his present position much longer, his chances of getting back to Mechanicsville would be slim, and was now quite certain that Captain Jewett was surrounded. Major Stone, at this critical period, rode up and led Company B. out of the trap and succeeded in bringing them safely into the camp at Beaver Dam creek. They were shortly followed by Captain Jewett and his Company, who had been given up as captured, but had made an almost miraculous escape.

Captain Irvin, with Company K., had been waiting for the appearance of the enemy in his front, the firing was getting nearer and nearer every minute. In the meantime the Fifth regiment and the three Companies of Bucktails had been withdrawn from the picket line and joined the line of battle forming near Mechanicsville. Lieutenant Patton now rode up and told Irvin of the crossing in his rear, at Meadow bridge, of a very large force of Infantry, Artillery and Cavalry, and that this force was marching rapidly up the river to attack him in the rear, and cut off his retreat. Captain Irvin, not knowing that the pickets had been withdrawn from Meadow bridge and the line occupied in the morning, asked why there had not been some firing when the enemy crossed, Lieutenant Patton told him he did not know anything about that, that he was not acting under orders, but that he did know that there was a large force in his rear and any delay in getting out of that would be dangerous, and said for his part he proposed to go now. Captain Irvin then sent a man back to ascertain the exact situation. This man had not gotten out of sight before the balls began to fly thick around him and he turned back and coming up to Captain Irvin told him Lieutenant Patton's story was too true. Captain Irvin at once formed his Company and attempted to get out; just in the rear of his position, the road leading to Meadow bridge, ran through a dense growth of small oak and when Company K. came to this road the enemy was formed in line of battle in it with their pieces ready, those who were foremost heard the officers cautioning their men to be very careful on whom they fired at their own troops were advancing down the river. Finding this place blockaded, Captain Irvin made a detour to the left hoping to get around the flank of the enemy, but when he attempted to cross near the junction of the roads named he found the line of the enemy there. On the extreme right the firing was getting farther and farther away proving that our troops were being driven in the direction of Mechanicsville.

Captain Irvin then led the Company into the swamp along the river, in sight of at least a Brigade of the enemy. To this day it is a mystery to every man of that Company why the force in their front and a good part of the time within one hundred yards, did not kill or capture the entire Company.

The firing on the right soon ceased and the enemy's line began to move, Captain Irvin and his Company lay hidden in the swamps and saw a continuous line of rebels passing along in their front until late in the evening. When they ceased to march, Captain Irvin reconnoitered the situation but found that there was no hope of his getting through. Sometime during the afternoon the battle of Mechanicsville began and Company K. was forced to listen to the terrific cannonading and the sharp firing of the rifles without having a chance to take part in it and only the faith the men had in the success of our troops in that engagement, and the hope that after night they would be able to make their escape and join their comrades, kept them quiet. The writer was one of that party, and knows that every one of the fifty, officers and men were as confident that our army would drive the enemy back, as they were that they were in that swamp. They did not entertain any thought but that before next morning they would be with their comrades who were so bravely doing their duty.

When the night settled down scouts were sent out in every direction to find some place where they could get through. They all came back with the same report. "The whole line of the road is lit up with camp fires." By day and night this was repeated until the night of the 30th of June. The firing each day was farther away, now nothing but the heavy roar of Artillery could be heard. It was evident that McClellan's army had either been defeated and was retreating down the river or a "change of base" was taking place.

On June 28th a rebel straggler was seen running through the swamp, and a file of soldiers were sent after him, they soon captured him and brought him in. From him we learned that our troops had fallen back, and that General Lee expected to capture the entire army. It is well enough to state here that this Company had not a mouthful of food of any kind. When they were ordered forward on the 26th they left knapsacks and haversacks behind. After holding a council of war it was determined, for the best interests of the service, to hold the prisoner and starve him with the rest. Many plans of escape were discussed, our prisoner whose name was John Robb, lived in or near Fredericksburg, and was very anxious to get home, advised this route, offering to be our guide. That was not in the direction of our army, and we could not give up the idea, that, in some way or other, our troops would be victorious. Our only and sole object was to rejoin our own Brigade. Hunger soon began to press her claims and officers and men were forced to stare unpleasant facts in the face. Something must be done. Captain Irvin refused to listen to any proposition looking to surrender. One day Captain Irvin, Lieutenants Welch and Dale took two or three men and went out on a scout, leaving the balance of the Company in charge of the First Sergeant.

During the absence of the officers the men concluded to go out and give themselves up, the Sergeant tried to pursuade them out of it, and sent a man in pursuit of the officers. The men formed in line declaring that they would not remain there and starve, they had then been five days without food, this being on the evening of the 30th, their last food was taken at daylight on the 26th. Fortunately, just at this time, the officers appeared. A council was held and an agreement entered into, by all parties, that we were to make an attempt to get out by following down the river keeping in the swamp. If we succeeded in crossing the Mechanicsville road, it was agreed we were to fight our way through. If attacked before we got here, we were to surrender.

We had moved every day and from our hiding places, we could see from one to two thousand rebels, and the country was swarming with stragglers and camp followers.

The swamps of the Chickahaominy were from two to three hundred yards to one-fourth or half a mile wide on each side of the river, the land down to the edge of the swamp was most all cleared. Our only chance, therefore, was to keep in the swamp. We had been making our way down and had come to the railroad crossing at Wilkinson's bridge. Trains were constantly running over the road, and guards were stationed at close intervals and were required to constantly pace up and down the road. This was a serious obstacle, and had caused us to halt. By the agreement we were that night to make an attempt to get over the railroad. Through the swamp there was a fill of some eight or ten feet, and bushes and briers grew close up to the side of the railroad.

We were laying but a short distance above the railroad and on the night of the 30th of June, when we were ready to move a terrific thunder storm was rising in the Southwest. The night was so dark that it was almost impossible to travel in the swamp. Captain Irvin, therefore, moved out to the edge of the swamp and took the dark line of the woods as his guide. Every man had been cautioned to securely fasten everything about their accoutrements that would rattle or make the least noise. When we reached the railroad the storm had burst in all it fury and the vivid flashes of lightning, gave us the location of the guards, who were not giving as much attention to watching for an enemy as they were to shield themselves, as best they could, from the fury of the storm. To our great delight we discovered that the edge of the swamp was about midway between two sentinels, who at this time were stationary. With great caution Captain Irvin, who was in the lead, approached the fill and in a few minutes he was on the road, and signaled the men behind him to cross over one at a time. Our great danger was that the lightning would discover us to thc sentinels. When, perhaps, half the Company had got safely over, we heard the boom of a cannon from the Richmond side, followed by one from the other side of the river. We had learned what that meant. It was the sign of an approaching train. We knew the sentinels would be aroused to greater vigilance and we must wait until the train passed. We crouched down in the thick bushes close alongside of the embankment and on both sides. Very soon the train came along, and stopped with the head-light of the engine shining fair on our line of crossing, and, those near the railroad, could plainly see the engineer and fireman. The two sentinels had come together, as though directed to do so, and a few words passed between the engineer and the sentinels, when the train, to our great relief, passed on. The sentinels then exchanged a few words, and, turning their backs to each other, soon resumed their former positions. The greatest danger seemed to be past, and the men again dropped over the railroad one by one, and oh, what a relief it was when we found, by count, that all had gotten safely over, but we had no time for congratulations, as it was very necessary that we should make as much progress as possible that night. Following the line of woods we moved on as rapidly as we could, and, after we had traveled some considerable distance, we found we were going up quite a grade, this excited a suspicion that we were out of our course, and, after a short consultation, it was decided to move on a little farther. The darkness was intense and the rain poured down in torrents. Only an occasional flash of lightning appeared and that apparently too far off to be of any use now when it would have been very welcome. We had not gone very far before we were satisfied that we were going out into the high ground and away from the river. A few feet in front of the advance, some one broke a cap but his gun failed to go off and in an instant every man was flat on the ground. After waiting a few minutes some one of our men said in a low tone, "Who goes there!" but go no answer. This challenge was repeated a little louder; still no reply. Two or three men were ordered by Captain Irvin, to move cautiously out and ascertain, if possible, who was there. After diligently searching we concluded it was some straggler who had broken a cap and got himself out of the way. We now retraced our steps, and went back until we were satisfied we were at the edge of the swamp, and, taking a fresh start with every one cautioned to keep a look out for the point where we had left our course. To our astonishment we came out at the same place. We then returned and tried it again with the same result. It was now near morning and it was thought best to wait until it was light enough to see, before we made another attempt. Soon as it was light we found that the woods extended in a point from the swamp out on the hills quite a distance from the river. This was the first day of July and the wants of the inner man admonished as that delay was dangerous. So we concluded to try the swamp by daylight. We recognized the country and knew that we were but a short distance above Mechanicsville bridge. There was a place opposite the village of Mechanicsville and but a short distance above the bridge where the woods was cleared to the bank of the river. When we came to that point we had another consultation. On the hill above us we could see quite a considerable camp of rebels. Desperate cases require desperate remedies, and, it was determined that we try to steal over this gap of two or three hundred feet, one by one, hoping we might not be discovered. All but a few did get over before the men were discovered, and then it was two stragglers who saw us. They soon notified the troops and it was the almost unanimous opinion of that little party that the only thing left for us was to surrender. We were only five miles from Richmond and in plain sight was eight or ten times our number. We had tried to take good care of our guns, but were not sure of the condition of our ammunition. The fact that we must surrender without firing a shot caused strong men to utterly break down. A handkerchief was waived from the edge of the woods, and a squad of soldiers approached within hailing distance, and asked what we wanted. After being informed who we were and what we wanted, they were worse scared than any one in our party. They reported to an officer, who assembled a Company of Cavalry and about one hundred Infantry. We then marched out and stacked arms. They surrounded us and marched us to Mechanicsville, where our captors were informed that we had fasted since the morning of the 26th when they set about to get us something to eat. Before they had the things ready we were ordered to fall in, and were marched to Richmond, where we got about three fourths of a bushel of soda crackers at dark. We will leave Company K. for the present and go back to Mechanicsville, and to the afternoon of the 26th of June.

No. 12

General Reynolds formed an advance line at Mechanicsville which was composed of the Fifth, Second and Bucktails. The object of this movement was to check the advance of the enemy and develop his line. This was soon accomplished and our troops fell back slowly to our rifle pits along Beaver Dam creek where the line of battle was formed in the following order: On the extreme right seven companies of the Second regiment, Colonel McCandless; five companies of Bucktails, Major Roy Stone; Fifth regiment, Colonel Simmons; First regiment, Colonel Roberts, and the Eighth regiment, Colonel Hays. This was the line of Reynold's First Brigade. About 3 P.M. the enemy's skirmishers were pushed forward to the attack and when they came in close range, our line opened a murderous fire of Artillery and musketry, which caused them to fall back upon their line of battle. General Lee, who was present and personally directed the battle, ordered the line forward and the advance of the rebel line was as steady as though the troops were marching in review. Our men were cautioned to hold their fire until the line got within close range. In front of the Bucktails was open ground, and the enemy were in plain, open sight. To stand and calmly watch an enemy, three or four times larger in numbers approach, with the air flying full of shells and shot, and to hear them crashing through the tree tops was a time to try what men were made of. This was a sight to which our men were not then familiar. Not a man quailed, but, with a look of determination on their faces that told more than words can tell, the fearful price which must be paid before that line of rifle pits would be occupied by the vastly superior forces now moving to the attack. The rebels, on this occasion, made what the Bucktails voted was a senseless movement. They advanced in two lines, four ranks deep, the second line but a short distance behind the first; when this first line came in close range our Artillery opened with grape, canister, shot and shell, and each discharge from the Artillery mowed swaths in their line; the brave fellows closed up their servered ranks and pressed on, the rifles commenced firing as soon as the Artillery opened, and now the engagement has become general, the rebels push on down the hill, soon they are at the edge of Beaver Dam creek and within one hundred yards of our line of rifle pits, the ground behind them is strewn with their dead and wounded, they are forced to retire over the same ground. What a terrible slaughter of human beings as they retreat up the hill. There is a short lull, the almost distressing silence of a few minutes is only the calm before another terrible storm, a new line marches out in the same determined manner, our men now have the utmost confidence in their ability to hold their position, the charging line, with a yell, came forward on the double quick, on the extreme right they gained the solid ground by wading the creek in places above the waist, Colonel McCandless made a counter charge and the two lines met in an almost hand to hand encounter, the gallant Second, knowing that everything depended on their driving the enemy back over the creek, nobly rushed to the charge, a charge that was simply irresistible, and the poor, shattered and bleeding line was again forced to retire with terrific slaughter, and the right wing was saved. At the same time, the battle was pressed in front of the Bucktails and Fifth with desperation, night was coming on and success or failure for the day depended on a few minutes work, and, General Lee knowing this, threw his troops, and all that he could muster, in our front in this last attack. The line was pushed forward more rapidly, the gaps made by the Artillery were closed up, and soon the line had reached a point as far in advance as the former, when a sheet of flame leaped forth from the Batteries and the rifle pits, the line reeled and staggered, cries of "Murder" were plainly heard by the Bucktails, when the smoke lifted what was left of the line was rapidly retreating. The roar of the Artillery, the shouts of our boys and the groans of the wounded men was terrible. The battle, at last, was over, the last effort to break our line ended in a complete repulse at about 9 P.M. The Bucktails had fired away all their ammunition, and had received fresh supplies during the battle. Now, their cartridge boxes were all refilled, and each man set about cleaning his gun, some of the gun barrels had been so heated as to burn the hand. All night long the wounded would cry out for water and for help, one poor fellow called out for Lieutenant Welch repeatedly. He, no doubt, had picked up Lieutenant Welch's baggage, near Mechanicsville, and had gotten his name from some article which he had marked.

On the left of the brigade the fight had been equally severe during he latter part of the afternoon, Lee finding General McCall determined to hold the right, pushed a strong force down the Ellerson Mill road and made a vigorous assault on the left, but was repulsed with a very heavy loss. His punishment had been very severe; the loss in general officers had been unusually large, and some of the best blood of the South had been spilled that day. On our side the loss was comparatively light. Protected by rifle pits, receiving the attack instead of making it, will account in measure for the difference, the much larger number of the enemy engaged, the manner in which they made the charge, in four ranks, all helped to contribute to the enemy's fearful loss in killed and wounded. Our loss was 33 killed and 150 wounded, the number engaged did not exceed 7000. That portion of Lee's army engaged with McCall that afternoon numbered not less than 25,000. Hill's Division, General McCall in his official report, says alone numbered 14,000. Their loss was something over 2000 more than ten times greater than ours.

Before 7 a.m., on the morning of the 27th of June, all our killed was buried, our wounded removed, the men had received rations, the arms were all cleaned and put in order and the Penn'a Reserves were ready and waiting for the enemy to renew the attack, or to be ordered to follow up the repulse of the night before by in turn attacking them. But during the night General McClellan had determined to change his base and move to the James river. About this time, (7 a.m.) the order to retreat, or rather to fall back was given, the men were quietly withdrawn; Capt. A.E. Niles with 70 or 80 men, was left in our rifle-pits. He kept up a brisk fire until he found that the rebels were coming in on his right and rear, when he withdrew and fell back towards the Chickahominy. The enemy came in with a rush and drove Niles and his little band into the swamp, where they were all captured during the day; Sergeant Ludlow, of Company E, the color bearer hid our flag in a hollow tree in the swamp, thus avoiding the humiliation of handing over our colors to their captors.

The troops that had swung around on the right of our position at Mechanicsville, were a part of "Stonewall" Jackson's corps, which had marched down from Gordonsville. They did not take part in the fight at Mechanicsville. General McCall says, General Jackson himself was present, and that his artillery was engaged; but that his infantry was several miles away. If that be the case, then the troops which attacked our cavalry at Atley's station, were either from Branch's Division, or if they were Jackson's, they must have made a circuit to their left in order to pass McCall's right and come in on his rear.

General Fitz John Porter had established a new line of battle near Gaines Mill. General McCall's Division, by reason of the severe engagement of the day before and the sharp engagement during the morning in covering the retreat, were to be held in reserve. They therefore formed the second line, in rear of the right-centre, in a good position to reach any part of the field in case of emergency. General Porter's line was an arc of a circle, and covered the bridges which connected Porter's Corps with the main army. By noon our troops were all in position, the Artillery well posted and protected by the natural formation of the ground, everything was in readiness, and a battle was to be fought on a much larger scale than that of the previous day. Jackson's Corps was on the ground and in the attacking party. The battle began about 3 P.M., before four o'clock, the whole line was engaged and McCall's Division had taken its place in the line and were in the heat of the fight. The struggle was desperate, at every point the rebels fought with a determination seldom equaled on any field. Our troops, men as well as officers, seemed to fully realize the situation and to comprehend how much depended upon the result of this battle, and, with a heroism worthy of the best days of Rome, Porter's Corps withstood and repulsed the repeated attacks of a superior force; the brave Easton fell beside his guns after the horses were nearly all killed and most of his gunners either killed or wounded. Almost the last words of the noble Captain were "pour in the double canister, boys, this Battery can never be taken but over my dead body." Over his dead body four guns and two caissons fell into the hands of the rebels. Many of that heroic band were bayoneted at their guns. Captain Cooper's B. Battery was then ordered to the right of our Brigade and did splendid work until 8 o'clock that night when it was safely withdrawn. Several times during the afternoon Battery B. was almost alone, the Infantry support being pressed back but the guns were double shotted and each time succeeded in arresting the advancing party and the slaughter in front of the Battery was terrible. The lines surged back and forth as either party would gain a temporary success. On no battlefield during the war was there more stubborn and desperate fighting for five hours than at Gaines' Mill. The Bucktails and Fifth fought side by side on the right of Reynold's Brigade and each seemed to try with commendable zeal to outdo the other in acts of bravery and daring. In their front the loss was terrible, the men without noise or undue excitement stood up quietly and firmly and received shock after shock from the enemy in his desperate and determined . . . that part of the line. General Reynolds was present on this part of the line during the heaviest fighting, and fearing that the ever increasing numbers of the enemy, and their repeated efforts would finally succeed in making a breach, he started to procure relief. While he was on his way he heard heavy firing in the direction of the Eleventh and a New Jersey regiment, he at once rode up to the front when a Brigade of Sykes' Division, on the right, were forced back and the enemy came in on the rear of the two regiments named, about the same time the left was forced and the rebels closely following, soon met the party from the right thus completely surrounding the Eleventh and New Jersey regiment. General Reynolds, his Adjutant General, Colonel Kingsbury, and an orderly were also completely cut off from their troops. The General and party hid in the woods, but the next morning while trying to make their escape, were captured. The two regiments, after fighting so bravely and holding their position against the repeated assaults of the enemy in their front, met the hard fate of being captured by a foe in their rear. The battle closed about 8 P.M. and was certainly a victory, as General Porter succeeded in crossing his Corps to the right bank of the Chickahominy during the night. From Sypher's history of the Pennsylvania Reserves we take the following account of the battle of Gaines Mills, by a Confederate officer:

> The attack was opened by the columns of A. P. Hill, Anderson and Pickett. These gallant masses rushed forward with thundering hurrahs upon the musketry of the foe, as though it were joy to them. Whole ranks went down under that terrible hail, but nothing could restrain their courage. The billows of battle raged fiercely onward; the struggle was man to man, eye to eye, bayonet to bayonet. The hostile

Meagher's brigade composed chiefly of Irishmen, offered heroic resistance.* After a fierce struggle our people began to give away, and at length all orders and encouragements were in vain—they were falling back in the greatest disorder. Infuriate, foaming at the mouth, bareheaded, sabre in hand, at this critical moment General Cobb appeared upon the field, at the head of his legion, and with him the Nineteenth North Carolina and the Fourteenth Virginia regiments. At once these troops renewed the attack, but all their devotion and self-sacrifice were in vain. The Irish held their position with a determination and ferocity that called forth the admiration of our own officers. Broken to pieces and disorganized, the fragments of that fine legion came rolling back from the charge. The Nineteenth North Carolina lost eight standard bearers, and most of their staff officers were either killed or wounded. Again, Generals Hill and Anderson led their troops to the attack, and some regiments covered themselves with immortal glory. Our troops exhibited a contempt of death that made them the equals of old, experienced veterans; for, notwithstanding the bloody harvest the destroyer reaped in our ranks that day, no disorder, no timid bearing revealed that many of the regiments were under fire and smelt gunpowder then for the first time. But the enemy, nevertheless, quietly and coolly held out against every attack we made, one after the other. Notwithstanding the fact that solitary brigades had to stand their ground from four until eight o'clock, p.m., they performed feats of incredible valor; and it was only when the news came that Jackson was upon them in the rear, that, about eight, they retired before our advance. Despite the dreadful carnage in their ranks they marched on with streaming banners and rolling drums, and carried with them all their slightly wounded and all their baggage; and when the cavalry regiments of Davies and Wickham went in pursuit, repelled this assault also with perfect coolness.

"By this time night had come on and overspread the field of death and darkness, compassionately shutting out from the eyes of the living the horrid spectacle . . . only a feeble cannonade could be heard upon our furthest left, and that, too, little by little, died away. The soldiers were so fearfully exhausted by the day's struggle that many of them sank down from their places in the ranks upon the ground. Although I, too, could scarcely keep in the saddle, so great was my fatigue, I hastened with one of my aids to that quarter of the field where the struggle had raged the most fiercely. The scene of ruin was horrible; whole ranks of the enemy lay prone where they had stood at the beginning of the battle. The number of wounded was fearful, too, and the groans and imploring cries for help that rose on all sides had, in the obscurity of the night, a ghastly effect that froze the blood in one's veins. Although I had been upon so many battlefields in Italy and Hungary, never had my vision beheld such a spectacle of human destruction."

* (Meagher's brigade did not arrive on the field until night. The troops referred to were McCall's Division.)

No. 13

The loss of the regiment at Mechanicsville, in killed and wounded, was slight compared to the loss inflicted on the enemy; killed, two men; wounded, two officers and sixteen men. At Gaines Mill the loss in killed and wounded, was one officer and twenty-five men.

The right wing of McClellan's army had successfully withstood General Lee's desperate effort to destroy it. Almost the entire army of Lee had been concentrated in the attack upon Porter's Corps at Gaines Mills. Saturday morning, the 28th of June, found the Army of he Potomac all safely over on the south side of the Chickahominy. To General McCall, and his Pennsylvania Reserves, was now assigned the very important task of guarding the vast train of siege Artillery and conveying it safely to the new base on the James river. This Division had won a noble record in the battles through which they had just passed. General McCall had proven that he was a General of no ordinary ability, and the charge that was now committed to his care showed that the commanding General had the utmost confidence in him and his Division. This train was (as a historian expresses it) the jewel of the army. Old soldiers will at once appreciate the importance of this mission and fully understand the tiresome night marches, the wearing waiting along the road, by far more tiresome and wearying that marching at a rapid gait, halting for a few minutes, then start up only to go a few rods in the dark then halt again, to be repeated again and again, until the men who had but little sleep or none since the 26th would actually blunder along in their sleep. Some idea of the magnitude of this train may be formed when you are told that there were between three and four hundred vehicles making a line over seven miles in length. The regiments were distributed along the line, on either side, and lines of flankers were formed to provide against a surprise.

About nine o'clock, on the night of the 28th of June, this long line moved forward on the road from Trent's toward Savage Station. The night was very dark, and, to make it still more disagreeable, a heavy rain fell all through the night. Along about midnight an officer rode up to General McCall and told him he was on the wrong road, the General told him that he was upon the right road and would continue forward. A short time after the officer again appeared with orders from General McClellan to General McCall directing him to counter-march his Division and give up the road he was then on to another command. General McCall replied that the long and heavy train could not be countermarched on the narrow road in the thick darkness of that night, and the men being fatigued from excessive duties, must not be subjected to this unnecessary hardship. Very early on Sunday morning General McCall reached the army headquarters at Savage Station. When he arrived General McClellan, with his Corps and Division commanders, were standing around a fire discussing the situation of the army. I quote again from Sypher's history:

"When General McCall arrived General McClellan stepped forward and said: 'Here is General McCall the hero of Mechanicsville.' General McCall bowed, and without further ceremony, informed McClellan of the order received to move on another road, and reported his reasons for continuing his march. General McClellan approved his course and leading him aside said in a low tone of voice: 'General McCall it is my desire to reach the James river before I am attacked by the enemy; if I destroy all the train, including private baggage, we can reach James river in twenty-four hours; but if I attempt to take the train with me, it will take us forty-eight hours to gain the river. What do you advise me to do?' Now, it must be remembered that McCall's Division had done more fighting and had been subjected to greater hardships during the three days that had just passed, than any other troops in the army; also, that at that very hour of rain and darkness, his gallant Reserves were toiling through the mud guarding a numerous train of artillery; that General McCall, like his troops, had been three days and three nights without rest or sleep, and almost without food. All this the Major-General commanding well knew, and knowing, perhaps, expected General McCall would gladly clear the road for his Artillery by destroying the trains in his front. But never was man more mistaken. Shaking the rain from his waterproof coat, and removing his cap from his head, General McCall, stood . . . and looking on McClellan's half upturned face said: 'General McClellan I don't know that I sufficiently understand the situation of the army to advise you; but from what I do know, I would fight over every inch of the ground from here to the James, before I would destroy a wagon. The moment you destroy your trains, you demoralize the army.' To these heroic words McClellan made no reply, but the two Generals in silence returned to the company around the fire. Greater compliments could not have been paid to men in arms than were that night awarded to the Pennsylvania Reserves. The Major-General commanding had entrusted to them the casket of his army, indeed, of the nation; the General commanding the Division reposed such high confidence in his troops, that he was bold, without hesitation, to deliver a reply to General McClellan, regarding the destruction of the trains, that in itself did much towards saving the Army of the Potomac. He believed his men were able to march to the James with their baggage, and if necessary, fight the enemy at every step."

The troops arrived at Savage Station on Sunday morning, tired and weary. At this place had been gathered together the sick from the hospitals and the wounded. Soon as our troops got here, without resting, they sought their suffering comrades and ministered as best they could to their wants. Many soldiers, who had been bound together by the closest ties of friendship, cemented by that bond, which mutual sharing of danger side by side, binds men more firmly than aught else in this world, saw each other for the last time on earth, those who were able to march left for other fields and other sufferings, those who could not travel fell into the hands of a pitiless foe, and many languished, starved and died from neglect in the horrible prison pens of the South. They moved on in the direction of the James river and crossed White Oak swamp creek during the afternoon; the trains were parked on the first suitable grounds after crossing the creek and the Division formed in the line facing in the direction of Richmond, where they remained until five o'clock in the afternoon. The trust had been faithfully kept, the train had been brought safely through and was now considered entirely out of danger. General McCall, relieved of the charge, moved forward on the road leading to Turkey Island bend on the James river. Porter's Corps had received orders to move on what was known as the Quaker road to the James. Where the New Market road intersects, the head of the column turned to the right and marched direct toward Richmond. Before going far General Meade found he was on the wrong road, he at once sent word to General McCall and then to Porter, who directed the other Divisions to cut across into the Quaker road, by the time they had got through it was past midnight and General Porter ordered McCall to go into camp. The other Divisions, after marching some time found they were wrong, took another road and marched back and on to the river, leaving McCall in the rear to cover their march. This was, perhaps, an oversight in General Porter, as he certainly would not have left McCall's Division, which had done so much and severe service, to cover the retreat. It appears that General Porter, after McCall had been placed in charge of the train, claims he had not been notified of the return of his Division to his command, and, therefore, was not subject to his orders. There was a serious blunder committed. Either McClellan or Porter was to blame.

General Sumner's Corps, on the 29th fought the battle of Savage Station, the battle lasted from nine o'clock in the morning until dark. Against large odds the old hero fought all day and won a decided victory. Knowing that he was master of the field and that the enemy's punishment was much greater than his own he protested against the commanding general's order to fall back, instead he insisted on reinforcements being sent to enable him to assume the offensive the next morning. No calculations had been made, however, to take advantage of any success our troops should gain and the Old Hero was ordered to withdraw his victorious troops. He retired during he night of the 29th, and on Monday morning joined the right wing of the army, south of the swamp, leaving his killed and wounded in the hands of the enemy.

On Monday, the 30th of June, the trains were safely landed on the James river, and, under the protection of our gunboats. A great part of the army was also near them, McCall's Division was formed across the New Market road facing Richmond, Kearney's Division on his right and in front of the Charles City road; Hooker's Division on his left and rear; General Franklin's troops near White Oak swamp. The enemy had been taught some severe lessons, their repulse by Sumner the day before, caused them to advance very cautiously. It was after twelve o'clock, on the 30th June, before they opened the battle. Their first attack was made upon Franklin's troops at White Oak swamp bridge; they continued their attack upon this point until dark, but failed to gain any advantage. The First Brigade, of McCall's Division, now commanded by Colonel Simmons, of the Fifth, was thrown forward on the night of the 29th to watch the movements of the enemy. With picket lines and special countersigns the Brigade remained there all night. In the morning they returned to their place in the Division which was camped in the open field. After the men had prepared a scanty breakfast the Division was posted in line of battle on the most advantageous ground and waited the coming of the enemy. As this was an important battle and many controversies have arisen as to the disposition of the troops and the responsibility for the action of the various Generals in command of Corps or Divisions, I take the liberty of again copying from Sypher's history, page 262 as follows:

"When, on the morning of the 30th of June, General McCall received the order from General McClellan to form his Division on the New Market road, and to hold the enemy in check until the trains had passed the cross roads in his rear, he supposed other Divisions of the army would be formed on the right and left of his position to protect his flanks. The general in chief, however, was not present on the field, either to form the line or to superintend the battle, and the Corps and Divisions being without a common leader, took positions and fought independently. The only instructions given from headquarters were, that the several commands should resist the enemy, until the immense army trains, moving toward the James had passed all the cross roads, and arrived in camps on the bank of the river. Of these disjointed and independent Divisions McCall's held the centre, resting on the principal road from Richmond. The main body of the Confederate force advanced on this road it being Lee's object to break through the lines of the National army at New Market and Charles City cross roads. Had he succeeded in this movement, he would have divided McClellan's army, and utterly destroyed the two fragments in detail. From the disposition of General Lee's forces, it necessarily followed, that the brunt of the attack would fall on McCall's position. General Lee had sent forward his most powerful Divisions with orders to seize the Quaker road. One of these commanded by General A.P. Hill, had assailed McCall's troops at Mechanicsville in a battle in which the Confederate General acknowledged that 'they were repulsed at every point with unparalleled loss.' Now, again, these same troops, reinforced by Longstreet's Division, making a force of nearly twenty thousand men, were to be hurled against the remnant of the Reserves, numbering less than seven thousand effective soldiers."

This is a concise and no doubt a correct statement of the situation. Mr. Sypher has taken great pains to collect official records, and submitted his work to officers who were on the ground, and so soon after the events occurred, that the whole matter was fresh in their minds, his history was written in 1864 and '65.

General McCall in his official report says his Division did not number over six thousand in this battle. About three o'clock, on Monday afternoon, General McCall's Division was vigorously attacked on the left and very soon the battle became general and his whole line was engaged but the enemy made no impression on the gallant Pennsylvanians. They then concentrated a heavy force on McCall's left, hoping to turn it. The General directed Major Stone to move to the extreme left and form a line somewhat in advance of the general line of battle. The Bucktails had barely gotten in position when the enemy rushed to the attack. A spirited fight followed and General McCall, knowing by the numbers, and the determination of the attack, that the greater part of the enemy's force were massed on his left now threw his right forward and by changing front concentrated his whole fire upon the attacking party. A German Battery, temporarily attached to McCall's Division, at the first onslaught of the rebels, fled from the field, abandoning their guns, they cut the harness and rode off on their horses. This at first created considerable confusion, and, no doubt, with green troops would have caused a regular stampede. The battle raged with great fury until after dark, and, although the Reserves were forced back from their original line, the enemy could not claim a victory, as they were too severely punished to occupy the field of battle. General Meade was severely wounded, Colonel Simmons was killed, and General McCall captured. Just after the last and most desperate effort of the rebels, which was made on the right and was handsomely repulsed, General McCall, Major Stone, of the Bucktails, and two orderlies, rode out in front and to the right of the line when they were confronted by a body of rebels who commanded them to surrender. Major Stone wheeled his horse and rode off making his escape with two slight wounds though a number of shots were fired after him. General McCall and his orderly were taken prisoner. There was only four companies of the Bucktails engaged at Gaines Mill and New Market cross roads, Co. K. were in the swamp, and Captain Niles and more than a company were captured the morning after Mechanicsville. This would have not over one hundred and sixty or one hundred and eighty men in the battle at New Market cross roads. Out of that number there was killed and wounded two officers and ninety men. Major Stone in his official report says: "the loss in the command was unprecedentedly large, being nearly two-thirds of its entire number."

General McCall in his official report says: "The loss of the Division in killed, wounded and prisoners in the three battles of the 26th, 27th and 30th of June, was three thousand one hundred and eighty, the killed and wounded amounting to one thousand six hundred and fifty, out of about seven thousand who went into battle at Mechanicsville on the 26th of June."

Surgeon Marsh, of the Fourth regiment, was taken prisoner and was taken to Lee's headquarters on the New Market cross roads where he met General Longstreet, who asked him what troops had been engaged at that point, he replied that it was General McCall's Division. "Well," said General Longstreet, "McCall is safe in Richmond, but if his Division had not offered the stubborn resistance it did on this road, we would have captured your whole army." The loss of the Bucktails in this battle will be given at the close of this history.

About midnight, on the 30th, General Seymour, now in command of the Division and the only general officer left, ordered the withdrawal of the Reserves with as little noise as possible leaving the wounded behind. It is to the credit of the men that many carried and assisted their wounded comrades, thus enabling them to escape falling into the hands of the enemy. Our march was directed to Malvern Hill where was to end this sanguinary campaign. The line of battle at Malvern Hill was as follows: Porter's Corps on the extreme left, Sykes' Division on the the left, Morrill's on the right, on the right of Porter's Corps came Couch's, Kearney's, Sedgwick, Richardson, Smith and Slocum's Divisions. McCall's Division in reserve behind Porter's and Couch's troops. The left wing, from its location, would receive the attack of the strongest force of the enemy, the ground being favorable to concentration of the troops of the enemy at that point. About ten o'clock on the morning of July 1st the enemy formed their line and opened fire on our line. They were evidently feeling the strength at the various points. About three o'clock, as was expected, a vigorous attack was made on Couch's front. The Artillery of Couch's and Kearney's Divisions poured a murderous fire into the advancing line, doing terrible execution. The Infantry, which was concealed by lying flat on the ground, did not fire a shot until the enemy came within short musket range, when they poured in volley after volley which drove the rebels back in confusion, the Artillery keeping up its work of destruction on the retreating enemy. This attack occupied about an hour. The repulse seemed to have stunned he rebel army as they remained quiet until about six o'clock when they opened with their Artillery all along the line. It was still more evident by the number of pieces that had been massed on our left that the final attack was to be made on the left. Column after column was soon pushed forward and with the same recklessness rushed upon our lines. A number of the heavy siege guns had been placed in position, and our gunboats threw shells into the lines of the enemy. Charge after . . . effort to break our line, until after dark, when he was driven off the field and beyond the range of the gunboats. The battle of Malvern Hill was a complete victory to the Union army. Lee's army had not only been repulsed and driven back, but it was completely routed, in fact the organization was as good as destroyed for the time being.

A Confederate officer in an account of the battle says: "At Harrison's landing, where the James river forms a curve, General McClellan collected his shattered army under the guns of the Federal fleet. But on our side we had no longer an army to molest him." I again quote from Sypher's history, page 305: "When the order to retreat was promulgated to the victorious army on Malvern Hill, on the night of the 1st of July, shame, deep sorrow, and patriotic indignation filled the hearts of many of the brave officers and men. A major-general exclaimed; 'We ought rather to pursue the defeated foe than to be shamefully flying before him.' General Philip Kearney, who had for twenty-five years been a soldier in the United States army, and who had seen more field service than any of his associate officers, having served during two wars in the French army, was moved to the verge of insubordination. Surrounded by a group of general officers, to whom McClellan's order was read, this gallant soldier exclaimed; 'I Philip Kearney, an old soldier, enter my solemn protest against this order for retreat. We ought instead of retreating, to follow up the enemy and take Richmond, and in full view of all the responsibility of such a declaration, I say to you all, such an order can only be prompted by cowardice or treason.'"

The Pennsylvania Reserves did but little fighting in the battle of Malvern Hill, but were most all the time under fire of the enemy's Artillery. The Bucktails, when they landed at the White House, had four hundred and fifty-six men. Company K., with fifty men were cut off on the 26th of June, the regiment, therefore, had only about four hundred men in the battle of Mechanicsville. Only about one hundred and sixty men were with the regiment at Malvern Hill. Captain Holland, of Company A., was killed at New Market cross roads while rallying his men. Lieutenant W. Ross Hartshorn, of Company K., who had returned from Signal Service and was made Adjutant, was wounded. Captain A.E. Niles, Lieutenants L. Truman and S.A. Mack, all of Company E., were taken prisoners at Mechanicsville. About one hundred and twenty men were taken prisoners, many of them wounded, besides these the loss was one hundred and seventy-six. The loss in killed and wounded was over one-half of the whole number. While we lay at Harrison's Landing most of our prisoners were exchanged and returned to the regiment. Colonel McNeil had recovered from his sickness and joined his command during July. The prisoners were returned on the 8th of August. General McCall and Reynolds were greeted by the soldiers with heartiest expressions of joy, McCall made a brief speech in reply. General McCall was now in his sixty-first year, the severity of the campaign and the hardship of prison life had told on his health, by the advice of the surgeon he applied for leave to return to his home in Chester county to recuperate, his request was granted and the Division sorrowfully parted with him. His fine military ability and noble soldiery bearing had endeared him to the men, and they loved him as a father. He had made no mistakes. With the utmost confidence in him his troops would go anywhere he commanded them to go. He never returned to the army. His health was broken and he, in a few weeks after he left, resigned. General Reynolds, the ranking officer, then assumed command of the Division.

No. 14

The Peninsula campaign is over and what has been gained? Will the readers of these papers pardon the writer for a digression right here? Is it not singular that in all the campaigns of the Grand Army of the Potomac, that this campaign is the only one that requires, or seems to require, explanation. Nearly every officer, of any prominence in either the Federal or Confederate army, has written articles and made statements of their knowledge of it. The war articles in the *Century* magazine are nearly all written on the Peninsula campaign. In the July number we have "McClellan's change of base, and the Confederate pursuit," by General D. H. Hill, "Rear guard fighting at Savage Station," by General W.B. Franklin and "The seven days fighting about Richmond," by General James Longstreet. Why should this particular campaign call forth so many articles and why were they written? This may all be plain to those who are now living, and who were living during the years of the war. Future generations, however, will inquire what were the peculiar circumstances of the army at that time, and what in the conduct of the army or its leaders that should require so many explanations by so many able writers who were participants in the important battles about which they write. This fact alone is sufficient to awaken the inquiring mind.

General McClellan charges his failure, to capture Richmond, upon the Secretary of War, Mr. Stanton. Fitz John Porter, his particular friend, in an ably written article in the *Century* cannot as a truthful historian, cover up the fact that the lack of a head, with the ability to direct the large force under McClellan's command, was felt in every engagement from Mechanicsville to Malvern Hill.

In the June *Century* General Porter says, in his article on the battle of Gaines Mills, "believing my forces too small to defend successfully this long line, I asked General Barnard when he left me, to represent to General McClellan the necessity of reinforcements to thicken and to fill vacant spaces in my front line. He himself, promised me axes. This was my first request for aid but none came in response.

If this had been a general engagement, in which the whole army was taking part, the failure to send troops to Porter's assistance might easily be accounted for. It will be remembered that General Porter's Corps were the only troops then on the north bank of the Chickahominy and against that one Corps Lee had massed nearly all his army and the army of General Jackson. There was no general engagement of the army. A defeat of Porter's Corps that day would have been a disaster that could not have been overcome. Lee still thought McClellan would retreat by way of the White House, and all his plans were directed to intercepting him before he reached that point. If Porter had been defeated at Gaines Mills, the plan of McClellan to change his base to the James river would, most certainly, have been discovered. To General Porter's skill in posting and handling his Corps that day, and to the unflinching courage and heroic conduct of his men, McClellan owes the success of his movement. Had Lee then discovered that McClellan had abandoned the base at the White House he would have made an entire change of plan. Had McClellan sent sufficient reinforcements to Porter to not only enable him to hold the position but to take advantage of any break in the enemy's lines, and to assume the offensive, the campaign might have had a very different ending.

General D. H. Hill, in an article on the battle of Gaines Mills in the June number of the *Century* says: "Lee knew that McClellan depended upon the York River Railroad for his supplies, and, by moving up on that road he could have compelled battle upon his own selected ground, with all the advantage thereof. The lack of transportation and the fear of the capture of Richmond while he was making this detour to the Federal rear, constrained him to surrender the advantage of position to McClellan and his able lieutenant, General Porter, commanding the field. Never was ground more wisely chosen or more skillfully arranged for a defense. During Lee's absence Richmond was at the mercy of McClellan; but Magruder was there to keep up a 'clatter,' as Swinton expresses it. No one was better fitted for such work. When McClellan landed on the Peninsula he had 118,000 men, and Magruder had 11,500 to cover a defensive line of fourteen miles (see 'official Records, War of Rebellion' Vol. XI., Part III, page 77 and 436) But 'Prince' John (as Magruder was called) amused his enemy by keeping up a 'clatter,' and it may be, amused himself as well. No one ever lived who could play off the grand Seignior with a more lordly air than could the 'Prince.' During the absence of Lee, he kept up such a 'clatter' that each of McClelan's Corps commanders was expecting a special visit from the much-plumed cap and the once-gaudy attire of the master of ruses and strategy."

General McClellan did not select the ground upon which General Porter fought the battle of Gaines Mills. He was not on the ground during the battle. He must have known that the greater part of Lee's army was concentrated on his right wing. This was the supreme moment, an attack by his left wing would have taken Richmond. And as the result proved would not have weakened or endangered Porter's position. The same author, in the July number of the *Century*, says: "The capture of Petersburg would have been almost as disastrous to the South as the capture of Richmond, and for many days Petersburg was at the mercy of the Federal army. There were no troops and no fortifications there when General McClellan reached the James. Some two weeks after the battle of Malvern Hill the first earthworks were begun at Petersburg, by my order." Sumner wanted to attack the enemy after the battle of Savage Station. Kearney and others after Malvern Hill. General W. B. Franklin, in the July *Century*, gives the words of General Sumner when McClellan's order to retreat was communicated to him, as follows: "No General, you shall not go, nor will I go, I never leave a victorious field. Why, if I had twenty thousand more men, I would crush this rebellion." In the same article General Franklin says: "I bade farewell to the Prince de Joinville, who told me that he and his nephews were about to leave us and return to Europe. He had always been very friendly, and now expressed many good wishes for my future. Holding my hand in his, he said, with great earnestness, 'General, advise General McClellan to concentrate his army at this point, and fight a battle to day; if he does, he will be in Richmond tomorrow.'" This is the testimony of those who were with him. While it is not by any means all that could be produced, it is sufficient to satisfy almost any one, that General McClellan had not in his mind at any time the capture of Richmond. From the day he was attacked at Mechanicsville, all his dispatches, and all his movements show that he was completely overwhelmed by Lee's offensive campaign. The more we study the history of the seven days' fight and in fact the time from the landing at Yorktown to the fight at Malvern Hill, the fact is plain that at no time was there any preparation to take advantage of whatever success our army might win. No attempt was made to capture Richmond by the several Corps lying, practically idle, while General Porter was doing his noble work at Gaines Mills. General McClellan in his article on the "Peninsula campaign" in the *Century* for May says: "The Army of the Potomac was accordingly withdrawn and it was not until two years later that it again found itself under its last commander at substantially the same point on the bank of the James. It was as evident in 1862 that there was the true defense of Washington and that it was on the banks of the James that the fate of the Union was to be decided."

General Grant got there, however, by following Lee and fighting over nearly the whole distance from Culpepper Court House to the James. Had he taken his army by way of Fortress Monroe instead of fighting the enemy in his front he would be subject to the same criticism which has been so freely made on McClellan's operations. In other words McClellan at an enormous cost transported an army hundreds of miles to an suitable ground upon which to fight an enemy that was lying in his immediate front, for several months. When he at last arrived at his chosen point of attack, and after a desperate battle on ground by him selected, upon which his opponent made the attack and suffered a terrible defeat, in which General D. H. Hill admits in the July *Century* that the Confederate loss was double that of the Union army, he does not follow up his success, but instead retreats before a defeated foe to Harrison's Landing. Everything was favorable to a forward movement. Richmond would have fallen had there been an attack on the morning of July 2. The writer was a prisoner at Richmond at that time. All the prisoners were jubilant, they knew Lee had suffered a defeat, it could be seen in the downcast faces and the almost hopeless expression of the citizens, in the anger displayed by the guards about the prison, the officers hurrying to and fro and the long heavy trains of wounded brought in from the field. Every private house to be seen from the third story of our prison was turned into a hospital. These told us plainer than words could tell the awful punishment which had been inflicted on the army of Lee at Malvern Hill. Carriage after carriage left the city loaded with escaping citizens. In fact the utmost confusion reigned throughout the rebel Capital until the news was received and verified that the conqueror had voluntarily delivered the prize of the battle to the vanquished.

General Longstreet, in the *Century* for July, says: "General McClellan's retreat was successfully managed, therefore, we must give it credit for being well managed. He had 115,000 men, and insisted to the authorities at Washington that Lee had 200,000. In fact, Lee had only 90,000." General Longstreet, in the same article, claims that the Federal loss during the campaign was greater than the Confederate, including prisoners. McClellan, in his official report, makes the total Union loss 15,849, the captured or missing 6,053, many of the latter were wounded. In the same report he gives the Confederate loss at 16,749. The army of Lee being the offensive or attacking party their loss would consequently be greater in killed and wounded. The defensive party having the choice of ground would be better protected. General Longstreet, in the same article, says of the commander of the Union army: "General McClellan was a very able engineer, but hardly equal to the position of field Marshal as a military chieftain. He organized the Army of the Potomac cleverly, but did not handle it skillfully when in battle."

Had McClellan, whose army had not done more or severer service than Lee's, made a demonstration against Richmond, held his almost impregnable position at Malvern Hill, under protection of the gun boats, and held Lee's army there, Pope would not have been driven back. It is not too much to assume that it was highly probably that the armies under McClellan and Pope could have combined in an attack upon Richmond that would have resulted in its capture and the practical destruction of the Confederate armies in Virginia. The Yorktown and Mechanicsville farce was to be repeated again. Lee had read clearly the character of the leader opposed to him.

By pretending to attack, by moving his troops, and by shelling the camp at Harrison's Landing McClellan was made to believe that a general attack was imminent. At the same time Lee had sent a large portion of his army to assist in the attack on Pope. Again opening the way to the capture of Richmond. From what had been learned of McClellan, as a military leader may we not fairly assume that he would have remained inactive at Harrison's Landing, until Pope's army had been destroyed, had not the authorities at Washington, after urging him to activity, ordered the withdrawal of the army. After a careful study of the campaign of McClellan we conclude that, as an organizer, he perhaps has few equals on this continent. In the plan of a campaign, perhaps, as few. In the execution of his own, or another's plan, he lacks all the qualities requisite to military success. To make him an aggressive leader would require a complete transformation of the man. To charge him with treason is a crime that is not only outrageous but infamous. We believe that he did the best he knew to achieve success, and earnestly desired the success of the Union Army. Hesitation, timidity and fear of responsibility are the rocks upon which his fame was wrecked. These were constitutional disqualifications, and for which it is hardly fair to censure him. The attempt of his friends at this late day to endow him with all these qualifications, and to claim that he possessed military genius only make his failures more prominent.

No. 15

We are promised several articles on prison life in Richmond from officers of the regiment which will, no doubt, prove highly interesting to our readers; we will give only a brief history of the prison and Belle Isle as we say it.

We were located in the Barrett tobacco ware house, those of our regiment were fortunate in getting on the third and upper story. The rooms were so crowded that when the men lay down at night there was not room to lay in any position but straight. Scarcely room to turn over. Our rations consisted of a small, very small, piece of bread and a small piece of beef, both without salt, once each day. We were not permitted to look out of the windows, or talk to the guards, or to any one on the streets. This order was not always obeyed or rigidly enforced. We had not been in prison but a few days before we learned that there were some Union people in the rebel capitol. From our lofty position we could look down into the dormer windows of a row of houses hear by; the family were forced to live in the upper story, the lower stories being occupied by rebel wounded. In our room there was a corps of very fine singers, who helped us to pass the time. When they would sing our national airs we discovered one of the families mentioned would bring from beneath the carpet where they kept it hidden a small Union flag; they would stand back in the dormer window so they could not be seen by any below them, but in plain view from our room. They would kiss the dear, old flag and press it to their hearts and by such signs as they could invent proclaimed their loyalty. To see our brave boys standing with tears in their eyes and fighting back the cheers that were trying to force themselves out, showed how they were touched by this exhibition of faithfulness under difficulties, that cannot be fully appreciated by those whose only knowledge of their situation is derived from reading about them. In the evenings there would gather into this house a bevy of young girls; their appearance at the window would call out the singers, the national hymns would bring forth the little flag, with the silent kissing and pressing it to their warm loyal hearts. Another battle would then be fought with the cheers struggling for release from bondage.

After remaining in Richmond some two weeks we were moved to Belle Isle, the notice of this change was received with joy. Any change from the close rooms during the extremely hot weather to the open air, was desirable. Our only regret in leaving the Barrett prison was that we would miss our friends and their little flag.

We were marched across the bridge to Manchester, opposite Richmond, where we got sight of "Castle Thunder" on up the river, then over a ridge to Belle Isle. The camp was located on the lower end of the Island on low sandy ground. On the side next to Richmond and the lower end of the island this flat extended out from the main part which rose abruptly sixty or seventy feet above the water. Directly opposite our camp, on the Richmond side, was the Tredegar Iron Works where was manufactured a large part of the heavy ordnance for the rebels. We could witness the testing of the guns every few days. Here, in a small compass, was crowded at one time, while we were there, five thousand prisoners, and, among them, a great many who were wounded in the late battles, and some from the valley. The wounded had no surgeon to dress their wounds or look after them, and many a poor fellow died because of "Man's inhumanity to Man."

One instance, from the hundreds, will give an idea of the sufferings endured by our brave boys when they were so unfortunate as to be wounded and captured by a foe more cruel than the wild Indian of the plains. A young man, not more than eighteen years of age, tenderly reared by fond, loving parents, of more than ordinary intelligence and manly courage, at a call of his country in time of need, gave his services freely and voluntarily. In one of the battles, in front of Richmond his right arm was carried away by a cannon ball which struck him just above the elbow leaving a stump perhaps six or seven inches long. The wound was never dressed, the artery was closed or so clogged that no hemorrhage ensued; he was taken prisoner and every day while we were on the Island you could see that young man sitting on the bank of the river dipping water with his remaining hand and pouring it on the mangled stump; a soldier and comrade dressed the wound in the best manner he could with the material he had. The wound, when the writer last saw him, was healing with the bone protruding. He was afraid to attempt to remove the blackened bone for fear the artery might be opened and he bleed to death. The patient suffering of this young man, and he was but one among hundreds, showed a heroism never surpassed in any age of the world.

A number of the prisoners died and their last resting places are now doubtless unknown. The writer helped to bury Harry France, of Company K., one of the party cut his name, company and regiment on a board and placed it to mark the grave.

Disease, contracted in prisons during the war, has caused the death of many of our noble soldiers, while thousands today drag out a weary life of suffering, and almost long for death, victims of the cruelty of a people who knew better.

While we were on the Island an escape was planned, originating it is said, with Roger Sherman, of Philadelphia, then Sergeant Major, of the Bucktail regiment. This plan was arranged in all its details and the time was set for the attempt which was to be made at midnight on a certain night. The morning before the time set, we were awakened by the roar of artillery. During the night several heavy Batteries were placed in position on the Manchester side and on the Richmond side both covering the camp, and, the guards at the bridge from the Island to the main land, had been doubled and the reserve on the bluff above the camp had been largely increased. It was very evident that there was a traitor in camp, the enemy had been informed of the contemplated effort to escape, and had so increased their guards, and surrounded us with heavy guns as to make it utterly impossible for us to succeed. A few days of detective work fixed the treason on a soldier of the Second Massachusetts regiment. He was soon after thus allowed a great many privileges, permitted to go over to Richmond in the boat that carried our provisions, etc. After that trip he never entered our camp but once, and then, by a miracle, escaped death. Soon as it was known that he was in camp, there was a rush for him, he happened to be near the edge and made a rapid retreat in that direction. Blow after blow rained upon him; he, however, kept his feet and reached the guard line where the guards took him under their protection, and this was the last we saw of him. It is best just to the Second Massachusetts to say that upon inquiry it was found that he was of Southern birth, happened to be in the old Bay State when the war broke out, and enlisted. French Frank, whose name has been mentioned before, recognized among the guards an old comrade who served with him in the French army in Africa. Frank, who had become thoroughly disgusted with the Southern Confederacy, gave his old comrade a sharp lecture for serving in the rebel army. Before he was captured Frank boasted that soldiering was his business, and that he would serve the party who paid him the highest wages. It took but a few days in rebel prison to make him an inveterate hater of "ze whole lot." Many scenes and incidents of life in prison could be given which would, no doubt, be of great interest to our readers; hoping that our comrades will feel at liberty to use freely the columns of the HERALD in relating their experiences we will leave the prison and again enter the field.

On the evening of the 6th of August nearly all the prisoners from our regiment, who were able to be moved, arrived at Harrison's Landing. There was a warm welcome given us by those who were so fortunate as to survive the campaign in front of Richmond, and doubly fortunate in escaping capture. Colonel McNeil had recovered his health and returned to the regiment after the battle of Malvern Hill. The first thought of the returned prisoners and their comrades in arms was to ascertain who were killed. This was the first that the actual number of killed had been arrived at. As our killed and wounded were left on the field in all the battles except Mechanicsville, many a manly tear rolled down the bronzed and furrowed cheek, while notes were compared, lips were compressed, and in the clenched hand and determined faces could easily be read the resolve to visit fearful vengeance upon the enemy for their inhuman treatment of wounded prisoners.

The paymaster was in camp when the prisoners arrived, the men had not had any pay for four months, and, as in the case of Company K., the organizations which were captured intire, had no rolls made out. The First Sergeant of Company K., the officers not having been exchanged until several days later, worked all night and succeeded in getting the company paid. The next day in our weak and exhausted condition we were marched up and down the landing for three or four hours during the hottest part of the day hunting for arms. Failing to get the kind of arms wanted, Colonel McNeil returned to camp and the next day repeated the effort and was fortunate in securing Sharp's breech-loading rifles. The so much needed rest could not be found in the camp at Harrison's Landing. The army, with all its vast material and machinery, was closely packed together, the hot August sun, and the clouds of flies with which the air was sometimes filled, prevented rest by day or night. An immense swamp bordered one side of our camp, the air from which was poisoned with malaria. Had the army remained there very much longer, the fatal effect would have been terrible. The Sanitary and Christian Commissions did more to counteract the injurious effects of the camp than any one has or can tell. In the hearts of the soldiers the memory of these noble men and women, is enshrined and there it will live while there is a loyal soldier living. Under this scorching sun we sweltered dividing the rather light supply of blood we had, with the voracious and never satisfied ally of Lee, the Southern fly.

On the night of July 31st, the rebels having crossed a considerable force of Artillery to the South side of the James, took up a position opposite our camp, and, before our troops knew anything of their presence, commenced a terrific bombardment of the camp, the guns being fired as rapidly as they could be handled. This was kept up for some time, or until our Batteries got into position, when they soon silenced the enemy and drove him from the field. The only death on our side reported was a negro laborer. The escape from serious loss to the army in men and material and the shipping lying in the river can all be credited to the imperfect aim of the rebel gunners. It must have been the cause of great mortification to General Lee that a movement, well planned and finely executed should be robbed of fruitful results by the inaccuracy of the aim of his Artillerists. This was the last attempt of Lee and was intended, in addition to the destruction of shipping and material, to blind McClellan as to the movement of the greater portion of his army to attack Pope.

On the 30th of July General Halleck, then commander-in-chief, ordered McClellan to remove all his sick from the Peninsula preparatory to removing the army. On the 3rd of August he was ordered to withdraw the army from Harrison's Landing. To convey it with all its material by transports to Aquia creek, then to march by way of Warrenton and join Pope's army. Although every facility was at hand the sick were not all removed until the 16th of August. The Pennsylvania Reserves were the first troops embarked, at ten o'clock that night Aug, 15th the day after embarkation General McClellan sent the following dispatch to General Halleck: "McCall's Division, with its Artillery, is now *en route* for Burnside." The Divisions of McCall and Kearney were the only troops from the Army of the Potomac that reached Pope until the 26th of August. Had the whole army been moved promptly as ordered by Halleck and reached Pope by the 10th of August he would have been enabled to have compelled Lee to retreat, or risked a battle against superior numbers on ground chosen by Pope. To the delay in forwarding that army to the assistance of Pope may be attributed the first cause for the defeat at second Bull Run.

No. 16

On the 22nd of August the Pennsylvania Reserve Corps, excepting the Second regiment which had been detached to guard transportation, arrived at Kelly's ford, on the Rappahannock river, having marched between thirty and forty miles.

On the 23rd the Division moved to Rappahannock Station where it joined the Army of Virginia and was attached to McDowell's First Corps.

On the 24th we camped near Warrenton where Colonel McCandless, with the Second regiment, joined the Division. The march, from near Falmouth, had been severe, the returned prisoners were in the worst possible condition to endure the forced marches in the hot August sun and the clouds of dust that lay waiting to be stirred up. Hot sun alone can easily be endured, but, when the mercury stands at 100 degrees with five or six inches of dust on the roads, the sufferings of men marching in ranks is very trying when they are in the best condition. The men who had been in Barrett, Libby and on Belle Island, half fed on unwholesome food and wasted by sickness were more proper subjects for hospital care than for active duty in the field. Only once did the brave men of the Pennsylvania Reserves complain.

They were marching as fast as they could walk in the hot sun and dust, up and down hill without a word, some stopping to drink from pools of stagnant water by the roadside, removing the green scum first. All at once, as though the Brigade had been seized with a sudden impulse, a murmur arose, the line halted and refused to move any farther. General Meade rode back and explained the situation of Pope's army, telling our boys that the safety of a portion of that army and the lives of thousands of brave soldiers expended upon our reaching a certain point that day and that he was painfully conscious of their suffering, after a brief speech he asked the men what they wanted him to do; a shout came ringing down the line, "all right, go ahead, why didn't you tell us this before," when the line immediately resumed its rapid march; not a murmur or a word of complaint was heard afterward, although every little while some poor fellow would fall by the wayside completely exhausted, to be picked up by the hospital or wagon trains.

We marched on the Warrenton and Alexandria turnpike, towards Centreville, when we arrived at Gainesville, where the Manassas gap railroad crosses the turnpike, the head of the column was fired upon by the enemy with two pieces of Artillery which were in position on the heights above Groveton, and to the left of the turnpike on which we were marching. General Meade, commanding our Brigade, immediately formed a line of battle. Captain Cooper's Battery of rifled guns were ordered in position, while they were getting ready, Lieutenant Bitterling, of Company F., was sent out with a party of skirmishers, he advanced rapidly within rifle range of the rebel gunners, when our boys for the first time, had an opportunity to test their new Sharp's breech-loading rifles, they got a good position and poured in several volleys in rapid succession with fatal effect, Captain Cooper then opened his Battery, his aim was perfect and a few shots silenced the rebel Battery which was withdrawn behind the hill. The column then resumed the march toward Manassas.

To attempt to follow, minutely, the operations of our division or Brigade would require a much more extended work than the writer contemplated or feels that he has the ability to perform; from this on our papers will be confined to the movements of the Bucktail regiment, save only when a more extended account is necessary to explain the position or movement of the regiment.

During the afternoon, of August 29th, while we were moving out the Centreville turnpike General Schenk, who commanded a Brigade in Sigel's Corps, rode up to General Reynolds and asked him to give him a a Brigade to protect his flank on that road, while he would charge up a ravine protected by woods and capture a rebel battery. General Reynolds, who was always ready to fight, at once consented and moved Meade's Brigade rapidly forward to a point opposite to and on the right flank of the battery about to be attacked, the road at this point ran through a strip of woods perhaps one hundred rods wide, on the farther side of these woods the road ran up a hill for near half a mile through cleared land, just over this hill was Groveton. Before Schenck got well under way the rebels opened with a battery which had been concealed behind these woods, the shells came crashing through the timber killing and wounding a number of our regiment, and doing fearful execution in the troops on Schenck's left.

The battery, for whose capture this movement had been planned, poured into Schenk's troops a murderous fire, causing them to abandon the capture of the battery.

A body of rebels were discovered advancing on the turnpike from the direction of Groveton threatening Meade's left flank, the Bucktails were sent out and deployed across the road. In skirmish line they advanced rapidly up the hill, before they got fairly started the rebel skirmishers opened up a sharp fire, with a yell they rushed forward and reached the top of the hill, on this ground there had been a severe fight the evening before and a small farm house was filled with wounded. Captain Irvin, with part of Company K., occupied this house and did good work. The enemy coming in on our left and rear in great numbers, a retreat was ordered when the Bucktails, fully realizing the situation, did some handsome running to reach the woods in advance of the rebels; under a heavy fire of Infantry, they kept on through the woods and on back to the point from which they started with General Schenk to make the attack upon the rebel battery, where we remained without any further engagements, until near dark when we moved to the rear and drew a few crackers, which were most welcome as we had been on short allowance for several days.

We remained at this point until about one hour before daylight on the morning of the 30th, when we moved out to the front and our Brigade was formed on the left of quite a large body of troops that evidently had lain there all night, they were in line of battle, with their batteries in position, but did not seem to be making any preparations for an attack, the men were lying down taking things, we thought, very comfortably. This was said to be General Porter's Corps. The Bucktails were at once deployed as skirmishers and charged forward in the direction of Groveton which was only about half a mile in front of us, soon as we neared the village the enemy's pickets opened a sharp fire on us, they were soon reinforced and quite a brisk engagement followed, our boys, however, steadily advanced on through the little town across a wide flat, where they captured a piece of Artillery, by this time the troops on the right were roused up and their batteries commenced firing, their shells fell in our line, we were in plain sight of the battery and some of the Bucktails fired into them when they ceased to annoy us, the force of the enemy in our front was heavily re-enforced and our advance was checked. Our breech-loading rifles enabled us to hold the enemy where we had them, part of the regiment was in an orchard and were well protected behind the trees, the others took whatever cover they could find and kept up a continual roar, and, from the fact that we were in close range and the men took careful aim, believe we did good execution.

We were expecting the line of battle to appear every minute, and wondered why they delayed so long to take advantage of the success we had won in what we supposed was the opening work of a general battle. To the surprise of every one on that line, the order came for us to fall back. The boys tried to haul the captured cannon with us but soon gave that up, they spiked it as well as they could with an old bayonet and left it on the field. When we rejoined the Brigade we were rapidly moved to the left to resist an attack from a large force of the enemy which had been massed there for the purpose of turning our left and doubling our Division back and come in on the rear of the troops, I have mentioned as lying on our right.

Our line was soon established and we were waiting the attack when an aide came up and gave an order to General Reynolds, we were hurriedly withdrawn and moved to the support of General Porter's Corps which had met a repulse and was retreating in some confusion. Forming in the rear our Division met the victorious rebels and after a spirited fight, they in turn wavered, but, re-enforcements arriving, they renewed the attack with great vigor but they had met the Pennsylvania Reserves and any advantage they got they were to fight for.

General's Reynolds and Meade were constantly with the line under the heaviest fire, encouraging the men and doing all they could to save the day. While our division was holding its own on this part of the field, our army was being flanked and our communications threatened. Our troops had been marching for many days on half rations and had been fighting for two days. When the break occurred in the lines they did not rally with any spirit. Our division continued to hold their ground until their ammunition was about all used up, when we got orders to fall back, which was done in good order; we supposed we were to be relieved to get a fresh supply of ammunition, and as we fell back were surprised that we did not meet the troops coming to take our place, not until we came out into the open country and saw the grand stampede, did the men of our division know that our army had suffered a terrible defeat. In good order and with ranks unbroken our brigade marched into camp near Centreville that night. This was the first sight we had of a routed and demoralized army, and no one will ever want to witness such a sight the second time. All night long could be heard men calling out the name and number of their companies and regiments. Some shameful scenes were witnessed, the greatest confusion and greatest fright was among the train men, drivers because so thoroughly panic-stricken that they would cut their harness, mount their horses or mules and ride off at full speed leaving their loads behind; it made no difference whether it was a load of wounded or dead or ammunition. This was not general. Among these could be seen the cool, calm teamster, working his way with his load through the crowd of men and wagons; a great many brave men drove teams that day, and deserve praise for their service. One of the mistakes many officers made was to select the very poorest men they had for extra duty, the reason for this in most cases was that good brave soldiers did not want those places while those least fitted to fill them were continually applying for them. None but the best soldiers should be put in charge of supply, or in fact any other train. The rebels did not follow this retreating army as closely as they might, yet when we take into consideration the severe duty Lee's army had performed and the terrible punishment that they suffered since the 26th of June, we can understand why they were well satisfied with the victory they had won. Had they followed up sharply they would have captured a great many prisoners. One writer claims that a vigorous pursuit by Lee that day would have driven the army across the Potomac; I do not believe one word of that. There was fight in the Army of the Potomac yet as the rebel found out at Chantilly the next day.

No. 17

On the morning of September 1st, we moved from Centerville; on the afternoon of that day, Lee attacked the right of the army, the most desperate effort was made by him to break the right wing and again throw the army into confusion. He was met by Hooker, McDowell and Reno, and Kearney's division of Heintzelman's corps. The fighting was terrific; in addition to the roar of musketry and artillery, the flashes of lightning and roar of thunder of a fearful thunder storm broke upon our ears. As we moved rapidly forward the battle was to our left, our pace was increased until we appeared to be directly opposite to the hardest fighting. Shells and solid shot were screaming through the air and tearing among the trees in the woods to our left. We received orders to move forward by line, facing to the left, and soon heard the zip of the minnies. Just then a wounded soldier, going to the rear, told us that the gallant Phil Kearney was killed. Major General Kearney was known all through the army as one of the best fighting Generals we had, and his death was felt by officers and men to be a very great loss just then. Soon we heard a cheer and recognizing the sound we knew, although we could not see our line, that success was ours, we were halted and marched out by the flank and resumed our march. Very soon we learned that another gallant Major General had been slain, Isaac I. Stevens. These two men whom the army could ill afford to lose, had been killed in the front of the battle, nobly striving to retrieve the misfortunes of the previous days fighting. The victory was a very decisive one, but the price paid for it was a fearful draft upon the army.

On the 2d of September, we camped near Arlington, on the Alexandria and Columbia pike. On the 4th, we marched to Munson's hill, where we went into camp.

The loss of the six companies, numbering perhaps 150 to 180 men was about thirty, of whom five were killed.

Was General Pope properly sustained by the corps commanders? Did the Army of the Potomac and its General render all the assistance they could? General Pope in his official report says:

"On the morning of the 30th, as may be supposed, our troops, who had been so continually marching and fighting for so many days, were in a state of great exhaustion. They had had little to eat for two days previous, and the artillery and cavalry horses had been in harness and saddle continually for ten days, and had had no forage for two days previous. It may easily be imagined how little these troops, after such severe labor, and after undergoing such hardships and privations, were in no condition for active and efficient service. I had telegraphed to the General-in-Chief on the 28th our condition, and had begged of him to have rations and forage sent forward to us from Alexandria with all dispatch. I also called his attention to the imminent need of cavalry horses to enable the cavalry belonging to the army to perform any service whatever.

About daylight on the 30th, I received a note from General Franklin, herewith appended, written by direction of General McClellan, and dated at eight o'clock the evening before, informing me that rations and forage would be loaded into the available wagons and cars at Alexandria as soon as I would send back a cavalry escort to bring out the trains. Such a letter, when we were fighting the enemy, and Alexandria was swarming with troops, needs no comment. Bad as was the condition of our cavalry, I was in no situation to spare troops from the front, nor could they have gone to Alexandrria and returned within the time by which we must have had provisions or have fallen back in the direction of Washington; nor do I yet see what services cavalry could have rendered in guarding railroad trains.

It was not until I received this letter that I began to feel discouraged and nearly hopeless of any successful issue to the operations with which I was charged; but I felt it to be my duty, notwithstanding the desperate condition of my command, from great fatigue, from want of provisions and forage, and from the small hope that I had of any effective assistance from Alexandria, to hold my position at all hazards and under all privations, unless overwhelmed by the superior forces of the enemy."

In the same report General Pope places the strength of his command on the morning of the 30th at forty thousand men, as follows: McDowells corps, including Pennsylvania Reserves, twelve thousand men; Sigel's corps, seven thousand men; Reno's corps, seven thousand men; Heintzelman's corps seven thousand men; Porter's corps, seven thousand men. Bank's corps, five thousand men, as at Bristoe Station guarding trains. Pope had been successful in the West, and against his wish, had been called East. After this unfortunate campaign he was relieved of the command at his own request and returned to the West. The four companies which had been detached from our regiment, and had went through a brilliant campaign in the Valley of Virginia, rejoined the regiment just after the second Bull Run battle. Col. Kane did not return with them; on the 7th of September he was made a Brigadier General and assigned to the command of a brigade in the Twelfth Corps. Our next paper will begin the history of the campaign of the four companies, after they left us at Falmouth.

On the 7th of September, we broke camp at Munson's hill, crossed the long bridge and marched through Washington to Meridan hill, where we went into camp. Our division had now been assigned to the First Army Corps which was under the command of Major General Hooker. The army was again put under the command of General McClellan, who was cheered by the troops whenever he made his appearance. The army that crossed the Potomac had regained the morale which distinguished it on the Peninsula. No one unfamiliar with its history during the past two months would have supposed it had suffered several defeats and had twice been forced from the offensive to the defensive, and had several times barely escaped destruction, and had once been driven from the field completely routed. General Lee finding that he could not capture the army, and knowing full well that delay would strengthen the Union army, determined to cross the Potomac and invade the North. He accordingly commenced to cross his army on the 4th, at a point near Poolesville, in Maryland. At Meridian hill we drew clothing, rations and ammunition. The regiment re-united, and, though greatly reduced in numbers, and recovered from the severe service they had seen during the month of August. The joy with which the men greeted each other when the four companies returned, showed how strong the ties were which bound them together as one family. Many sad tales were to be told, many noble men were missed, many manly tears were shed as the story of how a comrade fell fighting in the fore front of battle, was told. During this march we heard of Major Stone and Captain Wistar raising two regiments at home in old Pennsylvania, to be called the "Bucktail Avengers;" the regiments were the 149th and 150th Penn'a Volunteers, and were commanded by Colonel Roy Stone and Colonel Langhorn Wistar. They however soon found out that the old regiment was on hand and engaged in the avenging business on their own account. Many of the companies of these regiments were raised in the same counties from which the companies of our regiment came, and our relatives, in many cases our brothers, had joined them.

On the 8th of September we marched to Brookville, Maryland, from there we made easy marches and arrived at Monocacy Creek near Frederick city on the 12th. On that day we bade good bye to General Reynolds, who had been called to Pennsylvania to take command of the Militia called out to resist the invasion of our State. During the day we were filed off into a field where General Reynolds made us a short speech, telling us how sorry he was that he had to leave us just on the eve of a great battle, he said he would see if there was any fight in the militia and if he could get them into action we would hear from him. We knew full well that if any one could he would. To part with Reynolds at that time and under the circumstances was a sore trial to the Reserves, the men of the division had learned to love him, he was an ideal soldier. Gen. Geo. G. Meade, then commanding our brigade, took command of the division and General Seymore succeeded Meade in command of the brigade. On the 13th we crossed the Monocacy creek and marched toward Frederick City. On the morning of the 14th we marched through that place.

For the first time the Army of the Potomac are marching through a country where a large number of the citizens are friendly to the cause for which that army has so freely shed patriotic blood; the invasion of Maryland, by the rebel army, means a great deal to the citizens of that state, they are not ignorant of the terrible devastation which necessarily follows an army, some of them at least have seen the farms of Virginia laid waste by friend and foe; many citizens were converted to the Union cause by Lee's unfortunate movement. Our army was held under the strictest discipline. All property was respected and the severest punishment was promised to any Union soldier who disobeyed orders. The good citizens of Frederick City and other towns hailed our approach with demonstrations of joy. There was considerable rebel element to be found; it did not require much astuteness to discover who they were; the long face, the closed blind and the sullen silence marked the rebel sympathizer. Many acts of kindness by the ladies, and kind words of sympathy and encouragement to our sick recalled mother, sister and home. Many a "God bless you" is recorded above that was not heard on earth. We shall have more to say on this subject in a future number.

As the writer was with the six companies on the Peninsula, he must depend on comrades who were in the "Valley campaign" for the main facts of that part of our history; these are promised, should they not reach us in time for next week they will appear the week following.

No. 18

On Sunday morning, September 14th, 1862, our Division broke camp and marched out the Frederick and Hagerstown turnpike. Seven miles from Frederick we passed through Midletown, a short distance beyond the town we were filed off into a field, where the men made some coffee and ate their dinners. We were in plain view of South Mountain, which, at this point, rises to a height or elevation of about 1,000 feet. As you approach the main ridge you meet parallel ridges or rather a succession of hills broken up by deep ravines, in many places the sides being very steep. These may very properly be called the foot hills, and, with South Mountain rising high above these with a straight outline against the sky, presented a most formidable obstacle in our way and a grand defensive position.

The practiced eye of the old soldier soon took in the situation, and we quietly counted the cost of carrying that mountain against an enemy that possessed both courage and skill, the Artillery firing on our left had been coming closer, and the troops moving backwards and forwards getting position in line, gave evidence that a hard battle would be fought right here. It was a matter of great surprise to the Bucktails that they should be laying quiet while all these preparations were going on. Occasionally you would hear, "wonder if we are to be held in reserve," or "why don't Meade give us a chance." While the men were speculating on the strange conduct, that would leave the Pennsylvania Reserves in so comfortable a position, the order came to 'fall in' and when we marched a short distance out the Hagerstown road were turned square to the right and marched about one mile down a road running parallel with the South Mountain, when we faced to the left and moved in line of battle toward the mountain. Our Division formed the extreme right of the army and in line the Bucktails were the extreme right of our Division. We were to assult the enemy, and, if possible, turn their left flank. As we moved in line and soon as we came in view of the summit of the mountain, from which we had been hidden by he ridge running parallel with the road, the enemy opened on us with their Artillery from the top of the mountain, their sharpshooters also commenced to fire upon us from their position behind the succession of hills, which were also heavily timbered, forming excellent cover for a line of skirmishers.

As soon as the enemy's skirmishers opened up in earnest the Bucktails were deployed and went forward, calling forth a wicked fire, their usual tactics were resorted to, every man hunting cover when he could get it, and the most exposed parts of the line were left open; from behind cover, trees, rocks and depressions in the ground, our boys opened a rapid fire with their Sharps rifles which was kept up for several minutes, when, with a cheer which was started on the right of the line, we rushed forward and drove the enemy from their first line; back evidently upon a line in reserve and posted in a much stronger position near the base of the mountain. A rib-like line of rocks here formed a natural defense and from its irregular line and elevated position the enemy could command any part of our line, in fact, the position was much stronger than any line of earthworks could make it; when we reached this point we had passed beyond the range of the Artillery which now only fired on occasional shot that passed away over our heads, we had carried two of the ridges running along the base of the mountains by desperate fighting, but our advance was now checked by a most terrific fire and we knew the rebels were largely reinforced.

The terrific roar of musketry was the music General Seymour, commanding our brigade, was waiting for and he gave the order fort the Brigade to move forward, he rode ahead, found Colonel McNeil, and together, under the hottest fire, they rode along our line encouraging the men, when they came to Company K. General Seymour said "go in boys, we will take that mountain." When we took in the situation we almost despaired of being able to dislodge the foe from a position naturally so strong; we felt that if the situation was reversed, no foe could capture us, but there was no hesitancy or faltering on the part of our boys, they were fighting with a determination to win if human efforts could wring success from the unfavorable circumstances surrounding us. Just as we came in sight of the base of the mountain, and before we reached the line to which the rebel skirmishers had fallen back, a drove of colts and calves came running toward us, when they saw our line they turned and ran back, we watched them with great curiosity being anxious to see what they would do between the lines.

The ground, at this point, affording the boys partial shelter, we took advantage of it and poured our fire, at short range with telling effect, the rebels were armed with muzzle-loaders and those behind trees were more or less exposed while loading, the Bucktails were taking deliberate aim at these exposed portions of their persons, and, while holding our position here against a line of battle, our line came up. As it was the practice of our regiment to move forward with the line after the battle had been fairly opened, by us as skirmishers, were deployed in a single line at intervals of from ten to twenty feet. The Eleventh regiment came up behind Company K., and, when they reached our line, they opened fire. The shouts of the men and the roar of the musketry was almost deafening; the lines were not more than fifty to one hundred yards apart. The color bearer of the Eleventh regiment, was shot and one of the color Corporals instantly grabbed the flag but had hardly raised it from the ground when he, too, was shot, the third suffered the same fate, when the fourth bravely grasped the staff, Lieutenant J. M. Welch, of the Bucktails, who was close by, told him to let it lay that there was no use sacrificing life unnecessarily. The fight at this time, on account of our exposed position and the cover the foe had, was against us. Captain E. A. Irvin, of the Bucktails, realizing that we were losing a great many men and that to remain where we were only made it a matter of time when the enemy would destroy us, determined to make a desperate charge on their position. Stepping out in front of the line he turned around facing it and waiving his sword shouted, "forward Bucktails, and let us drive them from their position!" The boys sprang forward with a cheer followed by the Eleventh regiment. The gallant Captain Irvin had not time to again turn around before he fell shot in the head. He was sent back to the rear insensible, his loss seemed to fill the men with desperation, and they made an irresistible rush upon the enemy, capturing a great many prisoners and killing and wounding many more, they did not stop here but with cheers charged on up the mountain after the retreating enemy, who kept up a running fire but with little effect as they seemed to be completely terror-stricken and their bullets nearly all passed over our heads, on up the mountain, which in places was so steep as to be difficult of ascent, on we went capturing prisoners, taking advantage of every opportunity to pour a deadly fire into the broken and scattered line. Our breech-loading rifles gave us a very decided advantage, as we did not have to halt to reload, but kept right on to the surprise of the rebels who could not understand it. At the summit the rebels attempted to make a stand and had brought up fresh troops but the right of our line had pushed forward and was doubling their line and threatening their rear, their resistance to the enthusiastic line, that had driven them up the mountain, did not amount to much, we were continually capturing prisoners and sending them back. When we reached the summit a deafening cheer was started on our right, and, like a great wave of joy, was taken up by regiment after regiment along the line of the Brigade, to the Division, through the Corps. On, on, until a hundred thousand voices were proclaiming our victory.

We pursued the enemy until dark when we dropped upon the field to take a much needed rest. After the excitement of the battle had passed away the unusual exertion put forth climbing the mountain, left the men completely exhausted, and tired natures sweet restorer was welcomed as never before.

Colonel McNeil was present everywhere on the line watching every movement. Adjutant W. R. Hartshorn was also seen as he moved backward and forward along the line. Lieutenant Charles Bitterling, of Company F., killed; Captain E. A. Irvin, of Company K., and Lieutenant S. A. Mack, of Company E., wounded, were the only casualities among the officers.

The drove of colts and calves mentioned were entirely lost sight of, the attention of the men being called to objects of deeper interest. Just before the desperate and successful charge by our line, a rebel sharp-shooter, who had sent a bullet through the coat of another, when the attention of private DeBeck, of Company G., Bucktails, was called to it. He said "I will get that fellow," and, taking cover from a raise in the ground, he approached cautiously until he got close to the enemy's line where he waited quietly until a puff of white smoke from the tree top located the position of the sharpshooter, DeBeck then raised up, and, just as he was taking aim, the rebel finding that he was discovered sang out, "don't shoot I will come down and surrender." DeBeck replied, "don't put yourself to that trouble," then took deliberate aim and fired and the lifeless body came tumbling down through the limbs.

At one point on the left of Company K. a squad of the Company had pushed ahead to get under cover but found the enemy too strong and had to fall back to the line. One of the party, Manning S. Dunn, told the boys when they got back that he had shot a rebel over seven feet long, who had rushed out and demanded his surrender, and that he fell forward down the hill after he (Dunn) had shot him. When our line charged forward, Dunn's comrades found the long rebel just as Dunn had told them he fell.

On the top of the mountain, just over the crest, was a small field in which there was a stack of hay. Here rebels were behind it and were keeping up a fire at our boys who were behind trees close by the fence. French Frank concluded to use a little strategy and capture the whole lot. By pushing his cap out past the tree he would draw their fire, in this way he kept on until he was satisfied that all their guns were empty, when he made a rush upon them with fixed bayonet and bagged his game, Frank formed them in line in front of him and marched them back, meeting General Meade he sang out, "General see ze d---n rebels, caught zem behind straw stack!" The General told Frank to take them back and turn them over to the Provost Marshal, when Frank asked, "where is ze Provost Marshal?" just down at the foot of the mountain the General answered. "General, I so tired I cannot go down ze big hill, so nearly done for." General Meade smilingly replied, "turn them over to some of those stragglers, and let them take them back," he then asked Frank if there were any more rebels out front, and Frank said, "by gollee, General, capture whole lot more so soon I get out there." Frank did not forget his treatment when a prisoner and upon a slight provocation would have shot these prisoners, one of them, as he was taking them back, did attempt to get away when Frank drew up his gun and told him to come back. "I not run after you, I shoot you dead, I not like you anyhow." The prisoner took the hint, returned and marched quietly back.

No pen can tell the satisfaction our boys felt at the result of this days fight; after the route at Bull Run and the reports of a certain class of newspapers that magnified the defeat, and told a shameful story of utter demoralization of our army, and this in the face of the brilliant victory at Chantilly, had created a desire in our army for an opportunity to prove that they still retained the fighting qualities that had distinguished them at Mechanicsville, Gaines Mills, New Market Cross roads and Malvern Hill. How nobly they sustained that reputation.

The visitor to the scene of the battle of South Mountain as he approaches from Middletown on being told that our army had driven Lee's army from the foot hills up and over the mountain would involuntarily exclaim, impossible.

Our hospitals were established in Middletown where the good citizens threw open their houses and gave every attention to our wounded, every luxury the country afforded, prepared in that manner most tempting to the appetite was bountifully supplied, and many a poor boy, while dreaming of home, mother and sister, had his eyes closed in death by the kind hand of one of Middletown's noble women; fair girls and kind faced mothers did all they could to alleviate their suffering.

A great many wounded Confederates were here lying, side by side, with those with whom they had been engaged in deadly conflict, a good feeling was maintained and many good jokes passed between these grim and blood stained soldiers.

(NOTE.—We hope to be able to give a history of the campaign of the four Companies, C., G., H., and I., that were detached but have not up to this time received the information necessary.)

No. 19

The loss of the regiment in the battle of South Mountain was one officer and fifteen men killed and two officers and forty-five men wounded, total sixty-three.

On the morning of the 15th of September the troops were called into line very early, a dense fog enveloped the mountain completely shutting from our view the position of the enemy. Skirmish lines were formed and moved forward cautiously. They expected to encounter the enemy, and it was some time before the Bucktails realized that Lee had quietly retreated during the night. General Pleasanton's Cavalry was pushed ahead and overtook the Cavalry rear guard of the enemy in Boonsboro, a small town some five miles from the South Mountain battlefield. General Pleasanton charged upon the rebels and drove them through the town, capturing a great many prisoners, two pieces of Artillery, and killed and wounded a great many. The enemy had taken up a position on the west side of Antietam creek. Our Division moved through Boonsboro on out the Williamsport road.

General McClellan, in his official report, says: "My plan for the impending engagement was to attack the enemy's left with the Corps of Hooker and Mansfield, supported by Sumner's, and if necessary by Franklin's; and, as soon as matters looked favorable there, to move the Corps of Burnside against the enemy's extreme right, upon the ridge running to the south and rear of Sharpsburg, and having carried this position, to press along the crest towards our right; and whenever either of these flank movements should be successful, to advance our centre with all the forces then disposable."

Hooker's Corps was on the right, Meade's Division, of Pennsylvania Reserves, formed the right of the Corps and the Bucktails were on the right of the Division.

The afternoon of the 15th, and the forenoon of the 16th, were occupied in getting in position of the enemy. About two o'clock, in the afternoon of Tuesday, September 16th, our Division led the advance of Hooker's Corps, on the Williamsport road, after crossing Antietam creek, turned to the left, and moved in the direction of Sharpsburg. A body of Cavalry, which was in the lead, encountered the enemy in a strip of woods in front of the now famous Dunkard church. They reported to General Meade that a strong force of Infantry, supported by Artillery, were immediately in our front. General Meade directed Colonel McNeil to deploy the Bucktails as skirmishers and to advance and occupy the piece of woods in our front. In the meantime the Division was formed in line of battle and everything gotten in readiness to follow up and take advantage of any success the line of skirmishers should win.

The Bucktail's line was to charge across an open field in plain view of the Division, and, when the signal was given, the men responded with a will, they were soon met by a murderous volley of Infantry from their front while a battery of Artillery, on their right, raked their line with shell, grape and canister. They, however, got within seventy-five yards of the woods, when the fire getting too heavy, they threw themselves flat upon the ground and opened up a terrible fire from their Sharps rifles. While they were in this position General Seymour, who was only waiting for the skirmishers to reach the woods to order the Brigade to charge, was sitting on his horse in the rear of the line when an aid is said to have rode up to him and reported: "General, they have opened a Battery of ten pounders on the right of the Bucktails." The General quietly replied; "Well you don't suppose they can scare a Bucktail with a ten pounder, do you?" The Bucktails continued to pour their destructive fire into the woods for fifteen or twenty minutes, when the word was passed along the line, both ways from the centre, to charge the woods, night was just beginning to cast her sable garment over the blood-stained earth as a shrill cheer gave the rebels warning that the Bucktails were upon them. The skirmishers reached the fence, just on the edge of the woods and behind which the front line of rebels were posted, where a struggle for the fence ensued, the cheers from the Brigade now advancing rapidly to their support, inspired them with a determination to enter the woods before the line came up. The fence soon disappeared and a roaring cheer announced to the troops, in their rear, that they had gained their object. The firing had not ceased, but the Bucktails were now on equal grounds, they were protected by trees as well as their enemy. By the time the line came up it was quite dark and the location of the men could only be determined by the stream of fire from the muzzle of the guns, this was kept up for some time with the lines only a few yards apart, when the firing ceased. Demands to surrender could be heard from both sides. When a soldier, on either side, would call upon the soldier in his front to surrender his voice would locate him and call upon him the fire of those on either flank. A constant watchfulness was kept up all through that long night. Our line had barely penetrated the woods and that there was to be some hard fighting in the morning was well known to every soldier on that field. Thus far our line had been successful, but, at a fearful cost, for in the charge on the woods the loss of the Bucktails was two officers and twenty-eight men killed and sixty-five officers and men wounded.

During the night General Seymour reported that "his men were lying feet to feet with the rebels, and that the battle must begin as soon as it became light enough to distinguish friend from foe."

The Pennsylvania Reserves had not had anything to eat since noon on the day before, and, as they would necessarily have to open the battle the next morning, General Hooker determined to have them relieved early in the day, and with this object in view he reported the situation to General McClellan, who directed Mansfield's Corps to move up during the night to a position about one mile in the rear of Hooker's Corps, to be ready to relieve these troops at the earliest opportunity.

The battle opened the next morning, Wednesday September 17th, just as soon as the watchful soldier could distinguish objects in the forest, there was no preliminary to this battle, but with greatest fury the contest was brought on by the firing of one rifle, whose owner peering through the mist, discovered the outline of an enemy's form and sped a death-dealing missile on its short but certain errand, in an instant every man was awake to the importance of the first advantage that could be wrested from the foe, and the stubborn resistance of the rebels to our furious attacks, gave proof that he who fought longest and best would be victor.

While our Division scored the opening we were not alone engaged, with daylight, even above the roar of musketry we could hear the roar of Artillery on our left. The Pennsylvania Reserves, as was stated before, had not eaten anything since noon the day before, and, they knowing the circumstances which made it necessary for them to fight and not eat, without a murmur rushed on the foe, inch by inch the rebels contested that field, but they were finally driven from the woods, our troops closely pursuing them, when they reached a corn field, through the centre of which ran a ridge or elevated ground. Behind this ridge was a reserve line which met our now thinned line and forced it back. General Meade saw this and directed a Battery, which was situated on our right, to open on the advancing column, the fire of the Battery, which was well directed, cut great gaps in their ranks and arrested their advance. Here, in this cornfield, was fought one of the most stubborn contests of the war, for hours the battle raged without cessation, while thus hotly engaged the cry rang out through our regiment our ammunition will soon be exhausted, details from each Company were sent back in great haste to bring up fresh supplies. General Hooker had been wounded and Meade was in command of the Corps, Seymour of the Division, the brave Colonel McNeil, of the Bucktails, had been killed and the regiment though nominally in command of Captain Magee, the senior officer, was really being directed by Adjutant W. Ross Hartshorn. The battle continued with unabated fury until 2 o'clock, p.m., when Sumner's Corps relieved our troops and the Pennsylvania Reserves were formed on the ridge in the rear of the cornfield, where they were supplied with ammunition. The arrival of Sumner's troops was most opportune as in less than ten minutes the Reserves would have been entirely out of ammunition, for only a few of those sent back had found the ammunition wagon and returned. The Pennsylvania Reserves were not again taken into action, but were allowed to take a much needed rest.

The total loss in killed and wounded, on the 16th and 17th, was one hundred and ten. Colonel Hugh McNeil fell in the front urging his men forward, Lieutenant William Allison, of Company B., was also killed and Lieutenant Frank Bell, of Company I. and Lieutenant Jas. M. Welch, of Company K., were wounded.

The loss of the regiment, in the death of Colonel McNeil at that time, cannot be fully appreciated by the readers of this history. Captain Dennis Magee was the senior officer left, Major Roy Stone had resigned to accept the Colonelcy of 149th Pa. Vols., Captain Holland's place had not been filled, Captain Wistar, of Company B., had resigned to accept the Colonelcy of the 150th Pennsylvania Volunteers, Captain Gifford of Company C., had been wounded, Captain Jewett, of Company D., had been sent to general hospital from the Peninsula and had not returned, Captain Niles, of Company E., was taken prisoner on the Peninsula and had not returned. Captain Magee was unfit to command a regiment and would not give way to the only Captain besides himself left in the regiment, Captain Hugh McDonald, of Company G. Adjutant W. Ross Hartshorn was again called to the Signal Corps which left us in even worse condition, as he was able to keep Magee within bounds.

No. 20

After the battle of Antietam our Division went into camp near Sharpsburg. The army was poorly supplied with clothing, rations, and camp equipments. No soldier of the Army of the Potomac can look back on the two months following that battle without a sense of relief that it is all past and that the deprivations of that time are never, in their life, to be repeated.

Since the 26th of June the records of the regiments had been sadly neglected, all these had to be overhauled, and, in many cases, the Company books had been lost with much valuable information that can never be replaced. Our regiment, by reason of an incompetent commander, was in a most unfortunate situation. Generals Reynolds and Meade were never in favor of the method of electing officers by a vote of the men, and since Company officers had been elected, who could neither read or write, they forbid by general order, the holding of elections for that purpose. The Governor could not commission officers for our Division except they were elected by a vote of the Company or regiment. As has often been stated we had been very fortunate in our regimental officers, at this time, under the command of Captain Magee, a man who was not respected even in his own Company we earned to appreciate more highly our old commanders.

At one time while we lay in this camp there were only three commissioned officers on duty in the regiment. Most all the Companies were commanded by Sergeants. General Meade, knowing our situation, realized the importance of a change in the commanding officer. To avoid the order referred to and to meet the requirements of the law he permitted a petition to be circulated in the regiment, asking that Capt. Chas. F. Taylor, of Company H., be commissioned Colonel, Captain E. A. Irvin, of Company K., Lieutenant-Colonel, Adjutant W. R. Hartshorn, Major. This petition was signed by nearly all the men present.

Some of the men objected to the appointment of Hartshorn over Captain A. E. Niles and Hugh McDonald. This petition was approved by General Seymour and Meade and forwarded to the Governor, but the commissions were not made out until the next Spring. This act of gross injustice to men who were not only worthy of this promotion but who had fairly earned it and were justly entitled to this recognition, is one of those unfortunate orphans that has failed to find its father.

Our regimental drills were the attraction, and, when the Bucktails were taken out to the drill ground, all the sick and extra duty men were sure to be on hand. Captain Magee had picked up an old horse somewhere that was neither handsome or swift of foot. The Captain's favorite movement was the bayonet charge, and, when he got tangled up in the mysteries of battalion evolutions, he would give the command, "charge bayonets, forward double-quick, march!" and he invariably rode in front of the line.

One day the men having got tired of this so often repeated movement, concluded to vary the execution, they, at the command march, started on a run and prodded the old horse clear across the large field in which we were drilling, paying no attention to the oft repeated command to halt. At the farther side of the field there was quite a sharp raise in the ground, and, just at the top of this, was a high fence, the men were out of breath by the time they reached the fence and were glad to halt. The entire Brigade had halted to see the show and encourage the boys with cheers. As soon as the line halted, Captain Magee gave the command, "about face, charge bayonets, double-quick march! Now, d---n yees, I've got yees." His commands and his field lectures were as good as a minstrel show. Many of his commands were entirely original, and his pure Irish wit, of which he had an unlimited fund drew a "full house" every time.

While we lay in camp the papers at home were filled with complaints at McClellan's inactivity and the government repeatedly urged upon him the necessity of moving before the enemy would recuperate their wasted strength, both in men and materials. Lee's army was in a rich farming district, a region which could furnish subsistence for some time and the President and his Cabinet were anxious that the immense supplies of that region should be consumed by our army instead of the enemy.

McClellan had received considerable reinforcement, and ample time had been given him to thoroughly equip his troops. Notwithstanding all this there was a sad lack of organization, the Quarter-master and Commissary departments seemed to be without a competent head, rations and clothing were scarce in the army, while the depots at Washington were full. General McClellan, when urged to move, made this an excuse, and was repeatedly informed that both subsistence and quartermaster supplies would be sent him at any time he would make his requisitions for them. Much precious time was wasted. On the 1st of October, President Lincoln visited the army and reviewed the troops. On the 6th of October General Halleck sent the following order to General McClellan:

> "I am instructed to telegraph you as follows: The President directs that you cross the Potomac and give battle to the enemy, or drive him South. Your army must move now while the roads are good. If you cross the river between the enemy and Washington, and cover the latter by your operation, you can be reinforced with 30,000 men. If you move up the valley of the Shenandoah, not more than 12,000 or 15,000 can be sent to you. The President advises the interior line between Washington and the enemy, but does not order it. He is very desirous that your army move as soon as possible. You will immediately report what line you adopt and where you intend to cross the river; also to what point the reinforcements are to be sent. It is necessary that the plan of your operations be positively determined on before orders are given for building bridges and repairing railroads. I am directed to add that the Secretary of War and the general-in-chief fully concur with the President in these instructions."

On the 10th of October the rebel General, J.E.B. Stuart, crossed the Potomac at McCoy's Ferry with two thousand Cavalry and one light Battery of Artillery, crossed the railroad, between Harrisburg and Chambersburg, burned the railroad buildings and captured a large quantity of government clothing. After doing what damage they could they rejoined Lee's army crossing the river at White's ford without losing a man.

On Sunday morning (the reader will notice how frequently important movements were commenced on Sunday) October 26th, the Pennsylvania Reserves left their camp at Sharpsburg and camped that night near South Mountain. The army commenced to cross the Potomac on the 26th at Berlin and Harper's Ferry. The Reserves crossed at the latter place on the 30th of October, camping that night at Lovetsville. We marched slowly up the Loudon Valley to Warrenton. General Lee, from the leisurely manner in which the Army of the Potomac moved, had ample time to gather up all the forage in the rich valleys that abound in that portion of Virginia. With an immense train of cattle, and an army that had fattened on the country for over a month, he was in excellent condition to undertake an active campaign.

Not caring to risk his valuable stores in a battle with an army that had been largely reinforced since it had defeated him, he leisurely fell back toward Culpepper. The Cavalry had frequent skirmishes during the march up the valley, but the Reserves were not engaged, or did they have an opportunity to shoot at a rebel until they came to Warrenton, November the 6th.

When about one mile from the town the Division, which was marching left in front that day, was halted and opened ranks, the Bucktails being in the rear, were ordered to the front on double-quick, and, when they got to the head of the column, they learned that a body of the enemy occupied the town of Warrenton which is situated on high ground. One half of the regiment was deployed as skirmishers and charged forward, they soon discovered that there was only a small body of Cavalry there, and, after a few shots, they retreated through the town. The skirmishers were called in and the Bucktails led the column once more through that beautiful but intensely rebel town.

On the 7th of November, and while we were camped near Warrenton, General McClellan was relieved of the command of the army and General A. E. Burnside appointed to succeed him. This change of commanders was not only a surprise to the rank and file, but met with their bitter disapproval. General Halleck was severely censured and the Secretary of War came in for a full share. The selection of Burnside was a surprise to the men, he had been with the Army of the Potomac but a short time and was not so well known as many others, such as Sumner, Heintzelman, Franklin or Hooker.

During our march the same orders that were in force on the Peninsula were re-issued, we were not permitted to disturb the property along the route, not even to the burning of a rail to make coffee. One night the regiment was halted in a field four or five hundred yards from a strip of woods, when we filed off into the field the men sang out: "Take us to the woods where we can get wood to make coffee." It was no use, however, and as soon as the guns were stacked a rush was made for the nearest fence which was soon in the arms of men who had determined they would not suffer in order to spare the property of rebels.

Captain Magee made frantic efforts to prevent the burning of the rails but in vain; before an hour there was scarcely enough rails left on that farm to make coffee in the morning. Just back of Warrenton, where the Bucktails were on picket, General Meade rode along the line, when he came to Company F. he saw the Orderly Sergeant, Ernest Wright, chasing a pig. The General commanded him to halt but Wright was after some fresh meat and paid no attention to the command. General Meade rode up to him and asked him if he knew he was disobeying orders. The sergeant told him he knew very well that he was, but that he had but little respect for orders that required him to go hungry to guard the property of the enemy. General Meade had him arrested. That evening he sent to regimental headquarters to ascertain the record of Sergeant Wright, and on learning that he was a brave and faithful soldier, he released him from arrest and ordered him to duty.

While we lay in camp at Warrenton, General Seymour was sent to South Carolina and Colonel St. Clair, of the Sixth regiment, succeeded him in command of the First Brigade. General Reynolds had returned after the Maryland campaign and was assigned to the command of the First Corps.

General Burnside's plan was to make a feint to cross the Rappahannock so as to convey the impression that he would move in the direction of Gordonsville, at the same time to rapidly move the main body of the army to Fredericksburg. He had organized the army into four grand Divisions. The first or right composed of the Sixth and Ninth Corps was commanded by General Sumner, the second or center composed of the Third and Fifth Corps was commanded by General Hooker, the third or left composed of the First and Sixth Corps was commanded by General Franklin, the fourth or reserve, the Eleventh, was commanded by General Segel.

On the 16th of November we commenced our march toward Falmouth marching by Bealton Station on the Orange and Alexandria railroad and Stafford Court House to Brook's Station on the Acquia Creek and Fredericksburg railroad, where we lay two or three days. While at this place Captain Chas. F. Taylor, had been exchanged, and Captain E. A. Irvin who had been wounded returned to the regiment, Captain Taylor, by direction of General Meade, took command of the regiment relieving Captain Magee his senior. The arrival of these officers was hailed by the men with delight. Captain Taylor in relieving Captain Magee relieved the men of the uncertainty of the result of an engagement of the regiment under the command of one in whom they had no confidence.

From the preparations going on we knew that a battle was soon to be fought, and when on the night of the 11th of December, we marched out to the heights overlooking Fredericksburg and saw our army in position and the army of Lee strongly fortified on the semi-circular ridge behind the city, we knew that a desperate struggle would ensue and that many a poor fellow would find his last resting place on the banks of the Rappahannock.

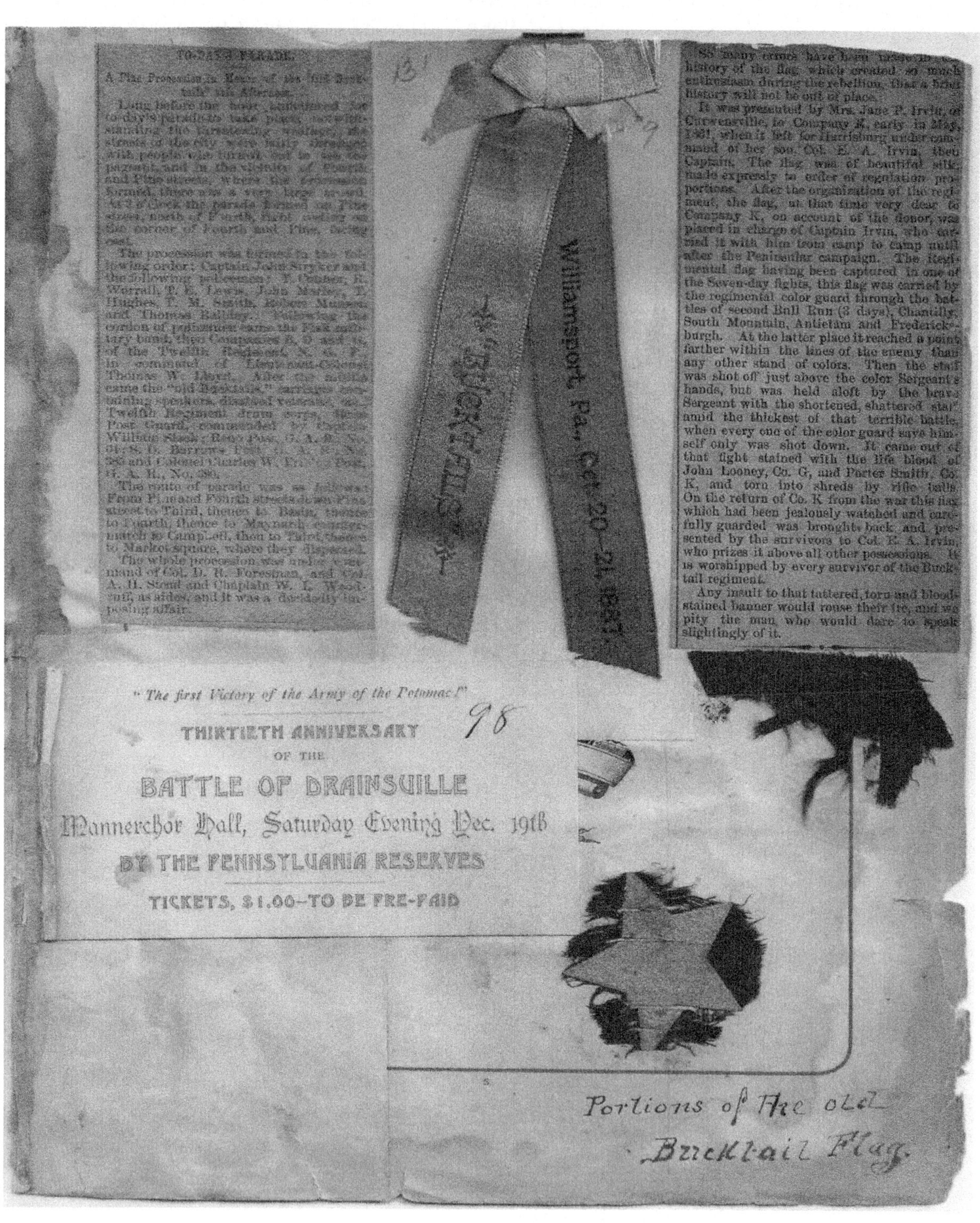

TO-DAY'S PARADE.

A Fine Procession in Honor of the 'Old Bucktails' this Afternoon.

Long before the hour announced for to-day's parade to take place, notwithstanding the threatening weather, the streets of the city were fairly thronged with people who turned out to see the pageant, and in the vicinity of Fourth and Pine streets, where the procession formed, there was a very large crowd. At 2 o'clock the parade formed on Pine street, north of Fourth, right resting on the corner of Fourth and Pine, facing east.

The procession was formed in the following order: Captain John Stryker and the following policemen: [illegible], R. Worrall, T. E. Lewis, John [illegible], T. Hughes, T. M. Smith, Robert [illegible] and Thomas [illegible]. Following the cordon of policemen came the Fisk military band, then Companies B, D and [illegible], of the Twelfth Regiment, N. G. P., in command of Lieutenant-Colonel Thomas W. Lloyd. After the militia came the "old Bucktails," carriages containing speakers, disabled veterans, etc., Twelfth Regiment drum corps, Reno Post Guard, commanded by Captain William Slack; Reno Post, G. A. R., No. 64; S. D. Barrows Post, G. A. R., No. [illegible] and Colonel Charles W. [illegible] Post, G. A. R., No. 36.

The route of parade was as follows: From Pine and Fourth streets down Pine street to Third, thence to Basin, thence to Fourth, thence to Maynard, countermarch to Campbell, then to Third, thence to Market square, where they dispersed.

The whole procession was under command of Col. D. R. Foresman, and Col. A. H. Stead and Chaplain W. L. Woodruff, as aides, and it was a decidedly imposing affair.

So many errors have been made in the history of the flag which created so much enthusiasm during the rebellion, that a brief history will not be out of place.

It was presented by Mrs. Jane P. Irvin, of Curwensville, to Company K, early in May, 1861, when it left for Harrisburg under command of her son, Col. E. A. Irvin, then Captain. The flag was of beautiful silk, made expressly to order of regulation proportions. After the organization of the regiment, the flag, at that time very dear to Company K, on account of the donor, was placed in charge of Captain Irvin, who carried it with him from camp to camp until after the Peninsular campaign. The Regimental flag having been captured in one of the Seven-day fights, this flag was carried by the regimental color guard through the battles of second Bull Run (3 days), Chantilly, South Mountain, Antietam and Fredericksburgh. At the latter place it reached a point farther within the lines of the enemy than any other stand of colors. Then the staff was shot off just above the color Sergeant's hands, but was held aloft by the brave Sergeant with the shortened, shattered staff amid the thickest of that terrible battle, when every one of the color guard save himself only was shot down. It came out of that fight stained with the life blood of John Looney, Co. G, and Porter Smith, Co. K, and torn into shreds by rifle balls. On the return of Co. K from the war this flag which had been jealously watched and carefully guarded was brought back and presented by the survivors to Col. E. A. Irvin, who prizes it above all other possessions. It is worshipped by every survivor of the Bucktail regiment.

Any insult to that tattered, torn and blood-stained banner would rouse their ire, and we pity the man who would dare to speak slightingly of it.

"The first Victory of the Army of the Potomac!"

THIRTIETH ANNIVERSARY

OF THE

BATTLE OF DRAINSVILLE

Mannerchor Hall, Saturday Evening Dec. 19th

BY THE PENNSYLVANIA RESERVES

TICKETS, $1.00—TO BE PRE-PAID

BUCKTAILS REUNION ITEMS
RAUCH'S SCRAPBOOK
Ronn Palm Collection

Ronn Palm Collection

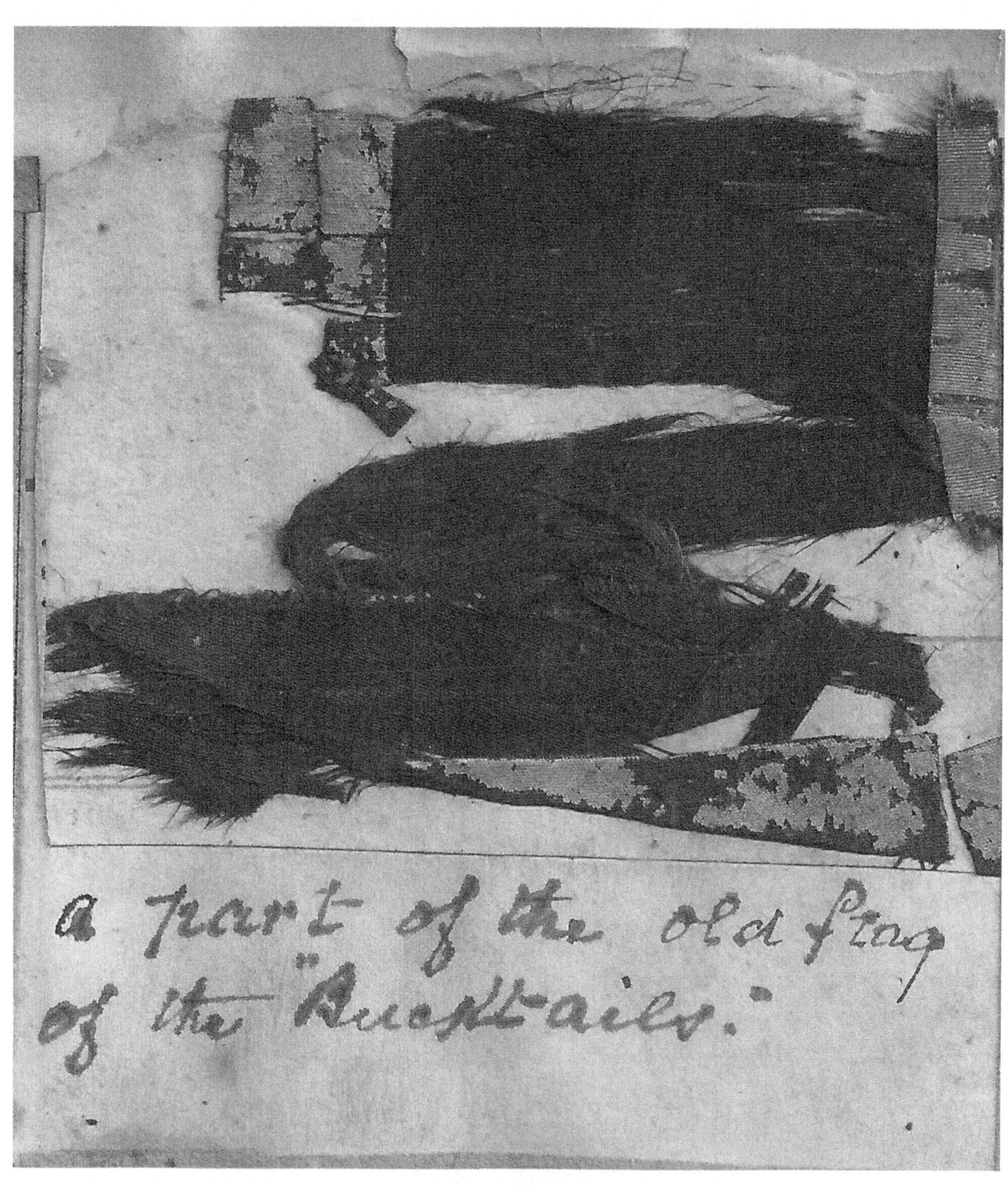

BUCKTAILS FLAG REMNANT
RAUCH'S SCRAPBOOK
Ronn Palm Collection

LT. COL. THOMAS L. KANE
42nd PA.
JUNE 13, 1861
Ronn Palm Collection

COL. CHARLES J. BIDDLE
42nd PA VOL. INF., 13th PA RES.
1st PA RIFLES; "BUCKTAILS"
Ronn Palm Collection

Ronn Palm Collection

CYRUS B. LOWER (SEE APPENDIX 'B')
CO. K. 42nd PA.
AWARDED MEDAL OF HONOR
ACTIONS AT THE WILDERNESS
Ronn Palm Collection

CYRUS B. LOWER
CO. K. 42nd PA.
AWARDED MEDAL OF HONOR
ACTIONS AT THE WILDERNESS
Ronn Palm Collection

1st SGT. THOMAS J. THOMPSON
CO. K, 42nd PA VOL. INFANTRY
13th PA RES.; "BUCKTAIL REG'T"
Ronn Palm Collection

LT. JOHN H. NORRIS
CO. K, 42nd PA VOL. INFANTRY
13th PA RES.; "BUCKTAIL REG'T"
Ronn Palm Collection

Ronn Palm Collection

SGT DANIEL BLETT CO. K
Ronn Palm Collection

1st Rifles, P. R. V. C. First Annual Re-union,

"BUCKTAILS." Williamsport, Pa., October 20th and 21st, 1887.

E.A. IRVIN
Clearfield County Historical Society

Clearfield County Historical Society

HON. JOHN PATTON
Clearfield County Historical Society

JAMES GLEN CO. K
Clearfield County Historical Society

JAMES GLEN POST WAR
Clearfield County Historical Society

JOHN ELLIOTT KRATZER
Clearfield County Historical Society

LT. DALE'S TOMBSTONE

SGT. JAMES F. ROSS
Clearfield County Historical Society

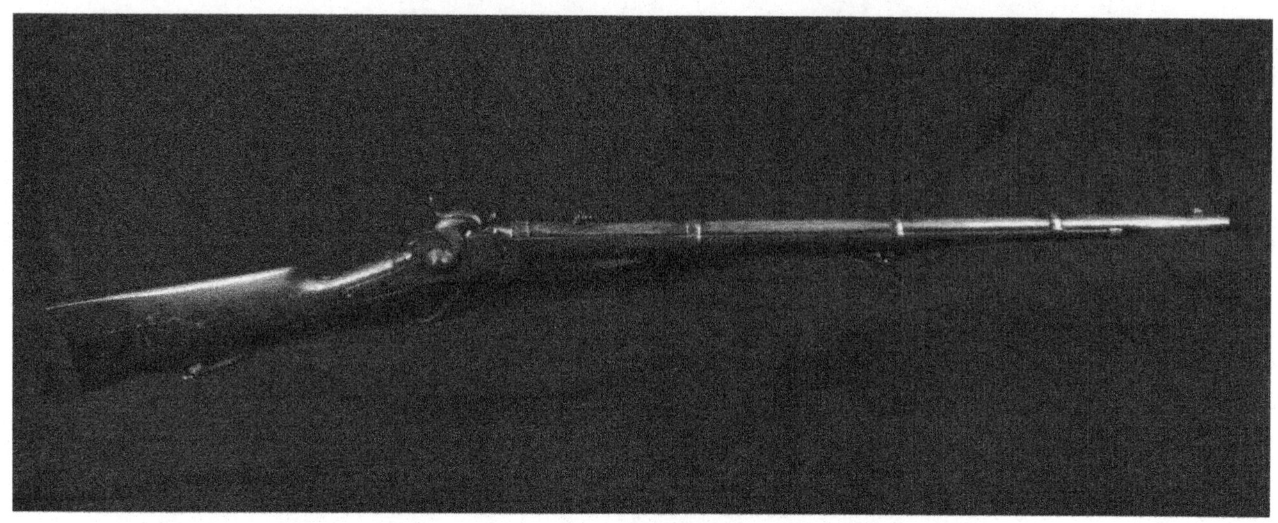

SHARPS RIFLE - SHAFFNER COLLECTION
Clearfield County Historical Society

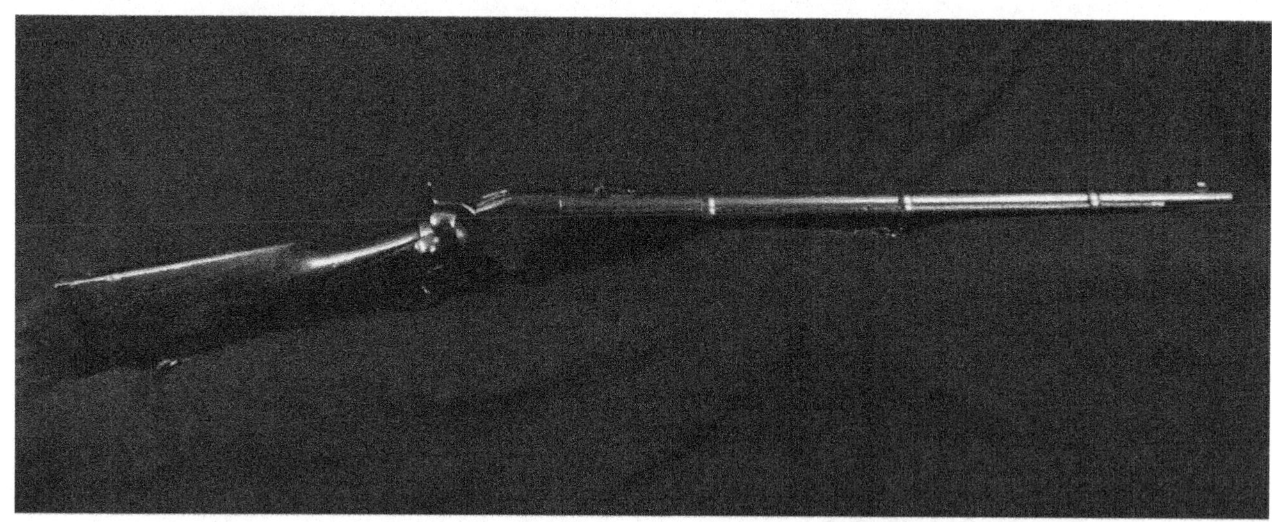

SPENCER RIFLE - SHAFFNER COLLECTION
Clearfield County Historical Society

This photograph was taken during a Bucktail reunion at Williamsport, in 1876. Seated from left to right: James Glenn, John Lemon, Edward A. Irvin, Cyrus Lower, William R. Hartshorne. Standing from left to right: Thomas Humphries, Zachariah Bailey, James Spence, and John Patton Bard.

No. 21

While we lay at Sharpsburg the 142nd and the 121st regiments, Pennsylvania Volunteers, were assigned to our Division, the 121st to our Brigade. These were new regiments and each had as many men for duty as one of our old Brigades. They were largely composed of young men and were very anxious to gain the favor of the old soldier; that they merited the highest praise the reader will soon be well satisfied.

As we lay on the height overlooking Fredericksburg, on the 12th of December, we saw the largest body of men preparing for battle we ever had a view of. The ground was so situated that from our position we could overlook perhaps one-half the Army of the Potomac. The rebel sharpshooters held the city and from the windows of the front row of houses they drove back our engineers every time they attempted to lay the pontoons. General Burnside had in position on the bluffs opposite Fredericksburg, one hundred and seventy-six pieces of Artillery, these were opened at one time, at the same time a party of volunteers crossed the river in boats and drove the rebel sharpshooters out of the houses near the river and the pontoons were soon laid.

In the meantime two pontoon bridges had been constructed by General Franklin near three miles below the city. On the lower bridge General Bayard crossed with his Brigade of Cavalry, which was immediately followed by our Division, which was to form the extreme left of the army. We moved rapidly down the river after crossing and took our position, the left of our regiment resting on the south bank of the river. We were shelled as we marched down, but did not encounter the enemy's Infantry.

By the time we got into position it was dark and we lay on our arms. This was Friday, December 12th, 1862. On the morning of the 13th of December, as soon as it was light our regiment, with the rest of the Brigade, were marched to our right down along our line of battle perhaps one-half a mile, when we were again formed in line of battle behind several Batteries already in position. We marched to this position under a heavy Artillery fire from several Batteries of the rebels which were in position in a woods some one thousand or twelve hundred yards from our line. Between these Batteries and our Batteries, which were in advance of our line perhaps two hundred yards, the rebels had a line of sharpshooters which were annoying our gunners. Our regiment was then moved forward in advance of the Batteries where a fine display of rifle practice took place between the rebel sharpshooters and the Bucktails, after a few minutes our breech-loading rifles gave us another victory and the enemy only fired an occasional shot, the Bucktails then turned their attention to the rebel gunners and in a short time their fire slackened.

The ground upon which the front line of the rebels was formed, was on the heights, the ground sloping off toward our line to a point near midway where the ground raised gently toward the river forming a hollow. Through this hollow and parallel with the lines of battle was the Richmond railroad, in our front the road ran through a cut from five to ten feet deep in this railroad cut the rebel sharpshooters were stationed.

On the heights the ground was one or two hundred feet higher than the bed of the railroad and was heavily timbered and in the rear of these woods, on still higher ground was a line of rifle pits. From the heights to the river was an open plain, and in our front the ground sloped off so gently toward the railroad as to appear almost level, between our Batteries and the railroad there was a deep ditch, at this point running parallel with the railroad which was dug to drain the low ground between the hill and the river. The ditch was six or eight feet deep and about the same width. I copy from the history of the Pennsylvania Reserves by J. R. Sypher the following description of the field:

"The plan of attack involved the initiatory advance of the left wing. A great work was to be accomplished there, before the army would advance in full force to battle. Franklin's grand Division numbered nearly forty thousand, Reynold's Corps contained about sixteen thousand and Meade's Division four thousand five hundred. From this grand Division, numbering in the aggregate about forty thousand of the best troops in the army, the remnant of the Reserve Corps, General Meade's Division of four thousand five hundred, was designated to lead the charge that was to break through the enemy's lines. Once more the Pennsylvania Reserves must lead the Army of the Potomac to battle. The troops on the left were drawn up on a plateau near the river; immediately in their front there was a depression several yards in width, which extended to the base of the heights beyond; the Richmond railroad track lay through this hollow, on its western slope. East of the railroad the ground was clear and mostly cultivated fields, but beyond the road, and up the slope to the heights, it was covered with woods. The enemy occupied these heights and the wooded slope, and posted a strong line behind the railroad embankment in the hollow. From the nature of the ground, the movements of the rebels were completely screened from view, whilst every position of the National troops was clearly visible to the enemy."

As our troops were moving into position in plain view of the enemy their Artillery did fearful execution until our skirmishers pushed forward within range, when they commenced picking off the gunners, which soon slacked their fire, this was kept up until about one o'clock. At this time one of our gunners threw a shell that exploded one or two caissons of a rebel Battery, when our line was ordered forward. The Bucktails were near the left of the Brigade and divided in several parties in support of as many Batteries. Colonel Sinclair directed Captain Taylor to remain in his position, but soon General Meade rode up and inquired what we were doing there. Captain Taylor replied that he was directed by Colonel Sinclair to remain in support of these Batteries. General Meade told him to form his regiment and take its proper place in line.

By this time the line had advanced two or three hundred yards to our front, and the rebels had opened on our troops with all their Artillery and Infantry. Our proper place being some distance along the line, we started on the double quick to the right of the Brigade, when we had gotten over about one-half the distance, the terrific fire of a rebel Battery caused a gap in the left of our Brigade and we were ordered to fill it. This necessitated a movement under a terrific fire. When the order was given we were marching by the flank. Captain Taylor then moved us forward in line by a left oblique into the gap. In advancing we had to jump the ditch described before. Just after crossing the ditch our line halted and opened a wicked fire on the enemy, and our Batteries in our rear, throwing shell over our troops into the rebel line; the halt was only for a few seconds when, with a yell, we reached the railroad, driving the enemy's line out and into the woods beyond, when in the railroad cut the Fifth regiment and the Bucktails found themselves side by side, our ranks had been terribly thinned crossing over that valley of death; the firing continued until the brave Major Harvey Larimer, of the Fifth, called for volunteers to go with him and charge the woods in our front in an instant the two regiments responded with a cheer, they made a noble effort but were driven back with fearful loss.

The right of our Brigade had reached the woods before we reached the railroad, the woods at that point extended down some distance across the road. When they heard our cheer the gallant 121st, which had born itself with remarkable coolness, the men fighting like veterans, now with a cheer charged forward forcing the rebel line back on our right, our boys at once took advantage of this and again charged the woods in our front, this time driving the enemy from their position and gaining the heights.

The line of rifle pits, though desperately defended, were captured and all that was expected of us had been fully accomplished. To gain this advantage we had strewn that plateau with dead and wounded. A fearful price to pay.

This charge is graphically described by Mr. Sypher as follows: "The men rushed forward, leaping over the ditch along the railroad, over the abandoned entrenchments, and fell upon the enemy in his second line before his forces had time to reform. The rebels threw down their arms and fled in confusion from the wooded hill. The Reserves dashed after the panic stricken enemy, until they came upon the third line, where they found the stacked arms of whole regiments, that had fled in hot haste from before the victorious troops of the First Brigade."

The rebel line was broken and General Lee at once perceived his danger and threw every available man into the breach. The line of our Division was advanced beyond those of the right and left, thus leaving our flanks exposed. The rebels came pouring in upon our front and pressed our flanks back, General Meade knowing that our ammunition was almost exhausted, sent repeatedly for reinforcements, but none came up. He then went back to General Birney, whose Division had been lying idle and in supporting distance, and assumed the authority of ordering him up to the support of the Reserves.

It was too late an to save themselves from being surrounded and all captured, the Pennsylvania Reserves with their cartridge boxes empty again crossed that open plain in the face of the fire of an enemy, by this time, three or four times their number.

The loss on the retreat was fully equal to that on the advance, and, by the time we got back to our Batteries there was but a sorry remnant left of the gallant line that had so bravely charged but a few hours before. The Division of General Birney did not get farther than our Batteries, consequently were really not engaged to any extent that would warrant them to the claim of having taken part in the battle. Had that Division promptly moved to General Meade's relief when he first sent word for reinforcements there can be no doubt that Lee would have been compelled to abandon his position in the rear of the city of Fredericksburg and the battle of December 13th, 1862, would certainly have had a very different ending.

When the Division marched back to the rear they were formed in close column when General Meade rode up and spoke to the men. He told them they had accomplished more than had been asked or expected of them, that they were not defeated but were victors notwithstanding the fact that they were compelled to abandon a battlefield so nobly won. While he was talking General Reynolds rode up, and, when Meade saw him he said, "My God, General Reynolds, did they think my Division could whip Lee's whole army, there is all that is left of my

Reserves." Tears flowed freely down the cheeks of both these Generals, as they looked in vain for familiar faces among the powder-stained heroes who had escaped.

Out of the four thousand five hundred, one thousand eight hundred and forty-two were killed, wounded or missing. The loss of the Bucktail regiment alone was over two hundred out of less than three hundred that went into action. Among the officers Lieutenant W. B. Jenkins, of Company C., was killed Captains Taylor and Irvin, Lieutenants O. D. Jenkins, D. G. McNaughton, Thos. Benton Winslow and R. Fent. Ward were wounded. Total, killed 24; wounded about 180, a number of the wounded were taken prisoners. The Reserves captured quite a number of prisoners and brought them in.

The regiment, with the other regiments of the Division, remained on the south side of the Rappahannock until the night of the 15th when they re-crossed the river and in a few days were marched to Belle Plain, on the Potomac, where they went into camp.

Captain E. A. Irvin was unfortunate, it just lacked one day of being three months since he was very severely wounded in the head, and he had joined the regiment but a few days before this battle and was again severely wounded, although commissioned Lieutenant-Colonel he never returned to the regiment but was soon after mustered out.

French Frank was shot in the hip when in the act of jumping the ditch and landed on the bottom on his head and shoulders, a comrade jumped down, raised him up and asked if he was much hurt, to which he replied: "go way, Bob, I is killed deader as h---l!" This wound left Frank a stiff leg and he was discharged. His soldierly bearing had won him many friends in the general hospital in Washington who got him a position as sutler at the end of the long bridge across the Potomac. Joseph Hayter, of Company I., just before going into action, called Lieutenant R. Fent. Ward to him and said: "Lieutenant, I want you to help me eat a little dinner I have here, this will be the last meal I will ever eat, I know I will be killed to-day." He said this in a sober manner with a tone of voice more cheerful than sad, when Lieutenant Ward said to him; "Joe this is all foolishness you will come out all right," but Hayter insisted that he would be killed.

In the charge on the railroad cut he was killed almost instantly, on his person was found a pass book and in it he had left some directions for Lieutenant Ward about some property he owned, and a statement of some money owed to him by some of his comrades, with authority for Lieutenant Ward to collect the same and send home to his mother and sister. He also stated that he would be killed in that battle.

No. 22

The Bucktails, with the rest of the Division, took part in the "Mud March" under General Burnside, after than they went into winter quarters. Owing to the fearful decimation of our ranks efforts were made by the State authorities to have the Reserves taken back to the State for the purpose of filling their Companies and regiments with volunteers. Recruiting officers had been sent out from time to time but so far as the Division of the Pennsylvania Reserves were concerned the effort to fill up the ranks proved a failure. Other regiments had been at different times filled up, but our readers will remember that the volunteers could choose the regiment and company in which they were enlisted; for some reason or other recruits did not choose the Pennsylvania Reserves, and particularly the Bucktail regiment, after the first season the only recruits that came to the regiment were men from the counties where the companies were raised and who had friends or relatives already in the regiment, and the number that came to us, even from the homes of the men were very small compared to the number that went to other regiments. The Secretary of War refused to grant the request. Any similar cases were before him, and, as he dare not grant all, he concluded to refuse all.

The situation of the Pennsylvania Reserves, however, required more careful consideration. From our thirteen thousand that entered the service, exclusive of the Cavalry and Artillery regiments, after the battle of Fredericksburg, there were less than fifteen hundred present for duty. In the Bucktail regiment there was less than one hundred, immediately after the battle.

After investigating the report and finding that the actual condition of the Division was even worse than represented, the Secretary of War had the Pennsylvania Reserves transferred from the Army of the Potomac to the defenses of Washington.

General Meade had been made a Major-General and was assigned to the command of the Fifth Corps, General Reynolds had been assigned to the First Corps, Generals Ord and Seymour had been sent to other armies and the Reserves were now without a general officer. Colonel Sickel, as the senior Colonel, was placed in command of the Division, the First Brigade, under command of Colonel William McCandlass, of the Second regiment, embarked on transports on the Potomac and on February 7th, 1863, arrived at Alexandria, Virginia, followed by the other Brigades, the 121st and 142nd regiments remained with the Army of the Potomac. The First Brigade was sent to Fairfax Court House, the Second Brigade was left at Alexandria, and the Third Brigade went into camp at Upton's Hill.

The night before the Bucktails reached Fairfax Court House, Moseby's Geurrillas captured General Stoughton, the commanding officer there, and twenty guards. They succeeded in passing the pickets, capturing or evading the guards around headquarters, and captured the General in bed. The next morning after that the Bucktails went on guard at Fairfax Court House and Colonel Mosby found it impossible to pass the picket line.

While we were in this camp there were several cases of small-pox in the regiment, one death, Austin Irvin, of Company K. The citizens of the village of Fairfax and the surrounding country were rebels, but as they were inside of our line, and their subsistence to a certain extent came from or through the officers of our army, they treated the soldiers hospitably, unless the right of secession was questioned, any reflection on their army would bring out the real sentiments of the natives, there were but few men left, but the soldiers soon learned that the men did not take all the "cuss words" with them to the rebel army. We remained in camp, at this place, until the 28th of March, when we broke camp and marched to Fairfax Station on the Orange and Alexandria railroad about five miles from Fairfax Court House.

While we lay here the following promotions were made in the regiment: Captain Charles F. Taylor to Colonel; Captain E. A. Irvin to Lieutenant-Colonel; Captain A. E. Niles to Major. Lieutenant-Colonel Irvin's wounds prevented him from returning in time to be mustered in with the others and he resigned when Maor Miles was made Lieutenant-Colonel and Adjutant W. R. Hartshorn Major. Sergeant-Major Roger Sherman was promoted to Adjutant. In Company A., First Lieutenant John G. Harrower to Captain; Second Lieutenant N. B. Kinsey to First Lieutenant; First Sergeant E. B. Leonard to Second Lieutenant. Lieutenant Kinsey was very shortly promoted to Captain of Company C. vice Captain L. W. Gifford mustered out on account of wounds received with the four companies in the Valley campaign. Lieutenant Leonard was then made First Lieutenant and Daniel Orcut promoted from the ranks to Second Lieutenant. Company B. Second Lieutenant Thomas B. Lewis to Captain vice Captain Wistar, resigned; Sergeant Philip E. Keiser to First Lieutenant vice William Allison, killed at Antietam; Sergeant Joel R. Spahr to Second Lieutenant vice Lewis promoted to Captain. Company C. Sergeant J. W. Craven to First Lieutenant vice William B. Jenkins, killed at Fredericksburg; Corporal Moses W. Lucore to Second Lieutenant vice Oscar D. Jenkins mustered out. Company D. First Lieutenant D.G. McNaughton to Captain vice J. T. A. Jewett, resigned; Second Lieutenant Ribero D. Hall to First Lieutenant; Sergeant Robert Hall to Second Lieutenant. Company E. First Lieutenant Lucius Truman to regimental quartermaster vice Lieutenant Harry D. Patton, promoted to captain and assistant quartermaster U.S. Volunteers; Second Lieutenant Samuel A. Mack to Captain vice Captain Niles, promoted to Major Sergeant George A. Ludlow to First Lieutenant; Sergeant William Taylor to Second Lieutenant. Company F. Second Lieutenant Jno. A. Wolfe, of Company G. to Captain vice Dennis Magee, mustered out; Sergeant Ernest Wright to First Lieutenant vice Harry D. Patton, appointed quartermaster; Sergeant Daniel Blett, of Company K, to Second Lieutenant vice Charles Bitterling, killed at South Mountain. Company G Sergeant John L. Luther to Second Lieutenant vice Lieutenant John A. Wolfe, promoted to Captain Company F. Company H. First Lieutenant John D. Yerkes to Captain vice Captain Taylor, promoted to Colonel; Sergeant Thomas J. Roney to First Lieutenant; Sergeant Robert Maxwell to Second Lieutenant vice Joel J. Swayne, killed at Harrisonburg. Company I. First Lieutenant Frank J. Bell to Captain vice William T. Blanchard, resigned; Second Lieutenant R. Fent Ward to First Lieutenant; Sergeant Richard A. Rice to Second Lieutenant. Company K. First Lieutenant Jas. M. Welch to Captain vice E. A. Irvin, resigned; Sergeant John P. Bard to First Lieutenant; Sergeant J. E. Kratzer to Second Lieutenant vice David C. Dale, died in general hospital.

Surgeon S. D. Freeman had resigned, and Assistant Surgeon William T. Humphrey had been appointed Surgeon of the 149th regiment Pennsylvania Volunteers. Jonathan J. Comfort, of Philadelphia, was appointed Surgeon and D. O. Crouch, of Clearfield county, Penn'a., was appointed Assistant Surgeon. At Fredericksburg while assisting in the amputation of the legs of Henry Jackson, of Company E., Dr. Crouch was wounded in the head by a shell which exploded close to the table, the nurse, Lewis Jordan, was killed and several wounded, and when they found

Jackson he was dead. Dr. Crouch soon after resigned and went home. Besides being a good surgeon and physician Dr. Crouch, by his kindness and unremitting labors for he men, had won their love and they were very sorry to part with him. Freeman and Humphrey were both skillful surgeons and faithful officers. Our Chaplain, Rev. W. H. D. Hatton, resigned and his place was never filled. Rev. Hatton found the Bucktails a pretty hard lot to manage, spiritually, but on the field of battle he could testify to their fidelity to their country. There was no place of danger where our Chaplain would not go, he was always to be found where the fighting was thickest, taking care of the wounded, bringing up ammunition or doing anything he could to contribute to our success.

Colonel Taylor, from the moment he took command of the regiment on the eve of the battle of Fredericksburg, won the respect and love of the men and soon the old-time discipline was restored and everything went along with military precision. Our ranks were slowly filling up with the wounded who had recovered, but the daily "official notice" of men being "discharged on account of wounds," and "died from wounds received in action" conveyed the sad intelligence that new men would have to fill their places, if they ever were filled. Lieutenants T. Benton Winslow of Company G, and Lucius Truman, Quartermaster of our regiment were sent home for recruits but their mission failed so far as our regiment was concerned.

Many amusing scenes were witnessed while we were encamped at Fairfax Station. This station was made a post, Captain Huff was commissary of subsistance and Captain Harry D. Patton quartermaster. Passes were granted to the men to go to Alexandria and Washington, and, although all orders were rigidly enforced, this was a genuine holiday to the Bucktails and they enjoyed it. Many officers brought their wives to camp and the many little changes made about the quarters; a boquet in the window, a canary encaged sending forth its morning song of praise, white collars and cuffs, with other changes, seemingly of no importance in themselves, all together gave a home-like appearance to camp that in the absence of the daily papers might have led the Bucktails into the delusion that "grim visaged war had smoothed his wrinkled front."

The movements of the Army of the Potomac were studied with the deepest interest by the officers and men. As was stated before, the appointment of Burnside to the command of the army was very unsatisfactory to the rank and file, but his honest assumption of all the responsibility for his failure at Fredericksburg had won for him the respect and admiration of the soldiers and, when relieved of the command, although at his own request, there was just as much dissatisfaction among the soldiers as there was at the removal of McClellan. The appointment of General Hooker to succeed him pleased them as Hooker had won the reputation of being a hard fighter. Whether General Hooker was competent or was possessed of all the requisite qualifications of a commander of an army or not others may determine. That the Army of the Potomac never was a complete organization until he assumed command the soldiers of that army knew full well. This was especially noticeable in the quartermaster and commissary departments and in the machinery like movement of the various departments in the routine of camp life.

When the army made the first move in the spring of 1863, the men in the regiment watched it with the deepest interest, and when it was known that Chancellorville was a disaster and that the Army of the Potomac was again compelled to recross the Rappahonnock, there seemed to be a settled conviction that the time of the Penn'a. Reserve Corps furlough had about expired; orders to move to the front were looked for every day. When the news came that Lee had crossed the Potomac and threatened to invade the North, and that Hooker's army was falling back toward

Washington, the Penn'a. Reserves were satisfied that they were soon to join their fortunes with the oft defeated but never conquered Army of the Potomac. The order to get rid of all surplus baggage and camp equipment, draw extra rations, prepare five days cooked rations, draw a full supply of ammunition and send all sick to general hospital, did not surprise the troops composing the Reserves. When it was announced that General Hooker had been superceded by General Meade, there was some disappointment among the Reserves; not that they doubted Meade's ability to command an army, but by military law, General Reynolds was Meade's senior, and was also looked upon by the Division as a great General. It was a current report about that time that the command of the army was first offered to General Reynolds, and that he made certain conditions upon which he would accept it; the General-in-Chief not willing to grant the conditions demanded then gave the command to General Meade. No mistake was made by placing George G. Meade in command; none would have been made had General Reynolds accepted. The Reserves were pleased that their first battle after their long rest was to be fought under the leadership of him who commanded the Division in their last battle.

On the 26th of June the regiment broke camp at Fairfax Station. We marched to Edwards Ferry where we crossed the Potomac river, thence by Frederick City to Uniontown where it arrived on the 30th.

Our Division had been assigned to the Fifth Corps forming the third Division. Now for the first time we wore that badge that has since become dear to every member of the old Reserve Corps—the Blue Maltese Cross.

No. 23

Some time in May General Samuel W. Crawford was assigned to the command of the Pennsylvania Reserve Corps, and our Brigade was under the command of Colonel William McCandless of the Second regiment.

General Lee crossed the Potomac at Williamsport and marched into Pennsylvania, his Cavalry getting as far as the Susquehanna river, a sharp skirmish took place at Wrightsville between the rebel Cavalry and the Militia. The rebels drove the Militia across the bridge which was fired from the Lancaster side and burned down, thus preventing the enemy from making a raid through the rich valleys of Lancaster county. After an attempt to shell Columbia they fell back toward the main body of the army, which was in the Cumberland valley. They occupied Carlisle and York, and were threatening Harrisburg. At this time the Army of the Potomac was encamped at Frederick City and Middletown.

On the 28th day of June General Meade assumed command of the Army of the Potomac, and, with great promptness, moved it on the most direct route from Frederick to Harrisburg. The First Corps, under the command of General Reynolds, was ordered to take the lead. General Meade assumed command under the greatest difficulties, he was not made acquainted with the situation of the enemy, or the plans of his predecessor, his knowledge of the splendid qualifications of General Reynolds, and knowing that he could place implicit confidence in his loyalty to him, caused him to assign him the important position he did.

The Eleventh Corps, under command of General O. O. Howard, was assigned to General Reynold's command. On the evening of June 30th General Howard, by direction of General Reynolds, moved forward and took position on Seminary Ridge, near Pennsylvania College.

On the morning of July 1st, General Reynolds arrived at that place and found our Cavalry, under Buford, sharply engaged with the enemy, west of the town, as General Lee's whole army was then directed toward this place, and knowing that a battle must soon be fought, General Reynolds determined to engage the enemy at once and check his progress until the Army of the Potomac could arrive. There can be no doubt that the forming of the line on Seminary Ridge, by Reynolds, was only intended to hold the enemy there until Meade came up, the soldierly eye of Reynolds would not have taken into consideration the advantages that Cemetery Ridge offered, but would have pushed any success he might have gained.

The First Corps passed through Gettysburg and formed on Seminary Ridge where they encountered Hill's Corps.* General Reynolds rode to the front to direct the forming of the line, and, while placing Batteries in position, the rebel Infantry opened a sharp fire followed by a charge on the Batteries. General Reynolds then ordered Wadsworth's Division to charge the enemy, he riding boldly forward with the line, when he was shot by a rifle, the ball passing through his neck and killing him almost instantly.

---

* Editor's note: Ambrose Powell Hill

General Reynold's death, at that time, was a loss of the most serious character. He had, by hard fighting and his readiness at all times to engage the enemy, won the reputation of being one of the best Generals, and among the foremost, military men in our army. To General Meade the loss was irreparable. With Reynolds in the field he could feel that but half the responsibility of the coming battle rested upon him. As Grant said of Sheridan after the visit he made to him in the Valley he did not need looking after, Meade could depend upon Reynolds doing all that he could direct him to do, were he present with him. When Reynolds fell, Meade lost his first Lieutenant, and felt that a much greater responsibility rested upon him. General Howard succeeded General Reynolds on the field. The charge of Wadsworth was successful in repulsing the enemy they, however, soon reformed and Ewell's Corps joining them they once more charged our line and drove it back.

General Reynolds had taken the precaution to station Steinwehr's Division with the reserve Artillery on Cemetery Hill, and this wise precaution was the means of checking the enemy and enabled Meade to occupy the fish-hook shaped line with his right resting on Culp's Hill and his left on Big Round Top.

On learning of the death of General Reynolds, General Meade sent General Hancock, to whom he had confided his plans, to the front to take command there. General Hancock hastened to the front when he and General Howard both agreed that the position the army then occupied offered as many advantages as any position in that vicinity. General Hancock promptly reported the situation when General Meade ordered all the forces of the Army of the Potomac to concentrate at Gettysburg. During the night of the 1st of July the commanding General rode forward, and, in company with General Howard, surveyed the position, he fully approved the report of Hancock and Howard and gave directions for posting the troops.

The line of battle was not completed until after noon on the 2nd, and was as follows: the Twelfth Corps, General Slocum, on the right; the First, General Newton, on the right centre; the Second, General Hancock, on the left centre; the Third, General Sickels, on the let; the Fifth, General Sykes, (who had succeeded General Meade) was held in reserve; the Sixth, General Sedgwick, had not arrived on the field when the battle began, but was directed to move toward Round Top, and, by moving in this direction from where it was, upon arriving on the field it could be directed to any part where it might be needed.

During the night rifle pits had been dug and earthworks thrown up to protect the Batteries from the rifles of the enemy's skirmishers. From Round Top, on the extreme left to the extreme right near Culp's Hill along our line of battle, was very near five miles, from the extreme right or inner point of the fish-hook to the extreme left or end of the shank of the hook, in a direct line was not more than three miles.

General Lee formed his line on Seminary Ridge and a succession of ridges or hills fronting our line his line was of necessity longer than Meade's, the ground between the two armies, which was from twelve hundred to fifteen hundred yards wide, was mostly cleared, in front of Cemetery Ridge the lowest ground was near midway between the two lines, on our right and left the ground was very much more broken.

Shortly after 3 o'clock General Meade rode out to the left where he found General Sickels had taken a position very much farther to the front than he directed, Sypher says "three quarters of a mile in advance of the prolongation of Hancock's line, and wholly disconnected, by an intervening ravine, from the proper line of the army." The right wing of Sickel's Corps was, therefore, unprotected by the troops on his right. Longstreet, with the flower of the rebel army, was opposite Sickels, forming the right of Lee's army, before Sickels had time to prepare to fall back to the proper line Longstreet's Batteries opened a terrific fire, and, under cover of that fire, his troops charged upon the Third Corps, his line covering Sickel's front and extending some distance beyond his right flank. General Meade was present, and, seeing the danger of Longstreet's long line doubling up the right of the Third Corps and forcing through the gap, at once ordered the Fifth Corps forward to take the position intended to be taken by the Third.

While the Fifth was getting into position a terrible battle was fought in their front, the "Peach Orchard" lay almost in front of Little Round Top, there the fighting was of the most stubborn character, the Third Corps fought gallantly but were not able to resist the furious assault on their front and flank, they were driven back behind the line of the Fifth. During the charge several of Hancock's guns opened on Longstreet's troops and made fearful slaughter, the enemy charged these guns and captured them, but several other Batteries opened on them and the troops of Hancock's Corps charged at the same time and recaptured their guns.

The victorious troops of Longstreet must be checked, General Meade, being still at this point, ordered his old command forward. The First Brigade formed in the rear of Little Round Top, the Third had moved off to the left and was in the rear of big Round Top; at the foot of little Round Top there is quite a swamp across which at the foot along the slope of the opposite hill is a cluster of rocks called the "Devil's Den," these rocks are large and formed a complete protection to the rebel Infantry.

The Brigade was formed in two lines the Bucktails forming the left of the second line, in this position they charged, our Artillery was posted on Little Round Top and when our line reached them they had about given up their guns, a large force of the enemy appearing on the left of the Brigade Colonel McCandlass directed Colonel Taylor to change front charge over Little Round Top across the swamp and try to drive the enemy from the "Devil's Den." With a yell the Bucktails charged forward down over the rocky side of the hill, across the swamp, up the rocks, the Brigade on their right gallantly charged at the same time. During this charge Lieutenant-Colonel Niles was wounded, at the foot of the hill a hand to hand fight for several minutes was kept up when Colonel Taylor ordered another charge and the rebels were driven from the rocks on over the hill, to a stone fence where they made a stand. The Reserves did not halt but drove them on through a wheat field where they were halted, during this charge several hundred prisoners were captured by the Bucktails.

Their position being considerably in advance of the rest of the line Major Hartshorn directed his men to fall back to the stone wall. During the charge from the "Devil's Den" to the stone fence Colonel Taylor was shot through the heart in the front line. The command then devolved upon Major Hartshorn, who held his position until the afternoon of the 3rd, when Colonel McCandlass formed the Brigade in close column by regiment with the Bucktails in front. In this formation the Brigade charged through the wheat field where the Bucktails had fought the day before, a large force of the enemy appearing on the left of the column, McCandlass halted the Brigade, changed direction to the left, and directed Major Hartshorn to charge the enemy. The Bucktails, with their usual vim, led the charge, closely followed by the other regiments, the enemy stubbornly resisted the attack and the Bucktails had another hand to hand encounter but succeeded in driving the enemy in confusion from the field, capturing the colors and all that was left of a Georgia regiment, the pursuit was kept up for some distance and many more prisoners were captured. When night came on the Brigade rested on their arms fully one mile in front of the position they occupied in the morning. This ended the fighting of the Bucktails at Gettysburg, the next morning the Brigade was relieved and marched to the rear.

Victory again perched upon the banners of the Army of the Potomac. Meade and Lee had fought a desperate battle with nearly equal numbers, otherwise the advantages were with Lee, in the last two engagements Lee had been victorious, he knew his men. On the other hand Meade had been appointed to the command just on the eye of battle and had lost the one on whom he depended most, before the real battle began.

The loss of our regiment was very severe, Colonel Taylor, Lieutenant Robert Hall, of Company D., and nine men were killed; Lieutenant-Colonel Alanson E. Niles, Captains Hugh McDonald, of Company G., J. D. Yerkes, of Company H., Frank Bell, of Company I., and Lieutenants Thomas J. Roney, Company H., Joel R. Spahr, Company B., and J. E. Kratzer, Company K., and forty enlisted men were wounded.

Charles Frederick Taylor was a brother of Bayard Taylor, had been highly educated, and was one of the most winning and attractive officers in the Corps. He was but a little past twenty-three years of age; a bright future awaited him; in him a most valuable and precious sacrifice was offered on the altar of our country. It is the purpose of the writer to give a short biographical sketch of the killed as far as can be gotten, at the close of the history.

During this battle, at the time Colonel Taylor was killed, Lieutenant Kratzer and a few, perhaps five or six men with him, were very close to the enemy's line. Kratzer seeing a rebel taking aim at the Colonel, who was close by, called to him but it was too late, just as he turned, he received the shot and fell into Kratzer's arms. But a few minutes later Kratzer saw a rebel officer but a short distance from him and ordered him to surrender, the rebel answered by shooting at him with a revolver. Kratzer, not being hit, returned the fire, he also missed, when the rebel fired again and missed, Kratzer also missed his mark the second time, the rebel then shot Kratzer through the arm; after he was wounded Kratzer shot the rebel officer who fell to the ground, while this shooting was going on each was calling upon the other to surrender.

No. 24

During the march to Gettysburg, Captain Welch, of Company K., was compelled to leave on account of the wound received at Antietam, he was shortly after transferred to the Veteran Reserve Corps. Captian Welch had a big heart, his bravery had won him the highest esteem of the regiment and it was, with sorrow, they saw him taken from us.

The first spy, executed in the Army of the Potomac, was hung near Frederick City on the 4th or 5th of July. His name was Richardson and he was well known in the Bucktail regiment.

During the winter of 1861 and 1862 he sang and sold Union songs all through our army, gathering information for the enemy at the same time. He was captured by the Cavalry of General Averill, they coming upon him so suddenly as to prevent him from destroying the carefully prepared description of the situation of the wagon train of the Army of he Potomac. The evidence found on his person revealed his true character. General Averill, therefore, hastily summoned a court martial when he was found guilty as a spy and immediately hung to a shade tree standing in a large field. A guard was stationed over the body which remained hanging for several days, by order of General Averill, as a warning to all others that the time had come when the extreme penalty of military law would be visited upon all spies.

Early Saturday morning, July 4th, our line was ordered to advance, when it was found that Lee had withdrawn from our right and had concentrated his forces on our left. General Meade was very anxious to prevent the escape of Lee, he knew that the armies were about equal in numbers, and that the odds would be against the attacking party. During the early part of the day a heavy rain began to fall, by noon the storm had settled down to a steady pour which lasted all through the day and night.

On Sunday morning, very early, our lines were pushed forward when it was discovered that the enemy was in full retreat toward Hagerstown. Our army was immediately ordered in pursuit, marching toward Middletown, Maryland, where it arrived July 9th, and halted one day to draw clothing and rations.

General Lee, knowing that Meade was close after him and would fall upon him the moment he attempted to cross the river, took a strong position near Williamsport and Falling Water, where he threw up earth works.

General Meade's army arrived in front of Lee's position on Sunday, July 12th, when the commanding General called a council of war composed of Generals Wadsworth, Hays, French, Sykes, Sedgwick, Howard and Slocum. General Meade stated to the council that he favored attacking the enemy along the entire line, but, that owing to his having but little means of gaining positive knowledge of the enemy's strength, he had called them together for the purpose of advising together. Generals Howard and Wadsworth favored an attack the others were opposed to an attack without first thoroughly reconnoitering the strong position occupied by the enemy. It was, therefore, determined to make a careful examination the next morning, the 13th of July.

The morning of the 13th was ushered in through rain and a heavy fog which made it next to impossible to ascertain anything about the disposition of the forces of the enemy. All that day the hero of Gettysburg chafed at what seemed to his restless spirit, unnecessary delay, and the bad fortune which brought clouds and rain when a clear sky was so much desired. That night he determined to attack at daylight on the morning of the 14th. He accordingly issued orders for the whole army to move forward and assault the enemy. The army in execution of these orders advanced when it was found that Lee had again made his escape. During the night he had crossed the Potomac and was again on his native soil.

Without delay General Meade started in pursuit or rather marched down Pleasant Valley in a southerly direction in order to cross the river at a point that would keep his army between Lee and Washington. On the 15th he commenced to cross at Berlin, where the Army of the Potomac crossed after Antietam. By examination of the map, it will be seen that the route taken by General Meade was considerable shorter to Washington or any point on the Orange and Alexandria railroad than the route Lee would have to travel to get there. Lee fell back rapidly by Strasburg and Front Royal, and concentrated his army at Culpepper Court House.

The Pennsylvania Reserves went into camp at Rappahannock Station where they arrived during the early part of August.

While we lay here the officers and men of the Pennsylvania Reserves raised, by voluntary contribution, several thousand dollars with which they bought and presented to General Meade a beautiful sword of the finest workmanship, with a sash, belt and a pair of golden spurs. On the occasion of the presentation Governor Curtin and many other distinguished guests were present. The presentation was made by General Crawford, commanding the Division, and accepted by General Meade in a speech of some length, which proved that our commanding General could talk as well, almost, as he could fight. In his speech he referred to the death of General Reynolds as follows:

"This re-union, gentlemen, awakens in my heart a new sorrow for an officer which it vividly recalls to my mind, for he commanded the Division when I commanded one of the Brigades. He was the noblest as well as the bravest gentlemen in the army. I refer to John F. Reynolds. I cannot receive this sword without thinking of that officer. When he fell at Gettysburg, leading the advance, I lost not only a Lieutenant of the utmost importance to me, but I may say that I lost a friend, aye, even a brother. I miss other faces which were familiar to me in your midst, McNeil and Taylor of the Rifles, Simmons of the Fifth."

Speeches were made by Governor Curtin, Morton McMichael, of Philadelphia, John W. Forney and Colonel Biddle Roberts, of the First regiment. For the occasion a grand banquet had been prepared and the headquarters of General Crawford, where the presentation took place, were handsomely decorated. Among the decorations the greatest attraction was an eagle with outspread wings, made of cedar boughs, by a member of the Bucktail regiment. This eagle was fastened to a crossbeam over the stand.

On the 26th of August, 1863, our regiment, with the other regiments of the Division, witnessed the execution of five deserters. The place chosen for the execution was a narrow valley or ravine with the hills sloping gently. Our Corps was drawn up in column on one side of the ravine, on the opposite side the five graves were dug. When the troops were all in position, the condemned men preceded by a brass band and each man preceded by four men carrying his coffin, were marched along in front of the Corps. A spiritual adviser accompanied each man. They passed along the entire front when they filed to the left and were marched down to the center where the graves were. The coffins were set beside the graves, the men, after prayer, each sat on the end of his coffin, facing the troops, their hands were bound behind them and a black cap drawn over their faces. Two, who were Jews, asked to have the cap removed so they might take a last farewell, their request was granted when they approached each other and kissed, then turned around and again took their seats on the coffins.

At a call of the bugle the firing squad marched out in front, the awful stillness was broken by the blood curdling command, "Ready," sharply followed by "aim," "fire," and five men fell over on their coffins dead. The stoutest heart was touched and the most hardened was made to feel. A large party of recruits and conscripts, just on their way to the several Corps to which they had been assigned, were drawn up to witness the execution. Many of these were quite young, and the horrible spectacle blanched many a cheek that had not been used to the terrible sight that had made the old soldier familiar with death in its most sickening forms. The history of the five men did not call forth the sympathy of those who witnessed their execution, they had been "bounty jumpers," enlisting for a bounty, deserting and enlisting again. Two were Jews and the other three were Italians.

While we were in camp here we received some recruits and many of our wounded returned to the regiment, so that we had present near four hundred men, present and absent over five hundred. Reports were circulated that our regiment was to be filled to the maximum number with conscripts, this created great dissatisfaction among the men, as there was much prejudice against drafted men.

About the 1st of September Meade's and Lee's armies were materially weakened. From the Army of the Potomac one Division was sent to North Carolina, and a considerable force to New York to enforce the draft. From Lee's army Longstreet's Corps was sent to Tennessee. As soon as General Meade learned, of this he advanced across the Rappahannock, drove the army of Lee across the Rapidan and occupied the winter quarters erected by Lee's army around Culpepper. Preparations were made to make a flank movement beyond the Rapidan, but Meade's plans were all frustrated by the withdrawal of the Eleventh and Twelfth Corps, they were sent to reinforce our army in Tennessee which had suffered a disastrous repulse at Chicamauga. This prevented Meade from taking the offensive, and he was obliged to wait the return of the troops sent to New York. They returned in October when the army was again placed under marching orders.

General Lee, however, knowing that the Army of the Potomac had been reduced in numbers deemed it a good time to assume the offensive, he, therefore, attempted to march around Meade's right flank, cut his communications, get in his rear and compel him to attack him on ground of his own choosing. Meade concluded to offer battle near Culpepper and disposed his army with that intention. Lee had no intention of risking a battle there, and pushed on toward Warrenton and from there toward Centreville.

It was now a race between the two armies for Centreville or the Bull Run battle field, a place where the enemy had twice defeated the Army of the Potomac.

On the 14th of October our Corps, now commanded by General Warren, had a sharp engagement with the Confederates under General Heath. The Pennsylvania Reserves, in this engagement, captured five pieces of Artillery and many prisoners, with comparatively but little loss. Meade had out-marched Lee, and had completely outgeneraled him. The noble old soldier was extremely anxious to fight the enemy on the battle-field that had scored two triumphs for the army opposed to him. I believe the Army of the Potomac, officers and men, were anxious to try again their fortunes on that historic field.

Lee did not wait for Meade to attack him but rapidly retreated towards the Rappahannock, the Army of the Potomac in close pursuit. At Kelly's ford the enemy held a strong position, but Meade, by a rapid movement surprised them, driving them across the river capturing several hundred prisoners and killing and wounding many more.

The rebels, in their retreat, destroyed the bridges and the railroad, crossed the river and established a depot of supplies at Brandy Station south of the Rappahannock. Lee took up a position on the line of the Rapidan.

On the 26th of November Meade, after being delayed two days by a severe snow storm, crossed the Rapidan. A movement intended to strike Lee's army and whip it in detail, was defeated by the tardiness, as charged by General Meade in his official report, of General French, commanding the Third Corps. Lee, by this delay, discovered Meade's plan and concentrated his whole army on a strong position on Mine Run, which he strengthened with earthworks, by this move he expected to compel Meade either to attack him in his strongly fortified position, or fall back across the Rapidan. General Meade prepared to attack the enemy on the 30th. General Warren was to assault the enemy's right, the Pennsylvania Reserves were to open the attack.

The evening before General Crawford sent for Major Hartshorn and told him to select several officers to make a reconnoisance of the ground over which they would charge the next morning, and report whether there was any favorable point at which the attack could be made. Major Hartshorn selected four or five officers and gave them their directions. The ground in front of the regiment was very rough and much broken, the enemy was strongly posted and well protected. Under a perfect storm of rifle balls these brave men coolly marched out to and along the line, carefully examining the ground, fortunately they all escaped with their lies. When they returned with one exception (Lieutenant J. E. Kratzer) they reported it impossible to successfully assault the position. General Meade himself selected the Reserve Corps to assault the strong position on the enemy right. Considerable fighting occurred for two or three days but no general battle ensued. Our Division was under as heavy Artillery fire as at any time during the war. The cold weather and the little promise of carrying the position of the enemy by assault compelled the withdrawal of the army. They recrossed the Rapidan on the 2nd of December and went into winter quarters along the line of the Orange and Alexandria railroad, the Bucktails, with the First Brigade went to Bristoe Station.

No. 25

Before finally locating at Bristoe Station for the winter, the Bucktails had a short campaign to Bull Run bridge and back. We were first ordered to occupy quarters vacated by other troops a short time before, and guard the railroad in that vicinity. We landed at the bridge during a very heavy rain storm, which continued all through the night. The old barracks were comfortable enough and the men were rather well pleased with their location. Shortly after our pickets were posted, firing commenced along the line, at first only an occasional shot, soon however it became more rapid, and the word came that Mosby had attacked our picket line. Mosby had been playing sad havoc along these lines, doing a good deal as he pleased; the Bucktails had had an experience with him at Fairfax Court House, and this night they looked upon his attack as very ungentlemanly, to say the least. The men from the camp soon reached that part of the line where the firing was the heaviest when they found that the pickets were driving Mosby and his guerillas in hot haste through the darkness. The gallant Colonel did not return that night, and soon all was still again. We only remained a few days at this camp, when we got orders to pack up; this was a surprise and a disappointment, as the men had prepared to stay all winter, they had overhauled the old quarters and were just getting everything in good trim when they had to leave. To obey orders without murmuring was one of the hardest lessons the Volunteers had to learn; by this time we had learned and well learned it. We could not tell by our preparations whether we were to march for only a short or long distance, and when we halted and were ordered to go into camp at Bristoe, where the other Regiments of our Brigade had already built comfortable quarters, the men were quite well satisfied. Another lesson the troops had learned was, that it paid in cold weather to erect comfortable quarters, even if they only occupied them a short time. The day after we arrived at Bristoe our camp was laid out in regular order, when without waiting for orders, every "mess" began work and in a few days we had the most comfortable quarters we ever had. In this camp during the winter of 1863 and 1864, the soldiers enjoyed themselves better than ever before. They knew better how to take care of themselves and the army was better supplied with clothing, rations and equipments, than at any former time. There was no relaxation of discipline. Orders were rigidly enforced, but there was no drilling, and as we were located on the railroad our mails arrived daily, and the papers were as eagerly looked for by the troops in the field as by our friends at home. The survivors of the old Bucktails will look back upon that winter with more satisfaction than any other period of the war. Many very amusing incidents occurred, practical jokes were so common that one had to be continually on the watch.

One afternoon our Adjutant, Roger Sherman, and Captain McNaughton, rode down to Manassas junction to visit some friends. They did not return until midnight. On their way home they concluded to have a little fun at the expense of the pickets. One of them rode ahead shouting, the other followed, firing his revolver, both horses on the run. The guards soon were in line, the alarm spread to the camps, and the men were called to arms and remained standing until it was found that it was not Mosby's troopers that had dared the Bucktail lion in his den. With imprecations on the man or men who would make a false alarm, and the wish that the penalty prescribed by Army Regulations, which was death; might be visited on the, the men returned to their quarters and to rest, after waiting half asleep, for two hours.

The next morning was Sunday, and when Major Hartshorn made his usual daily visit to Division headquarters, he learned from some one on the way, that the alarm the night before, was caused by the officers named. On his return to the Regiment he sent for the writer and told him what he had heard, and proposed to give those officers a good scare. General Sykes was then in command of our Corps. He was very strict, and at this particular time he was in no mood to be lenient to any one who, had been guilty of the least violation of orders or military discipline. Numerous cases of bad conduct along the line of the railroad had been reported to him, calling forth an order, breathing out threatenings against the next party that was found guilty of any conduct "unbecoming a soldier or prejudicial to good order and military discipline." This order had only been read at Dress Parade a day or so before. Hartshorn, after unfolding his plans to the writer, sent for the Adjutant, and in the most solemn manner told him that he had just come from Division Headquarters and that Col. McCoy, the Adjutant General, was writing out charges and specifications against him, (Adjutant Sherman) and Captain McNaughton, for false alarm of the camp, that General Crawford knew all about it and was very angry; the attention of the Adjutant was called to that paragraph in Army Regulations relating to this offense and the punishment. Sherman at once realized his unfortunate situation and was thoroughly alarmed. He said: "Major, my God, what will I do!" The Major told him the only thing for him to do was to have all his traps polished up, and his boots blacked, so that he would present a neat and soldierly appearance, then ride over to Division Headquarters before the hour for sending reports to Corps Headquarters, go at once to General Crawford, make a frank confession and throw himself on the General's mercy. While Sherman was getting ready, Hartshorn was hunting up some official business to call his attention to, but the hour for Corps reports was drawing dangerously near and the Adjutant rebelled against any further detention; his horse was ready, all his equipments were polished up, his boots blacked and he had donned a paper collar, but just as he was ready to mount, Major Hartshorn told him that he was only giving him a good scare. Sherman called his Orderly, told him to put "Pete" back in his place, went into his office and wrote a note addressed to "The Chaplain of the Christian Commission Chapel" which read as follows: "Dear Sir the prayers of yourself and congregation are earnestly requested in behalf of Captain D. G. McNaughton and the subscriber;" he signed his name as Adjutant and sent it by the Orderly on duty that day. The Chapel was in plain sight of the Regiment and but a few hundred yards distant, it was in session at this time, and when the orderly handed the note to the chaplain he read it aloud to the congregation and thanked God for this evidence of a spiritual awakening. A committee of good Christian men were appointed to wait on the officers and invite them to the Chapel. As soon as Sherman saw them emerge from the Chapel, he hunted up McNaughton and together they fled to the picket line and remained there until the congregation was dismissed. This cost the Adjutant several "set ups."

Sometime during the winter the Cooper Institute, of Philadelphia, presented the Second regiment with a beautiful silk flag. The committee sent to the army to make the presentation were nearly all rather elderly gentlemen. In honor of the occasion the Second regiment, which never did anything in a half-hearted way, their fighting not excepted, had prepared a grand banquet, and Colonel McCandless of the Second, then in command of the Brigade, ordered the Brigade out in review. To Captain Dick Henderson, an aid on the Division staff, was assigned the duty of furnishing horses for the committee to ride in review. Henderson had found out that these men were very poor horsemen, and that some had never ridden a horse. This was too good an opportunity for him to let slip; he, therefore, gathered up the most unmanageable horses he could get. The men were mounted and rode down to the end of the line where Colonel

McCandless, who was leading, gave his horse the rein, the band started up, the command "present arms" rang down the line. This with the rattle of the rifles in executing the command so thoroughly frightened the horses, ridden by the committee, that they became unmanageable by their riders. The men soon took in the situation when they made matters a great deal worse by the most unearthly yells, the group of horsemen soon passed out of sight and the regiments marched to their several camps. That evening at the banquet several of the committee, in a very humorous manner, referred to their appearance on horseback.

These men, flying over the field with their hair streaming in the wind letting go of their bridle reins and grabbing the saddle, their feet out of the stirrups, their pants above their knees, their white drawers appearing was one of the most laughable sights we had witnessed; very fortunately no one was hurt.

The officers servants were all contrabands that had been picked up here and there on our marches. These men were all very superstitious and afforded an endless amount of amusement to the men. Many of them were very anxious to learn to read and write; several classes were formed and soldiers nobly undertook the task of teaching them. One of these classes some ten or twelve in number, met in a tent belonging to the servants of a couple of officers, this tent was constructed by first digging a square hole in the ground about eight or ten feet wide and perhaps twenty feet long and three or four feet deep, a ridge pole was raised on forked posts and old tent cloths, gum blankets and anything else that could be used formed the roof, a square fire place would be dug in one side and a stick and wood chimney built from the surface up a sufficient height to secure good draft. One cold night when this class were very deeply interested in their studies, with a roaring fire in their fire-place, several soldiers cautiously approached the door and securely fastened it, at a signal two men brought a bag containing about a bushel of the old paper cartridges which they had gathered up somewhcre and poured them down the chimney, they had hardly struck the fire when they began to crack, the darkies yelled, the fire was flying all around the tent, they rushed for the door and when they found it fastened they walked off with the roof of their house, never stopping until they were well satisfied they were out of the reach of a rifle shot. It would be impossible to produce a more thoroughly frightened lot of darkies than literally picked up their house that night and fled for safety to the limits of the camp. After the boys had gotten all the fun they could out of them they turned in and helped the poor fellows rebuild their house and in a short time nothing but the tramp, tramp, tramp of the sentinel broke the stillness of that cold winter night. The remembrance of the scene and the frightened ejaculations of the poor darkies called forth bursts of laughter for many days.

There are also some very sad scenes associated with our camp at Bristoe, and among the saddest is the death of that elegant gentleman and brave soldier Maj. J. Harvey Larimer, of the Fifth, one Sunday morning, near Brentsville Court House, and of the soldiers of the 13th Cavalry killed with him. Major Larimer called to see the writer only the day before, he was looking remarkably well, and in fine spirits, in less than twenty-hours he was cold in death, pierced by five bullets, his body was recovered and sent home to Clearfield where it was buried. Colonel, afterwards General Martin D. Hardin, of the Twelfth, while riding along the railroad one day in the early part of the winter was approached by a small party of horsemen in the Federal uniform, he did not discover their real character until they were close on him, they fired at him one ball taking effect in the left elbow necessitating amputation. Major Larimer, at the time of his death, was inspecting officer on the Division staff.

The next Spring the time of many of the old regiments would expire. The government were loathe to part with these trained soldiers and as an inducement for them to re-enlist, they were offered an additional bounty by the general Government, the men were permitted to credit themselves to any State or district they chose, thereby enabling them to secure the largest local bounty offered. They were also granted a furlough for thirty-five days, and their new enlistment, which was for three years or during the war, was to date from their muster in under the re-enlistment. The unexpired term of the first enlistment being canceled. Where two-thirds of the members of a company re-enlisted they were allowed to keep up their company organizations and the officers could then retain their positions, the same held good with regard to regiments. Quite a number of the old Bucktails re-enlisted, many of them were credited to New Jersey, because that State sent their agents to the field and paid the men $480 in cash just as soon as they signed the muster rolls, while the most that was offered in our own, much more wealthy State, was $300. In County Bonds, which were selling then in the market at from fifty to sixty cents on the dollar, and by reason of an opinion by Judge Woodward, who declared them unconstitutional it was a question whether they would be worth anything.

This action on the part of those officers in command of men who accredited themselves to New Jersey seems to have offended the Chief Executive of the Commonwealth, as not one of them ever received promotion afterward, notwithstanding the fact that they were repeatedly recommended for promotion, and recommended by Major Hartshorn commanding the regiment, the Brigade, Division and Corps commanders, (the law only requires the recommendation of the commanding officer of the regiment). After repeated failures with all these endorsements, they were again recommended by the same officers with a strong endorsement by General Meade, then in command of the army, but all to no purpose, and First Lieutenants were mustered out of service with Captain's vacancy's hanging over their heads, and Second Lieutenants with just and honest claims to the rank of First Lieutenants. The mean injustice done these officers is a stain upon the State administration that time cannot wipe out, and that will not be forgiven by those who survive. Other officers in the same regiments whose men either did not re-enlist or were credited to Pennsylvania were promoted as fast as vacancies occurred.

In March General Grant established his headquarters with the Army of the Potomac. His brilliant victories in the West had won the admiration of the soldiers of the Army of the Potomac. There was, however, considerable feeling on account of his establishing his headquarters with this army.

On the 29th of April we broke camp and marched to Culpepper Court House. On the 3rd of May our Brigade crossed the Rapidan at Germania ford, and on the night of the 4th camped on the Wilderness road.

No. 26

Kane's battalion, composed of Companies C., H., I. and G., after they left the camp near Falmouth May 25th, 1862, crossed the Rappahannock at Fredericksburg and took the plank road to Hanover Court House, and bivouacked the first night twelve miles south of Fredericksburg.

During the night they received orders to return and march into the Shenandoah Valley. The battalion had been assigned to General Bayard's Brigade of Cavalry then in General McDowell's Corps. This Brigade was composed of the First Pennsylvania and the First New Jersey regiments.

The officers and men of Kane's battalion parted with the six Companies with great sorrow, some of the more thoughtful with fearful forebodings of the future. They knew, from the character of their commanding officer, Colonel Kane, that they would be called upon to undergo the severest duty, both on the march and in battle. They had learned that Colonel Kane never took numbers into account, but was just as likely to attack a Brigade, with his battalion, as a regiment. The branch of the service, to which they were assigned, was another indication of what was in store for them. It had been a favorite boast of Colonel Kane that his regiment could, on a long march, keep up with any regiment of Cavalry. This campaign proved that he was correct but did not demonstrate either the prudence or practibility of repeating the experiment, the novel idea of uniting riflemen and Cavalry, after a brilliant test, died with that campaign.

The Brigade of General Bayard entered the Shenandoah Valley at a small town above Winchester *(Strasburg)*; near the latter place they came upon the rear of Jackson's army as it was retreating up the Valley. General Bayard, with his accustomed promptness, at once fell on the retreating foe with his full force, and, for five days and nights, kept up a running fight in which Kane's battalion took a prominent part.

Several sharp contests took place during this time, the enemy taking advantage of every favorable position to punish the troops that were continually pressing them; quite a number of prisoners and arms were captured and a good many killed and wounded on both sides.

At Harrisonburg, on the afternoon of June 6th, the rebels got a Battery stuck fast in the mud; all their efforts to get it away proving futile they ambushed it, General Ashby's Cavalry Brigade was formed in mass to defend it. Colonel Wyndham, with his regiment of Cavalry, charged the Battery; he was allowed to close on it when they threw a deadly volley of grape and canister into his line. General Ashby's Cavalry, charging at the same time, his line was broken and fled from the field in the greatest disorder and confusion, leaving their killed and wounded behind. Colonel Percy Wyndham, commanding the First New Jersey Cavalry, was wounded and taken prisoner.

General Fremont, it appears, was very anxious to avoid a general engagement just at that time, and, after forming a new line of fresh troops, recalled them; it was then drawing towards evening. Generals Fremont and Bayard and Colonel Kane were in a group together with other officers when Fremont gave the order to recall the troops. Colonel Kane protested against leaving our wounded to fall into the hands of the enemy, and begged permission to take his Bucktails forward to a small piece of wood on the left of our line. His persistence secured the consent of General Bayard who gave him forty minutes to ascertain what was in the woods and come back.

From the position occupied by Generals Fremont and Bayard the movement of the rebel troops were plainly seen. Just as Kane's battalion entered the woods a long line of Infantry was seen approaching from the other side. Bayard at once ordered the Bucktails recalled, but, before an aide could reach them, the battle began. A Brigade of rebel troops on one side and just one hundred and five Bucktails on the other side.

As the enemy advanced Colonel Kane deployed his men as skirmishers and told them to take cover and give them h—l. The rapid fire and deadly aim of these practiced riflemen very soon arrested the advance of the enemy in their front, but the flanks of the long line of the Brigade opposed to them were thrown forward threatening to surround them. The watchful eye of Colonel Kane saw his danger, and, as soon as he checked the enemy in his front, he directed a portion of his line to drive back the line threatening his left flank. This was accomplished and as the rebel line doubled up, the effect of the fire of the riflemen was terrible and success seemed about to perch upon the banners of the brave handful of men who were so nobly contending against twenty times their number.

At this critical moment General Ashby came on the field and rallied the rebel line. While he was leading them in a charge he was killed. His efforts had saved the day for the enemy, and the Brigade engaged from a stigma that time never could have removed.

About this time Colonel Kane was wounded, and, as he lay upon the ground, Lieutenant John A. Wolfe approached him and said: "Colonel, shall I send two men to carry you back, we can't stay here any longer, if we don't get out right speedily we will all be captured." The gallant Colonel replied, "you are doing nobly, Lieutenant give them h—l." The command devolved upon Captain Hugh McDonald. The numbers of the little band had been greatly reduced, but, with undaunted spirit, they met the onset of the foe and slowly fell back toward the edge of the woods. Their slackened fire told the rebels that they had been sadly reduced, yet they very cautiously followed up the retreat; darkness had settled down upon the field and the survivors, only forty, got safely back to the line they had left less than two hours before numbering one hundred and five men. Captain Taylor was captured with Colonel Kane.

Nobler blood never stained the earth than poured forth in that little grove of pines on the evening of June 6th, 1862. After one hour and a half of the most brilliant fight on record, these men returned to their command amid the cheers of the troops who had watched their gallant fight; witnesses of the unequal struggle without the power to render them any assistance. The only regret that stirred the hearts of the brave forty that returned unhurt was that they were compelled to leave so many of their dead and wounded comrades in the hands of the enemy.

Thus ended an engagement that has no parallel in history and about which there has been many accounts written by both Union and Confederate officers.

When the writer was a prisoner in Richmond, after the battle of Malvern Hill, Jackson's troops passed through the city on their return to the Valley. As they passed our prison, some soldiers in the First Maryland regiment, noticed "bucktails" on the caps of the prisoners who were looking out of the windows. They got permission from the guards and came into our room to buy our "bucktails," offering as high as fifty dollars in Confederate script for one. Our boys declined to sell, and asked them why they were so anxious to buy them, they replied that they had fought our *Division* up in the Valley at Harrisonburg and had whipped them and that their regiment, which had led the final charge, had, by special order of General Ewell, been permitted to place a captured "bucktail" on their flagstaff. One of the boys asked them how many troops were engaged against the Bucktail division, they replied that only one Brigade was in the battle. After getting from them full particulars of the fight, which they described as being a hotly contested battle lasting over an hour and a half, but claimed that they won a decided victory, driving the Bucktails from the field capturing the commanding *General* Kane.

After drawing out this story the Bucktail told them that there was but one regiment of Bucktails in the world (the new Bucktail regiments, the 149th and 150th, were not then enlisted) and that six companies of the ten were on the Peninsula with McClellan and that there were but four companies in the Valley and they were attached to a Cavalry Brigade, and that, according to their own story, as the Bucktails were in a woods of course the Cavalry were not with them, therefore, with a whole Brigade they fought for over two hours, before they drove from the field, four companies numbering less than two hundred. A deep interest had been taken by the two or three hundred prisoners who had been listening to these stories, and a cheer arose when the Bucktail finished; and the Confederates left.

Colonel Kane, when captured, was taken to the headquarters of General Ewell who had been a class-mate of his at school. General Ewell soon ascertained the number of troops engaged on the Union side, and knowing that Kane would see how much greater the Confederate force was, he was very much chagrined at the result. While Colonel Kane and General Ewell were talking the officer commanding the Confederate force rode up and announced in a loud voice that "we have gained a glorious victory, the enemy have been completely routed and driven from the field." General Ewell turned upon him fiercely and said: "General, I am astonished that you should have the face to come into my presence and claim a victory, such victories would drive us to h—l before we are ready to go. Shame! Shame! That not over one hundred men should so nearly destroy one of my best Brigades, and worse, that I must lose the brave General Ashby who had to take command of your Brigade in person in order to prevent defeat. I would not have lost him for a regiment such as you."

Colonel Kane, who was present as a prisoner, related this conversation to an officer in command. This officer has given it from memory, and says Colonel Kane, after relating it, declared that he could not have borne the fierce manner and language of General Ewell, but would have shot him down in his own tent.

The loss of the four companies at Harrisonburg cannot be given at this time. Among the killed was Martin Kelly, whom our readers will remember was engaged with Jimmie Ward and others in the raid on the Hospital supplies at Manassas when three men were poisoned by drinking a preparation of laudanum.

The following report of the battle of Harrisonburg was published in the Philadelphia *Inquirer*, June 16, 1862, a copy of which was kindly furnished to the writer by the publisher. After an account of the repulse of Colonel Wyndham's regiment and his capture the article concludes as follows:

Colonel Kane and his Bucktails

News of what has occurred is rapidly transmitted to Head Quarters, and General Bayard is ordered out with fresh cavalry and a battalion of Pennsylvania "Bucktails," But the Sixtieth Ohio has already beaten back the guidon of the bold rebels from flinging its folds in our eyes. The evening is waxing late; General Fremont does not wish to bring on a general engagement at this hour and the troops are ordered back. "But not to leave poor Wyndham on the field and all our wounded remonstrated my brave Col. Kane of the "Bucktails" and besides, General, think how such a stampede as this will dishearten and demoralize the army; let me at 'em General with my Bucktails." "Just forty minutes I'll give you, Colonel," says General Bayard pulling out his watch; "peep through the woods on our left, see what's in there, and out again when the time's up."

It was my first introduction to Colonel Kane, but I was willing to do honor to him as brother of the man who pushed the prow of his adventurous ship far up into the icy seas. "Good bye" he said pressing the hand of each of our group; "I hope to see you again; but if I don't, take it for granted that I and my Bucktails have given a good account of ourselves." In go the hundred and fifty *(Major John A. Wolf who was a Lieutenant in Company G and was present, says that there was only 105 men in the battalion at the battle of Harrisonburg.)* at an opening in the pines and the badge they bear on their caps, and from which the battalion takes it's name is soon lost among the green leaves. Brave boys, you never showed the tips of those bucks tails to the foe while a round of ammunition remained in your cartridge boxes, nor until the dead of your brave battalion outnumbered the living. In plain sight, on an eminence opposite, the same squadron of cavalry is drawn up that pursued us before; but an officer with a field-glass cries out that he can see dark columns of infantry creeping down in the woods, and we can distinguish with a naked eye that a cannon is being placed in position.

"Ride over there, Wier, and call back the "Bucktails,"" shouts General Bayard, but the order is cut short by the rattle of musketry over where they lie—single shots at first broadening and deepening into volleys. And now the bullets come straying up the hill where we are posted with the cavalry. Did you ever hear a bullet from a rifled musket come singing over your head, reader? No. Then catch a large bee some day and hold it to your ear, open your hand a little to hear him buzz, and then suddenly shutting off his music into a sharp fiz-z-z. "The Bucktails will shove it into them," remarked an officer. Now, do you know I had heard this same thing said of the Bucktails a dozen different times since they were called out, and really began to wonder whether they would sustain their reputation or not, for the sad, demoralized retreat of the cavalrymen had rather shaken my faith in the mettle that men are made of. Well, the Bucktails did shove it into them.

Through the openings between the trees we could see our brave boys surrounded by a cordon of fire, flashing into them from the muzzles of more than a thousand muskets. But not a sign, nor the shadow of a sign of yielding. Their fire met the enemy's straight and unyielding as the blade of a matador. Oh! For reinforcements, but none came. Our cavalry that had been drawn up under cover of the woods rode out upon the open hill, but cannot charge the trunks of intervening trees. To heighten the amusement the cannon opposite opens its mouth, and deposits a shell close by the side of a squadron. The range is accurate, and now they come, shot and shell exploding around us like exaggerated firecrackers on the Fourth of July.

Now our "Bucktails" give back, and anon they break cover and retreat across the fields of waving green between us, firing as they go—but not the hundred and fifty that went in. The rest of them lie under the arching dome of the treacherous forest, and the night dews alone can go to moisten the lips of the wounded ones, for the rebels hold the woods, and we are not now prepared to dislodge them. To send a force for their support would bring on a general engagement, and this in our present unprepared condition would be ruin.

My brave Colonel Kane is reported wounded and a prisoner—shot in the knee. Fare you well great heart; a more gallant soldier, or a truer gentleman never wore sword by side, and if we meet not here let me share your fate hereafter what ever that may be. This evening forty of the Bucktails are reported from the hospital as wounded, and the Heaven that bends above them only knows how many are lying dead and wounded on the field, or how many are prisoners.

One man whom I noticed at the hospital, was shot in three places—the top of the head, the back of the neck and the side; is not here evidence of the fierce fire that my Bucktails stood under? "Why didn't you come out when you found they were in such force against you?" asks a bystander of a wounded officer. "Why, you see I was told to deploy some men as skirmishers and before we had moved thirty yards we were breast to breast with a whole regiment of Rebels. It was no use, of course, to fight, but as for retreat, I knew the Colonel would not hear of it, so we went in." And you did go in my Bucktails, and you did the bravest thing that has been done in all this sudden making of splendid names and poor wailing ghosts."

The following is taken from the history of one of the Maryland (rebel) regiments engaged in the battle of Harrisonburg which appeared in the Phila. *Times* some months ago. The date and name of the writer cannot be recalled:

"From the first Manassas to the surrender at Appomattox the Marylanders were in the thickest of every fight in which they were engaged, and when they were seen "going to the front" it was known that hot work was at hand. They were in Jackson's memorable run up the Valley in the spring of 1862, and were conspicuous in the fight with the Pennsylvania "Bucktails" on the 6th of June, when General Ewell issued an order directing that "in commemoration of the gallant conduct of the First Maryland Regiment, under Colonel Bradley T. Johnson, on the sixth of June, when they drove back the Pennsylvania Bucktail Rifles in the engagement near Harrisonburg, authority is given to have one of the captured Bucktails (the insignia of the Federal regiment) appended to the color-staff of the First Maryland Regiment." Colonel Johnson led his men in a dashing charge in the hottest part of the day, and drove the enemy off with heavy loss, capturing Lieutenant Colonel Kane, commanding the Bucktails. With their bravely won trophy on their colors the regiment marched gaily and gallantly into action on the morning of the 12th of June, the day of the battle of Cross Keys.

In alluding to the bravery of the Marylanders on the 6th of June, Ewell said: "Their gallantry on this occasion is worthy of acknowledgment from a higher source, more particularly as they avenged the death of gallant Ashby, who fell at the same time."

Addendum to Bard's Scrapbook with No. 26 written in pencil

The following is the introduction of an illustrated paper published at the time by Mr. Webb, correspondent of the New York Times.

We illustrate today one of the most heroic actions of the war, the attack of 150 of the famous Bucktails, under the gallant leader, Col. Kane, upon a portion of Stonewall Jackson's army, consisting of infantry, cavalry and artillery. Our artists, Mr. Edwin Forbes, says the spot where the deadly conflict took place is about a mile and a half beyond Harrisonburg, on the road to Port Republic, towards which places the rebels were in full retreat, closely but warily pursued by Gens. Freemont and Shields. On Friday, June 6th Col. Sir Percy Wyndham, of the 1st Jersey Cavalry, having been charged by General Bayard to reconnoiter, was led into an ambuseade, when his regiment was fearfully cut up and himself wounded and taken prisoner. So for our special artist; we will now borrow the description of Mr. Webb the special correspondent of the New York Times, who rode side by side with our artist amid the whistling of the bullets. It will be seen that the humanity of the brave Col. Kane led him into a similar trap.

(There follows the same article on preceding page which I have credited to Philadelphia Inquirer.

No. 27

Bates gives the loss of the battalion, in the battle at Harrisonburg, at fifty-two killed and wounded, and the loss of the enemy five hundred and fifty-nine. All this in less than two hours fighting, surely history gives no account of an action where one hundred and five men, without entrenchments, rifle pits or other protection than that afforded by trees, fought a Brigade of at least three regiments, the Forty-fourth and Fifty-eighth Virginia and the First Maryland, and killed and wounded more than five times their own number.

After the battle of Harrisonburg the numbers of the battalion was increased by men joining who had not been able to keep up on the march, but were enabled to overtake their command by the delay occasioned by that engagement. So, that on the 8th of June, at Cross Keys, the battalion numbered about eighty-five men. At this time they were temporarily attached to a Brigade in Fremont's Corps and were placed in support of the Pierrepont Battery commanded by Captain Buell. Fremont's line, during the battle, was driven back leaving this Battery exposed to the concentrated fire of the advancing line of the enemy, and, to make matters still more desperate, the enemy threw a strong force of Infantry almost in the rear of the position occupied by the Battery thus completely cutting off their retreat. Captain Buell changed position and loaded his guns with grape declaring that his parting shot would be one never to be forgotten, then, turning to the battalion he said, "boys, they've got us, but we will hurt some of them badly before they take my guns." The brave boys replied: "Oh, no, Captain, they havn't got us yet, we've been in worse scrapes than this and got out." Captain McDonald formed his battalion in line in front of the Battery and told them to lie down and wait the coming of the enemy.

They waited but a few minutes when the line of battle made its appearance. The Bucktails at once opened a wicked fire which caused them to halt when the battalion charged forward with a cheer and drove back the line in front under cover of the hill, Captain Buell all the time pleading with them to fall back behind his guns and give him a chance to get a shot at the enemy.

As soon as they succeeded in driving the enemy to cover the Bucktails returned to the Battery. A new line was formed by the enemy to attack them on the flank while the reformed line again threatened another charge on their front. Captain Buell now declared that there was no hope for his Battery but the Bucktails said to him "this Battery is not captured yet, Captain, and there is going to be lots of fun here before they get it." An opportunity was given when Captain Buell poured a murderous fire of grape into the enemy. Immediately after firing he limbered up his guns, and, with the battalion as a rear-guard, made a rush to reach our troops.

During this fight, which was witnessed by General Fremont and his chief of Artillery, our Artillery had been placed in position to give the enemy a warm reception as soon as he made his appearance. A strip of woods and a hollow lay between where Buell's Battery was in position and the line to which our troops had fallen back after their repulse. When Buell fired the volley and withdrew his Battery he passed out of sight and as long lines of Infantry could be seen moving down on both flanks General Fremont believed their escape impossible, and, when Captain Buell with his Battery and the battalion of Bucktails came in sight of our line our batteries, supposing them to be rebels, opened on them and shelled them until one man ran forward with the flag and convinced them that it was the Pierrepont Battery and the battalion of Bucktails, when they ceased firing. In a few minutes more they were safe and this ended the battle of Cross Keys.

The loss of the Bucktails was very small only some eight or ten killed and wounded.

The troops went into this fight without a mouthful of food in their haversacks; indeed they had been on less than half rations for several days. General Fremont, as soon as they got back into our line, ordered his staff to gather up all the eatables there was around army headquarters and send them to the battalion that had saved his famous Pierrepont Battery.

The next morning Colonel Pilson, Fremont's chief of Artillery, came over and asked to be introduced to every man in the battalion. He shook each one by the hand and thanked them for having saved his best Battery. While he was doing this great tears were rolling down the bronzed cheeks of Captain Buell who stood near by.

After the battle of Cross Keys the battalion marched to Mount Jackson where they remained several days; from there they marched to Bristoe Station remaining there some time. While in camp at this place, on July 4th, General Bayard was presented with a horse and equipments. The same day they were ordered to march to Warrenton Junction to head off the rebel Cavalry force, commanded by General J. E. B. Stuart, which was rapidly moving in that direction with the intention of capturing or destroying a large lot of lumber on cars at that point. Our troops and three locomotives fortunately arrived in time to remove it and it was safely conveyed to Alexandria.

The battalion, then attached to McDowell's Corps, marched back to Slaughter mountain. General Pope there detailed the Bucktails as his headquarter guard. This was a new business for the brave men who were left, and they naturally supposed that they would get some much needed rest, but the situation of the army and the condition of affairs at that time did not give them a chance to recuperated. After the battle of Slaughter mountain, in charge of the headquarters train they marched to Catlett's Station. Colonel Kane had returned August 19th about the time of the battle of Slaughter mountain and taken command of the battalion. Jacksons's Corps, with Stuart's Cavalry, came down on the right of Pope's army, and, on the night of August 22nd when the headquarter train arrived at Catlett's Station, Stuart made a raid on the train. The night was intensely dark and the rain was pouring down in a perfect flood. Colonel Kane had occupied a pine woods close by the road and the train was parked near by. Lieutenant Winslow, of Company G., was riding out a country road posting the pickets when two men rode up, one on each side, and asked him some questions. The Lieutenant, knowing at once that something was wrong, dropped his bridle rein and drew his sword with one hand and his revolver with the other, but, before he could use either, the men grasped his arms and commanded him to surrender. By this time a score or more rebels had arrived and Lieutenant Winslow was taken back a prisoner.

The rebels at once charged upon the train and began to set fire to the wagons. Kane called his men together and whispered to them to take six steps forward, stop and touch elbows, take six steps more and do the same. As soon as they saw the light from the wagon that had been set on fire they commenced firing soon driving the rebels away from the light. Whenever a torch was lighted with which to fire a wagon some watchful riflemen, directed by the light, fired and in every instance the torch was extinguished. The Cavalry then charged into the woods yelling and firing. Their shots, however, passed harmlessly over the heads of the men who were wasting no ammunition. The Bucktails had a decided advantage; they were on food and in the woods. They, in a short time, were surrounded by the Cavalry, but, in the black darkness that surrounded them, they were invisible to the foe. Corporal Looney, taking advantage of a glimpse he got of a Cavalryman fired, when his rifle cracked another Cavalryman, who was close behind him, struck him with his sabre cutting a terrible gash in his head and felling him to the ground, he, however, soon recovered and continued to take an active part in the fight. One unfortunate rebel was mounted on a white horse and as he was riding toward Lieutenant Wolfe and threatened to ride right over him the Lieutenant drew his revolver, which he thought he had kept perfectly dry, but six times in succession the hammer fell upon the cap without exploding it, he then caught it by the muzzle and threw it at the Cavalryman, who soon disappeared. The Cavalry, finding that they could not make any headway against the battalion and utterly failing to set fire to the train withdrew, disappearing in the darkness, having succeeded in burning just one wagon and robbing several others.

After the affair at Catlett's Station the battalion in charge of the train moved up to the battlefield of Bull Run. During this battle they were engaged in reforming broken lines of stragglers and did good service. At the time the grand stampede began Kane formed his battalion in line of skirmishers and halted every man that came back, among the number was a Brigadier-General who attempted to force his way through, Kane being near by drew his sword and riding up to him called him a coward, and beating him over the back with his sword bade him tear off his shoulder straps and go home, that it was a shame for an officer to be seen among a crowd of stragglers who were trying to see which could reach a place of safety first. The crowd of stragglers soon got so large that Kane's small force was overwhelmed and he formed his men and marched them back to Centerville.

At Chantilly the battalion was under fire but not actively engaged, and met with no loss. They then marched to Arlington Heights where they were again united with the six companies. The joy that filled the breasts of all the men at their reunion cannot be expressed, it was like receiving the long lost, or like the dead returned to life again. On September 7th Colonel Kane was commissioned a Brigadier-General for his conspicuous gallantry and assigned to the command of a Brigade in the Twelfth Corps.

After writing letters to officers who were engaged in the campaign of the four companies in the Valley and failing to get a reply from any one containing the information necessary to give even a . . . of it, each one writing me . . . could not trust their memories as to dates and places. I was obliged to attempt the story from information gathered from Major John A. Wolfe in a conversation lasting about three hours. These letters, relating to that campaign, have been submitted to him and received his approval and endorsement as being correct and accurate in the statement of facts. I am conscious that many things have been omitted that should have been mentioned, but am confident that there has been nothing stated but what is true. I am well aware that the affairs at Harrisonburg and Cross Keys will appear overdrawn, but the facts can be fully substantiated, by testimony from the writings of both Federal and Confederate officers. The following taken from the biography of Stonewall Jackson by John Esten Cooke, a Confederate, shows how desperate the engagements were considered by the rebels:

"Ashby witnessed this result, and the persistent stand of his opponents, with fiery impatience. He directed the 58th to cease firing and press the enemy with the bayonet, and, putting spurs to his horse, rushed forward shouting, 'Virginians charge,' when the animal was shot under him and fell. In an instant he was on his feet and again advanced. He had not, however, moved ten steps, and was still ordering his men not to fire, but depend on the bayonet, when a bullet pierced his body, and he fell dead almost instantly, at the very moment when the shout of triumph around him indicated the repulse of the enemy."

From "Memoirs of Ashby," by Averitt another Confederate, we take the following extract, relating to the battle of Harrisonburg:

"It was, perhaps, two hours after, that orders came for three regiments of infantry to retrace the steps they had taken in the morning, and we felt sure, from the command being accompanied by General Ewell in person that some serious work was on hand. The regiments selected were the Fifty-eighth and Forty-fourth Virginia and the First Maryland. After moving through the woods for some distance we were met by General Ashby, when the command was halted and two companies of the First Maryland thrown forward as skirmishers under the immediate eye, I may say command, of Ashby. The reserves followed closely, and in half an hour three or four shots announced that the enemy was near. The Fifty-eighth was ordered up and soon became engaged. The fire of the enemy was very deadly, and the Fifty-eighth recoiled before it."

Then follows an account of the killing of Ashby very much the same as given above after which the article continues as follows:

"After the fall of Ashby, the troops engaged fell back in great confusion, when General Ewell, rushing through a storm of bullets, ordered the Marylanders to charge. Under the gallant Johnson they rushed to the attack, and, after a short but sanguinary engagement, drove the enemy from the field. We then discovered that we had encountered the celebrated Bucktail Rifles, commanded by Lieutenant-Colonel Kane, who was wounded and a prisoner in our hands."

From a letter received from Major Wolfe I take the liberty of publishing the following extract:

PHILIPSBURG, PA., Oct. 22nd, 1885. Your description is all right and correct as to facts. I don't think you have overdrawn either of the engagements referred to and as an instance of the severity of the campaign would note here that at the battle of Cross Keys, General Bayard, a soldier who never cried "hold enough" had to report his Cavalry unfit for duty. His horses and men, as well as himself all being worn out. Our battalion had bivouacked with them every night during that memorable Valley Campaign as well as skirmished for them in every engagement they had in the Valley, save the one in which Colonel Wyndham was surprised and captured.

No. 28

On the 4th of May, 1864, General Meade issued an address to the army which was read to each regiment. I give the address in full, believing the surviving soldiers of the Army of the Potomac will be pleased to read it; it will call forth recollections of that memorable day and awaken their love for their noble leader, who is now laid to rest with many a noble hero whose remains lie scattered through that wilderness:

"COMRADES:--Again you are called upon to advance on the enemies of your country. the time and the occasion are deemed opportune by your commanding general to address you a few words of confidence and caution. You have been reorganized, strengthened and fully equipped in every respect. You form a part of the several armies of your country—the whole under the direction of an able and distinguished general, who enjoys the confidence of the Government, the people and the army. Your movements being in co-operation with others, it is of the utmost importance that no effort be left unspared to make it successful.

Soldiers! The eyes of the whole country are looking with anxious hope to the blow you are about to strike in the most sacred cause that ever called men to arms. Remember your homes, your wives and children, and bear in mind that the sooner your enemies are overcome the sooner you will be returned to enjoy the benefits and blessings of peace. Bear with patience the hardships and sacrifices you will be called upon to endure. Have confidence in your officers and in each other. Keep your ranks on the march and on the battlefield, and let each one earnestly implore God's blessings, and endeavor by his thoughts and actions to render himself worthy of the favor he seeks.

With clear conscience and strong arms, actuated by a high sense of duty, fighting to preserve the Government and the institutions handed down to us by our forefathers, if true to ourselves, victory under God's blessing, must and will attend our efforts."

GEORGE G. MEADE.
Major-General Commanding.

On the morning of May 5th, at daylight, the Bucktails took the advance of our Division and moved forward in the direction of Parker's store. About the middle of the afternoon we encountered the enemy. A regiment of dismounted Cavalry were engaged in a woods immediately in our front, we advanced rapidly across the open country and formed our line in and about twenty rods from the edge of the woods. We were situated on one side of a farm that was almost entirely surrounded by woods. Our dismounted Cavalry were doing good service, but the superior force of the enemy in their front, was slowly but steadily forcing them back. Major Hartshorn directed the Bucktails to lie down and conceal themselves behind trees and logs. He then informed the Cavalry of our presence and directed them to fall back behind our line, in order to draw the enemy up close to us before we would open our fire. The trap thus set for the rebels appeared to afford great pleasure to this line of Cavalry which had been fighting and slowly falling back since early in the morning.

This woods, was very favorable to us being clear from underbrush, and a man could be seen a very considerable distance. There was a small stream running through the woods nearly parallel with our line, and about one hundred and fifty or two hundred yards in our front, the ground sloped gently down on each side. We were thus able to see the enemy when they were several hundred yards distant. The Bucktails patiently waited their approach, and became deeply interested in the efforts their officers were making to get them to charge "and capture those Yankees, there are only a handful of dismounted Cavalry there anyhow."

These words caused a smile to pass along the line of the Cavalry skirmishers as well as the Bucktails.

After the Cavalry crossed the stream and began to ascend the hill, the rebels got a fair view of the line opposed to them. Their officers again ordered a charge, and, this time, it was heartily responded to. They came forward on a run with the well known rebel yell. When the Cavalry fell back past our line and the foremost of the enemy got within a few yards of us Major Hartshorn gave the command to fire when from our Spencer rifles we poured several deadly volleys into them in quick succession which utterly routed them, they did not stop or attempt to rally until they passed clear out of sight. One rebel, when his officer tried to induce him to stand, and repeated the assertion that there was nothing but a line of dismounted Cavalry in their front kept on running and shouted back: "Cavalry h—l, Cavalry don't carry knapsacks and wear Bucktails!"

Major Hartshorn had reported to General Crawford that the enemy appeared in considerable force in our front and that his line extended on past our right flank. General Crawford at once sent forward the other regiments of the Brigade. He at the same time directed Major Hartshorn to hold his position.

Some of the regiments, while moving into position, were attacked and thrown into confusion, and nearly all of the Seventh regiment was captured. Our right was threatened and the firing soon indicated that the enemy was in our rear. Our regiment had been engaged but about an hour when Major Hartshorn discovered that a large force of the enemy were massing on our left and he at once ordered companies E. and K., under command of Lieutenant Bard, to move forward to the left and deploy in skirmish line with the right of the two companies resting on the left of the regiment, and forming the short line of an L facing outward.

Our right flank being threatened, Major Hartshorn deployed a portion of the line to protect it, thus forming three sides of a square. The regiment was now in immediate danger, although not engaged, the line in our front evidently holding back until the flanking party should engage us in the rear. At this critical moment an aide rode up at full gallop and told Major Hartshorn that he was almost surrounded and to make his way out as best he could. The Major soon rallied the six companies in the centre and the companies on the right, but the word which was to be passed along the line to the two companies on the left failed to reach them. They remained at their post wholly unconscious of the fact that they were all alone, until a special messenger, sent by Major Hartshorn, told them that they had only one chance out of many of getting out of their unfortunate situation. The line was ordered to face to the left and move forward rapidly, and the word was passed along for the rear to close up double-quick; as soon as the companies were gathered together the order to run was given.

It was not necessary to repeat the order, as we could tell by he sound of the firing that the enemy was rapidly closing in on us, from both flanks and the troops on our first front were charging after the prey that had quietly gotten away from them. The two companies, on their retreat, passed into the woods from a small field as the rebels entered it from the other side.

We had now to run a gauntlet, down a ravine to a creek, fired into from both sides, we crossed the creek, which was literally bridged with knapsacks that had been thrown into it by the troops that preceeded us in their flight. We were soon in sight of our line and were met by Major Hartshorn, who had given us up for lost. Three cheers went up as we took our places in line.

On our left, Hancock's Corps had been severely engaged, and had failed to break the enemy's line. Our line was formed and some rifle pits were thrown up to protect the more exposed portions. Thus ended the first days fight under the leadership of General Grant. Every old soldier knew that we had met with a repulse; we had met the enemy, and he had driven our line with very considerable loss. It was the general opinion, as we lay on our arms that night, that our army would fall back across the Rapidan, and when the Bucktails were moved forward and placed in the front line with orders to lay with our arms in our hands, prepared at a moment's notice to resist an attack, you could hear along the line such remarks as "well the change in commanders has not changed the old order of things. Bucktails in front on the advance, and in the rear on the retreat."

Troops could be heard marching and Artillery moving through the night. This was supposed to be our army retreating and the men of our Brigade supposed they were the rear guard of the Corps and would have to cover the retreat. Just on our left was a regiment of Heavy Artillery numbering eighteen hundred men, under command of a very youthful Colonel. These men had been laying around Washington, in the Forts and doing guard and patrol duty, this was their first experience in the presence of the enemy. They supposed they were in the extreme front, and it was quite amusing to our boys to watch the moving around with great caution, they even spoke in a suppressed tone of voice. Colonel McDonaough, of the Second Reserves, was in their front, on picket. The Artillery were lying in a field close by the edge of a woods, the Second was in the woods, two or three hundred yards in advance of their line. Just after dark a rebel picket fired at one of the Second's pickets, his shot was answered by four or five shots from the Second which called forth a rattling fire from the enemy. When the first shot was fired the Heavy Artillery regiment sprung to arms and poured a volley into the woods. Colonel McDonough soon came riding up and wanted to know what they meant by firing into their own men, the young Colonel replied that he did not know that there was any Union troops in his front, Colonel McDonough replied, "Yes there are and if you fire into them again I will face about, march back, and kill every man you have." This settled them, and they remained quiet during the night.

Some time after midnight the moving of troops and trains ceased and everything was still; this was the calm that always preceeds the storm. Many comments were made by the men on Grant's first move, which they had determined was a failure, and as has been stated before there was considerable feeling against Grant on account of his being a Western man. Those who had encouraged this feeling felt a sort of grim satisfaction at his failure in his first encounter with Lee. The reader, being informed of this feeling, can form some idea of the astonishment greeted when as soon as the first streaks of light in the East gave notice of the approaching day, firing was heard, first away off on our right, soon Artillery firing was heard on the left, we were called to arms and in a short time the whole line of the army seemed to be engaged. There was to be no retreating, the Army of the Potomac had crossed the Rapidan for the last time.

All that day the battle raged with terrible fury. The two armies were, apparently, standing and shooting at one another, and it seemed to be only a question of the destruction of one or both lines. Charge and counter charges were made, the lines would surge back and forth, the same ground in many cases was fought over two, three and four times during the day. General Hancock's Corps on our left drove the enemy considerable distance in the morning, succeeding in routing the Corps of A. P. Hill but in driving them back encountered the Corps of Longstreet which in turn drove the Second Corps back to their entrenchments.

Our Corps, the Fifth, then commanded by General Warren, formed the centre, Sedgwick, with the Sixth Corps, formed the right, the woods surrounding and in front of Hancock's Corps was so dense that Artillery could not be used and indeed but little Artillery could be used anywhere along the entire line. The Sixth Corps, late in the evening, met with a repulse when the Reserves were hurried to their support marching in the dark guided only by the sound of the fierce battle that was being fought, when they arrived on the ground they found the gallant Sixth Corps had not only checked the advance of Ewell but had recovered the ground they had lost. Finding that his assistance was not needed there General Crawford marched his Division back to its place in line, by the time they reached there firing had ceased and the second day's fighting was over.

Both armies had lost heavily in killed, wounded and prisoners. Neither side had gained any advantage, although fighting had been of the most stubborn and determined character. Lieutenant-Colonel Dare, of the Fifth Reserves, was wounded during the day, and died that night. After we returned from the right and while we were making some coffee an officer brought us the dying message of Colonel Dare, he was well known in our regiment as a brave officer and noble patriot and the news of his death, accompanied as it was with his last message to his comrades in arms, produced a feeling of sadness and sorrow seldom witnessed among men who had become so familiar with death.

The second day's fight awakened the curiosity of the soldier who was studying the character of our new leader. We had held our ground, everything in the shape of supplies was on hand, ammunition well supplied on the line, rations were brought up and there was no indication that any preparations were being made for falling back. The army of the Potomac lay down to rest on the night of the 6th of May, 1864, with a feeling that the battle would be renewed very early the next morning; they were gaining confidence in the man who had made them no promises in general orders, or addresses, they were soon to learn that this silent man whom they had seen quietly riding along the line during the hottest of the fight that day intended to keep "pounding away" until the army of Lee should be destroyed. In general officers our army lost Wadsworth and Hays killed.

Two hundred thousand men had been engaged all day, and the air was filled with smoke, the sun shining through it caused a red glare which at sunset produced a scene never to be forgotten by those who witnessed it.

As the men were laying quiet at their posts, along about midnight away off on our right there came the sound of that rebel yell, it was taken up by regiment after regiment on both sides and swept down along the entire line of both armies. No soldier, of either army, will ever forget the thrill that went through him when the yell first broke the stillness of that midnight hour, or the strange sensation as of some indefinable fear that took possession of him as it swept down the line gathering greater power as regiment after regiment joined until two hundred thousand men were making all the noise they could. This yell however, was only to cover a fierce attack upon Sedgwick. Lee had determined to make a desperate night attack on our right and had concentrated a large force there for that purpose, hoping to be able to break through, thus turning our right and getting between our army and our line of retreat. The movement was not successful, although a portion of our line on the extreme right was turned.

Early on Saturday morning, May 7th, General Sedgwick discovered that the enemy had fallen back from his front, he at once pushed forward and soon discovered that that portion of Lee's army had withdrawn. The line in our front, however, showed no signs of a general retreat, and their position being naturally strong, an attempt to drive them from it promised but little hope for success but must cause a terrible sacrifice of life.

About noon our Cavalry reported Lee in retreat, Major Hartshorn was at once ordered to take our regiment out a country road, deploy on each side as skirmishers, and ascertain whether the rebels were in force. He was cautioned not to bring on a general engagement, but when he ascertained that there was a considerable force then to fall back.

Several regiments moved out in front in order to protect our flanks and prevent our capture should the line of the enemy be found in position. Major Hartshorn led his regiment about half a mile out the road, that ran through a dense forest, at right angles with the line of the army. He then ordered two companies to deploy on each side of the road holding the other six in reserve, those on the right G. and D. soon met the enemy in force when Major Hartshorn sent companies F. and K. to their support directing the officers to deploy their men in the intervals of the two companies then engaged,--making a double skirmish line,--and to push forward and find out what was there. When F. and K. got in position the line charged driving the rebels before them into a cluster of large rocks some of them ten to fifteen feet high, covering perhaps half an acre of ground. The rebels took refuge behind these rocks and checked the line immediately in front of them, the Bucktails took cover behind trees, and the word was passed along the line for the flanks to press forward and flank the position while the boys in front would hold them there.

Just as this movement was being executed with certainty of success and the capture of near three hundred rebels an aide came up and ordered the men back, the officers and men both plead for twenty minutes, but not one minute would be given the aide said General Crawford was fearful that we had gone too far, as it was of the greatest importance, in view of certain movements going on, that we avoid a general engagement just at that time. The officers had some difficulty in getting the men to fall back and leave the prize that was already within their grasp. This skirmish which only lasted a few minutes, was one of the hottest fights our regiment had during that campaign. Somewhere near thirty of the four companies were killed and wounded. The loss of the enemy was undoubtedly greater, as we had the very decided advantage of breech-loading rifles and poured a terrible fire into them as they ran towards the rocks for shelter.

We carried back our killed and wounded, and when we got back to our place in line received the highest praise from the other regiments of the Brigade for our success in finding the enemy and for the terrific fight which they declared surpassed anything in the way of a skirmish that they had heard.

This ended the fighting for that day, during the night the army began the flanking movement to the left which was continued until it arrived in front of Petersburg.

No. 29

Saturday evening, May 7th, the army began to march toward Spotsylvania Court House. The Fifth corps did not start until after dark, the Pennsylvania Reserves left their line about 10 o'clock and marched along just in rear of the ground fought over by the Second corps. The stench from the field was almost unbearable, it arose from the dead horses. The march was very slow and very tiresome, the column would start off at a rapid gait, go but a few rods, then halt for several minutes, just long enough for the men to fall asleep, when it would start again. The night was very dark and the men suffering for want of sleep, they had none but such rest as they could snatch in line since the night of May 4th.

The Reserves took the road leading to Todd's tavern and in the direction of Chancellorsville. Our Cavalry, under General Custer, had a severe fight with the enemy near Todd's tavern, encountering heavy lines of infantry General Custer sustained a vigorous attack and held his ground until Robinson's division of our corps arrived and relieved him. The Reserves, as soon as the firing indicated a battle, were pushed forward as fast as possible, when they came on the field, Robinson's troops were formed on the right and Griffin's division on the left. The battle was raging with great fury when the Bucktails entered a piece of woods, on the right of which, was Griffin; the left of his command extending across a farm to a point near these woods, the enemy were threatening his left flank, in fact under cover of the woods were moving a strong force for that purpose. The Bucktails came upon them as they were marching by the flank. Major Hartshorn ordered Captain Samuel Mack, with the first platoon of his company, to deploy as skirmishers to cover the regiment while we came in on right by file into line. Captain Mack sprang to the front and calling upon his men to follow him, charged upon the enemy. His wicked attack saved the regiment from a terrible loss; the enemy was there in force and punished the gallant little band severely, Captain Mack was wounded twice and every man that went out with him was either killed or wounded.

The enemy occupied a position in the woods on a slight eminence, in their rear, and in front of our regiment, there was a strip of cleared land, the ground descending from the woods to about the centre then rising more abruptly to a thick woods in which were the entrenchments of the enemy. As soon as our line was formed we were ordered to charge; we were then under a very hot fire from the troops in our front, and as soon as Captain Mack opened with his skirmishers a rebel battery, off to our right, opened on us with shrapnel, raking our line, this was calculated to make the men eager to get at the enemy, as the terrible execution they were doing would soon weaken us they, therefore, charged with a will, but they soon found that there was no easy job before them, the rebels stubbornly resisted and hotly contested every inch of ground. They were, however, forced back across the field into their earthworks, here they rallied and checked our advance. On the left of our regiment the low ground between the hill were we first formed, and the position to which we had driven the enemy, was a deep swamp, through this both lines were obliged to wade above the knees. We held our position but a short time when we were ordered to fall back to the woods behind the field. The enemy did not again venture out of their works, or attempt to interfere with us.

After getting something to eat, and about three o'clock in the afternoon, we were ordered to the right where we formed a part of the second line in a desperate charge made by the First brigade, under Colonel Tally, who was captured. Three times our troops charged the works of the enemy, after driving him nearly a mile, but they failed to carry them, night setting in it soon became too dark to distinguish between friend and foe, the Fifth corps was taken back and occupied a parallel ridge on which they dug rifle pits during the night.

Our loss in this day's fight was very severe, Lietuenant Daniel Orcutt, of Company A., was killed, Captain S. A. Mack and Lieutenant Daniel Blett, wounded, the latter died in hospital at Georgetown after suffering the amputation of a leg. The names of the killed and wounded in the separate engagements cannot be given as there was no time to make daily reports and the loss was given only when an opportunity presented itself. The names given here are from memory. In one of the companies two brothers were killed only a few yards apart. For four days we had been fighting and everything indicated a renewal of the conflict the following morning. We were now about three miles from Spotsylvania Court House the point to which our army was not directed. Lee had handled his army with great skill and had thus far successfully covered and defended every approach to it. Notwithstanding the hard fighting and severe loss, our army did not appear in the least discouraged, daily battles even this early in the campaign were looked upon as a matter of course; there was no more wondering whether we would fall back or advance, something of the spirit of our leader seemed to take possession of the rank and file, and to "keep pounding away" was accepted as the general line of conduct for the Army of the Potomac. This was war in real, dead earnest, every day war; no fighting to-day and resting to-morrow. We had seen Grant several times, always quiet, unassuming, but on the field, looking after the work in hand. The supplies, as I stated before, were at hand, rations were plenty, it was only a question of a chance to get them and prepare them. Ammunition was always at hand when wanted. This gave the army the greatest confidence in their leader, and taught them that arrangements had been made to "fight it out on this line if it took all summer."

On Monday morning May 9, we moved to the right relieving a portion of the Sixth corps. Our troops occupying their earthworks, it is hardly necessary to say that General Crawford requested Major Hartshorn to take his regiment out in front and deploy them as skirmishers. While in this position we had an opportunity to test our marksmanship. The river Po, a narrow, deep sluggish stream ran along in our front, the enemy were strongly entrenched on a heavily wooded ridge on the opposite side of the stream. Some distance to the right of our brigade the river made a sharp turn cutting through our lines nearly at a right angle, the rebel line, at the point at where the river made the turn, did not follow the course of the stream but continued on the ridge, the river cut across the low ground taking the other side of the narrow valley. The enemy's sharpshooters were about 800 yards away, and protected by rifle pits and trees, our regiment had no cover except what the inequalities of the ground afforded, except at one point near the centre of the regiment where there was a farm house surrounded by an orchard, this afforded fine shelter for one company. Their sharpshooters paid their respects to us while we were getting our line formed. When we got into position we got their range and for about an hour kept up a pretty lively skirmish, by that time both sides found it unsafe to expose any part of the body. At one point on the line occupied by Company K., the rebels had complete range and they were permitted to have undisputed control over the few rods upon which they had concentrated their fire. During the day a squad of Berdan's sharpshooters armed with very heavy rifles, globe sights and patent rests, were sent out to our line to try to pick off the gunners from a rebel battery. It took them several minutes to load and fire, their coming aroused the curiosity of the Bucktails and they watched them with great interest, they were particularly interested, because on several occasions they had heard of the wonders performed by these sharpshooters. A group of three or four general officers sat on their horses just behind our batteries who were also interested spectators. After they fired several shots without doing what they were brought there for, their attention was called to some rebels who were digging a rifle pit off to our right. The sharpshooters turned their attention at once in that direction, with no better result. An officer of the Bucktails signaled to Major Hartshorn who was with General Crawford, and when the Major came closer this officer told him if he would have the Berdan men taken away, that he would soon stop work on that rifle pit. Major Hartshorn reported this to General Crawford who had the sharpshooters recalled and told Major Hartshorn that his chance was good. Hartshorn then directed the officer to see what he could do. Estimating the distance at 1000 yards he directed the first platoon of his company to elevate their sights for that distance and shoot high; at the first volley two men were seen to fall, and the rest hunted cover. This caused rejoicing along the line, and several soldiers cried out "it will not be necessary to send heavy riflemen to assist us on the skirmish line." Shortly after this occurred, a body of horsemen was seen to ride out to the edge of the woods and examine our line, they were still farther to our right than the party that were working on the rifle pits, Major Hartshorn with the aid of a field glass made out that it was a general officer and his staff. He pointed out the one whom he supposed to be the general, and the platoon of 16 men all took careful aim and fired, when this man was seen to fall forward, and was taken back by those with him. A few days after we got hold of a Richmond paper which gave an account of General Longstreet being wounded while in the extreme front taking a view of our lines. This no doubt was him.

George Champlain of Company E., and a rebel sharpshooter were firing at each other, the rebel was aiming too low, Champlain called out to him to shoot higher, he did so, Champlain said that is better but still too low; the rebel finally shot Champlain dead. Lieutenant R. Fent Ward was walking along the line when a rifle ball struck his sabre near the middle cutting or breaking it in two, steel scabbard and all; the shock threw Ward down but did not hurt him. Major Hartshorn brought the piece with the handle home, and may have it yet.

By a general order all stragglers picked up by the Provost Guard, were sent to the extreme front and put in the most dangerous places. This day some thirty or forty men were sent to our regiment and distributed among the companies. Three were assigned to Company K. and were directed to the point mentioned before as being completely commanded by the enemy's sharpshooters, one of these men coolly marched up, took his place and began to load and fire, the other two as soon as they came in range and the rifle balls began to zip 'round them, threw themselves flat on the ground and would not move. They watched their opportunity and slipped off. The other was a brave soldier who had on the march fallen out to get a drink, and was picked up. He was taken from his dangerous position and put with the rest of the men. He done noble fighting that afternoon, went with us the next day, when he was given a certificate setting forth his bravery, and with a request for all guards to pass him to his regiment; Major Hartshorn approved the certificate and sent him on his way. We saw him once afterward as we marched by his regiment.

There was no general engagement in our front that afternoon. As soon as it got dark our regiment was cautiously advanced toward the river, when we had gotten about one third of the distance between our line and the distance between our line and the enemy's the regiment was halted and a detail of three companies sent further to the front; they were ordered to crawl up as close to the river as they could and ascertain if possible, what the enemy was doing. After they had cawled up close enough to hear them talk, they laid flat down and remained there until near morning. Major Hartshorn took an officer with him, crossed the river on a log, crept up to their earthworks inside their outer pickets, and in a quiet tone of voice commanded a sentinel to surrender. The sentinel replied, "If you want us, why don't you come up and get us." Major Hartshorn remained quiet until he was satisfied the sentinel was paying no attention to him, when he succeeded in getting back into our lines without even being shot at. Why the sentinel did not shoot or cause an alarm is a mystery that has not been explained. Soon after Major Hartshorn returned there came an order from General Crawford for our pickets of the Sixth Corps on our right. These troops had arrived after dark, and their exact location was not known, fires had been kindled across the river at the bend, before spoken of which we supposed belonged to the troops of the Sixth Corps. To Lieutentants, Bard and Kratzer, was assigned this task; they crept cautiously up the line until they came to the bank of the river, which was not over twenty feet wide. A dense fog had settled down in the little valley adding to the darkness of the night. Sheltered by a few bushes which grew on the bank, these officers saw a group of some ten or twelve men and one officer sitting around a fire, this was evidently the reserve post. (Old soldiers will understand that by a fire at night, one cannot tell gray clothes from blue.) Not being certain whether they belonged to the Sixth Corps or the enemy, they concluded to hail them; upon doing so and asking them what troops they were, they answered, "You will soon find out if you don't soon get out of that!" After a little parleying, they asked the Bucktails what troops they belonged to; they replied Fifth Corps. Army of the Potomac; they then asked them who commanded the Fifth Corps, and when told it was General Warren, they said it was a lie, that General Sykes commanded that corps. Lieutenant Kratzer then agreed to meet one of their number at a bridge a short distance above under an agreement that neither party was to be detained if they proved enemies. The result proved them to be just what the two officers supposed them—the Sixth Corps, and the lines were connected. On their way back the officers had to go some distance before they came to the first picket of their line, they hunted around in the dark for some time and at last stumbled right on Zach Bailey of Company K., who had taken his bayonet and dug a hole in the soft ground just large enough to admit his body. When he laid down in it he was even with the ground and completely hidden in the darkness. Continuing down the line they found that all the pickets had done the same. When they came to the reserve post, one man who was half asleep, jumped up in front of Lieutenant Kratzer and fired his gun, Kratzer grabbed the piece and raised the muzzle over his head, thus saving his life, all conversation was carried on in a whisper. At one time during the night, one of the rebel pickets called out, "Major Hartshorn, bring your Bucktails up here." How he knew Hartshorn's name and that we were there is another mystery.

Before daylight we were withdrawn and taken back to the line we occupied during the day. No doubt the minute account given of this night's experience will bring it back to the minds of all the survivors of the regiment that may read it and they will with the writer almost feel again the terrible strain of that night's work.

No. 30

On the 10th of May the regiment was moved to Mountain Run where the enemy had strongly fortified a position which nature had made an admirable defensive position. The Bucktails charged these works, taking their proper position, on the right of the Brigade. The first charge was repulsed with heavy loss, another line was formed or rather our line was reformed, to again assault the works. General Ward's Brigade from General Birney's command was formed on our right.

When the order to charge was given our line moved forward steadily. The men knew there was to be hot work, they had gotten a good view of the enemy's position when they made the first charge and they knew they would strengthen their line if possible. We were formed in a woods the ground rising gently in our front, just over the top of the hill was the entrenchments of the enemy.

As soon as our line appeared in sight, it was received with a terrible Artillery fire; the Brigade of Ward extended out to an open space and was first discovered, a heavy Artillery fire was at once concentrated on it causing it to double back, on our right, they suffered heavy loss, Major Hartshorn, taking advantage of the attention the enemy was paying to Ward's men gave the order to charge on the double-quick hoping either to break through or detract the fire from the Brigade of Ward to enable them to reform and participate in the general assault.

Just as soon as we came in sight we were met with a murderous fire of Infantry and Artillery, bravely breasting the awful storm of death our brave boys pushed on up in plain view of the fortifications, where they halted, sought such cover as they could find, and opened fire upon the enemy. The companies on the right of the regiment soon silenced the Battery that had poured the most deadly fire into Ward's troops. The enemy had their Artillery well posted and we suffered from Batteries posted on the left of our regiment, their shells came crushing down along our line while we could not get sight of them. The boys held their position here for half an hour during that time it was clearly demonstrated that any further attempt to take the position in our front by assault would be useless, and we were therefore ordered to fall back to our rifle pits.

Our loss in the battle at Mountain Run was severe but cannot be given at this time. During the night of the 10th we were again put on picket, and were engaged all through the night paying our respects to the rebel sharpshooters who kept up a rattling fire continually, they done us no harm during the night, and in all probability they suffered as little from our fire as we did from theirs.

On Wednesday, May 11th, an assault was ordered by the whole army the line was to advance at a signal agreed upon, the hour set was five o'clock in the morning. Owing to an attack by Lee on our right the movement was not made until half past six. Hancock's Corps had been quietly moved to the left and succeeded in capturing General E. Johnson's entire Division including the commanding General and both his Brigade commanders with four thousand men with their guns and equipments, their Artillery consisting of several field pieces were also captured. Lee made a desperate effort to retrieve this loss but in vain. Hancock was re-enforced and with dogged obstinacy held his position. The assault on other portions of the line including our Corps, was not generally successful, some advantages were gained, in our immediate front it might be called a drawn battle, the fighting on both sides was desperate.

Lee's army seemed determined to hold their position if it was in human power to do so. They were conducting a defensive campaign in a country well adapted to defensive operations, yet at times they came out of their entrenchments and charged our lines with a courage that would compel the admiration of any soldier. The gallant charge of Pickett's Division at Gettysburg was a sample of what these Confederate soldiers could do, and even when the tide seemed against them they would rally and with a seeming contempt for death charge our line leaving the ground behind them strewn with their dead and dying.

We were now, on the 12th of May right in front of Spotsylvania Court House, Colonel McCandless had been sent home being utterly used up, Colonel Tally, who had succeeded him in command of the Brigade, had been captured and Colonel Harden, of the 12th regiment, had been placed in command. On the morning of the 12th, Companies, F. and K., of the Bucktails were sent out to the extreme front and directly opposite the Court House.

The Court House is surrounded by cleared land, in the rear of the building there is a small stream. The ground upon which the buildings stand is, perhaps, one hundred feet higher than the stream and four to six hundred yards distant from it. On the opposite side of this little stream the ground rises more abruptly and to a height of perhaps one hundred and seventy-five feet from the stream, the top of the hill about five hundred yards or more from it. In front of the Court House the ground runs off level for a short distance then forms another bench. Surrounding the building were a number of Batteries, some heavy siege pieces among them. Between the buildings and the stream was a line of rifle pits, while across the stream about half way up the hill was another line occupied by the enemy's front line. Along the crest of the hill just above this line of rifle pits companies F. and K. were deployed, with instructions to pick off the rebel artillerymen. Company F. was on the right of K. the left of the latter extended into a large body of woods, which extended over the hill and down across the stream in their front and extended perhaps one-half mile in their rear. In the rear of Company F., and the major part of K., was cleared land, there being quite a hollow in their rear, beyond this, a mile distant, was our line of battle.

We were in plain view of the Court House, and soon discovered that it was occupied as the headquarters of some General high in command. The hill, on which our line was formed, ran parallel with the rebel line, the narrow comb forming a good cover for the Bucktails. The rebel Batteries were silent when we got into position, and as their advanced line did not appear to want to bother us our boys crawled up and quietly took in the view which was a grand one. Some of the men desiring a better chance to see the disposition of the forces of the enemy rose to their feet, hardly had they done so when there was borne on the air a sharp note of warning, "git down thar, Yanks," quickly followed by the vicious "zip" of the minnies.

This was sufficient provocation, and a sharp fire was kept up by both sides for some time. We suffered no loss, and could not tell whether we had done any damage to the enemy or not. The fire gradually slackened until again all was quiet. The Johnnies and our boys kept up quite a fire of words, but when ever one of either side exposed more than his head he was notified to "git down" and order that was instantly obeyed.

After we had been on the ground about an hour, an aide of Colonel Harden came to the line and told us not to fire unless the enemy advanced, or began firing on us, that it was the order of Colonel Hardin that we remain quiet if the rebels would permit.

As this also seemed the wish of the troops in our front, there was no firing for a long time. During the lull a group of officers from the line came forward to get a sight of the place we had been fighting so hard for several days to reach. Captain Wolf, of Company F., told them to creep up quietly without exposing their bodies and take a peep over the hill. The day was beautiful, silence reigned and the whole surroundings, particularly in our front, looked so innocent to these officers who had not caught a glimpse of a field covered with a courageous foe and all the machinery of war. They treated the warning of Captain Wolfe as a joke and marched boldly forward in a group, Captain Wolfe again told them to scatter, but without heeding him, they continued on and when their eyes first caught the sight they involuntarily gave an exclamation of surprise, the watchful pickets of the enemy saw them at once and this time the word of warning was preceded by the "zip" of a rebel ball, fortunately no one was hurt.

A rather amusing occurrence took place which I will relate. Pusey Chambers, of Company H., commonly known as the "coon" came out and requested permission of the officer in command of Company K. to meet a Johnny between the lines to exchange some coffee for tobacco and trade papers. The officer told him he had no objection to the exchange of produce but there must not be any exchange of papers. Pusey replied: "I have that all fixed," and drawing a paper from his pocket he showed that he had cut out all the news items and dispatches leaving nothing that could convey any information to the enemy.

The officer then told him that the paper was innocent enough and to go ahead. Pusey hailed the line and made his proposition which was promptly accepted by a Johnny, the conditions were soon agreed upon when the two met midway between the lines, sat down side by side and talked several minutes. After exchanging coffee and tobacco they shook hands and were about to return to their lines, when the same thought seemed to strike both at once, they each drew from their pockets a paper neatly folded, with the date outside, soon they were seen to make another trade after which they showed an eager desire to reach their lines as soon as possible. As soon as Pusey got safe under cover he hurriedly unfolded the paper in his hand when he found it also shorn of all news. Just then was heard a roar of laughter from the rifle pits in our front which was responded to by a loud ringing Yankee laugh.

Sometime during the afternoon an Artillery officer came to our line and took the bearing of the Court House, and made arrangements with one of the officers to signal the result of the shots that he proposed to make from Cooper's Battery B stationed in rear of our general line of battle. The hill we were on was a little higher than the Court House or the position of Battery B. Having made his arrangements he returned and fired seven shells, five of which struck the Court House, causing quite a panic for a few minutes; the Battery then ceased firing and the officers who had hurriedly vacated the Court House, returned as though nothing had happened.

Toward evening the rebels sent out a company or two of men to the edge of the woods, in front of the left wing of company K. with axes, picks and shovels, they at once began to fell timber and dig rifle pits. This must not be allowed and the officer in command of that company gave the order to fire, when several rebels were seen to fall, quite a brisk fire followed which lasted for twenty or thirty minutes. The firing had not ceased when an aide came out to inquire the cause, bringing orders to remain quiet as long as possible. He was told that the enemy had attempted to build a rifle pit right under our nose and that we apprehended an attack from these woods when night came on and did not propose to permit them to fortify themselves preparatory to that attack.

Colonel Harden approved the action and instructed the two companies to hold their positions as long as they could, and informed them that support would be sent.

Shortly after the attempt to build breastworks which was not repeated, a rebel soldier, under cover of some bushes, stole up to our line, coming to the posts of Levi Ennis and George McDonald of Company K., these men were busy digging individual pits with their bayonets, and did not see the man approach. He was only a few yards from them and was just in the act of raising his gun to fire when Sergeant James F. Ross, whose post was in the edge of the woods, discovered him, and fired at once without taking aim, this caused the daring rebel to beat a hasty retreat, and before the boys could understand what had occurred he reached his own line in safety.

There was quiet along the line from this until dark, which satisfied the officers of the two companies that the rebels, under cover of night, would attack them, and as there was not more than sixty or seventy men in both companies they would make but a poor show of holding their line.

The men were instructed what to do and every preparation was made to give the Johnnies a warm reception as possible. A messenger was sent to the rear to ascertain the position of the troops sent to our support. Some seven or eight hundred yards in our rear a New York regiment was found near one thousand strong, it having been filled up by substitutes and drafted men. The Colonel, who seemed to think he was in the extreme front, was informed of the situation and requested to hold his fire until our boys would either check the advance of the enemy, should they attack us, or fall back to his line. He, in a pompous manner, informed the Bucktails that he was not in the habit of firing into his own men. When his conduct was reported to Captain Wolfe, who was in command of the two companies, he told the officer in command of company K. to look out for that regiment.

Shortly after dark two or three men were pushed forward in the woods to watch the movements of the enemy, they soon discovered a line of battle cautiously advancing through the woods extending as far as they could see beyond our left flank. They returned with the information and soon a yell announced their attack, "aim low, fire" came the order, and from our Spencer rifles poured several shots as rapidly as the boys could handle their guns. The rapidity of our fire, no doubt led the enemy to suppose our numbers to be very much greater than they were.

They pressed forward without halting, and when they got very close the Bucktails quietly fell back a short distance and took cover behind trees, when the enemy reached the point where our line had been formed they halted and poured a volley into the trees above our heads.

This was just what the Bucktails were waiting for, the fire from their guns gave us their exact location, and our aim, guided by this, no doubt, made our fire more effective than theirs. At our first volley from this position, which was considerably nearer to our reserves than our first position, the regiment sent out to support us, poured a terrible broadside into the woods, this, like the fire of the rebels, passed harmlessly over our heads, some of the Bucktails turned around and fired back. The rebels were content with having driven us from the hill and did not pursue us.

During this little skirmish the two companies became separated, company K. fell back to where the New York regiment had been stationed but found that they had disappeared. Company F. took cover in a piece of woods to our right, and the night was so dark that neither party could see the movements of the other.

Both companies remained until morning when they were taken back and rejoined the regiment. The Reserves were not engaged during that day, Friday, May 13th. The next day the Division was moved several miles and formed on the extreme left of the army. From that time until the evening of the 19th the regiment was actively engaged on the skirmish line.

A terrible storm prevailed from Friday, the 13th, till Sunday night which compelled both armies to remain, so far as a general movement was concerned, inactive, it being impossible to move Artillery or ammunition trains over the roads.

On Thursday afternoon Lee determined to turn the right wing of Meade's army and to effect this the Corps of Ewell was directed to cross the river Ny and reach the Fredericksburg road in the rear of General Tyler's Division which occupied the extreme right of our army. General Tyler's Division was composed largely of new troops, several heavy Artillery regiments numbering from twelve to eighteen hundred men each being a part.

General Meade, who determined to make this a dear effort to Ewell sent General Crawford with the Reserves to try and force his way around the right of Ewell's Corps and get between him and the Ny, thus cutting off his retreat. The Reserves moved rapidly but did not reach the ground until night. A heavy rain had been falling all afternoon and the fog settling down in the woods caused darkness to come on earlier. On arriving at the edge of the woods, bordering the Ny, the Bucktails were deployed as skirmishers and marched into the woods which were very dense and full of sweet brier vines making it a difficult matter to make any progress, the line was kept in place by constant communication by the file closers.

In the woods we found the heavy Artillery very much scattered, they were firing in the right direction, however, and slowly falling back. We soon passed them and pushed on toward the Ny. We, in a few minutes, encountered the skirmish line of the enemy, our first notice of the presence was given by a Sergeant of company A. who sang out in order to warn his comrades, "there I am captured again." The rebel officer who captured the Sergeant was, in a few minutes, captured with several of his men, a good many prisoners were captured by us, our only loss was the Sergeant of company A.

The movement of Ewell upon Tyler's Division did not prove a success. The attack was repulsed and Ewell was in full retreat with the greater part of his force before we arrived. Learning this General Crawford halted our line and during the rain the men took what rest they could until daylight.

With the first streak of light the line was pushed rapidly forward to the Ny, the rebels had escaped, crossing the river during the night. We captured several hundred prisoners that morning, many of them soundly sleeping under their blankets. They lay down during the night in the rear of the pickets and when the picket line was withdrawn in the darkness they were left.

Lieutenant Maxwell of company H. received a wound at Laurel Hill on the 8th of May from which he afterwards died. As he was the only commissioned officer left with that company, Lieutenant J. E. Kratzer, of company K., was assigned to the command and continued in command during the campaign.

No. 31

In the fight on Thursday General Ferror's colored troops repulsed an attack by a brigade of Cavalry that was sent to come in on the rear of General Tyler's command. This was the first time colored troops were engaged in the Army of the Potomac. They conducted themselves in a manner to call forth the praise of the veterans and from that time on the prejudice against arming the colored man rapidly disappeared. General Ferrero's division belonged to General Burnside's corps.

Friday, the 20th of May, we were on the picket line, and were engaged during that day and Saturday until 12 o'clock when we broke camp. Our position, at that time, was on the extreme left of the line. After breaking camp we marched to the left in the direction of Guinney's Station on the Richmond and Fredericksburg railroad. About the middle of the afternoon we were ordered to quicken our pace, and soon we realized that we were making a forced march.

Men began to fall out by the roadside, our ranks were rapidly growing thin, and when we arrived at Guinney's Station there were just fifteen men and six officers in the regiment. General Meade was at the Station and had deployed his headquarter guard, the 100th Pennsylvania Volunteers, and attacked a body of rebel Cavalry in a piece of woods on a hill just above the Station.

Only a few shots were fired before we arrived. General Meade directed Colonel Harden to move his brigade, as soon as it arrived, in front of the 100th regiment, deploy a line of skirmishers, and occupy the high ground fronting the Station; just beyond in the woods the rebel Cavalry was posted. Colonel Harden directed Major Hartshorn to immediately deploy his regiment as skirmishers. As our little force of twenty-one officers and men passed through the line of the 100th regiment they encouraged us by exclaiming; "Go in, Bucktails, and give 'em fits!" This 100th regiment numbered, at that time, certainly over five hundred men.

The severe march we had made did not seem to dampen the ardor of those who had been able to keep up. Men fell out on that march who had never before failed to keep up with their command. The color Company, H., did not have a man when we arrived at the Station, the colors were carried by Lieutenant Kratzer then in command of that Company. Zach. Bailey and John Rish were the only two men the officer in command of Company K. brought in. The other companies were represented by one or two men each.

When we arrived at the point designated by General Meade we deployed along a fence. In our front was a large orchard, on the other side of the orchard, in an open woods, we could plainly see the line of rebel Cavalry. On our right and in front stood a large Virginia mansion, when we came in sight of this house we saw several officers ride rapidly away. An old colored woman, from a neighboring house near by signaled one of our officers who went to see what she wanted. When he got close to her she said: "Foh de Lawd, Masa, heah drink dis watah so's de ole Missus, who am watchin' me, won't suspect." While the officer was drinking the water in an agitated and excited manner she continued, "Youse gwine to be all killed dis blessed ebe'nin' dars a whole heap, thousans' and' thousans' ob our men jis blow de house dar an my old Massa, who am de Colonel, am wif dme an' dey am only waitin' fo' youse to come up, when diy kills youse ebery one." The tears rolled down the old woman's cheeks while she was giving this information. The officer assured her that we knew all about it and not to be alarmed for we were not going to be killed that night.

The temptation to steal out into the orchard in our front and get a shot at the enemy, from behind the large trees which promised good shelter, was too much for the Bucktails. We had been there but a few minutes when several of the men asked permission of Major Hartshorn to "just step out there in front a little piece to see what's in those woods." Their request was granted and one after another made the same request until there was no one left but the officers.

The boys soon opened up quite a lively skirmish, one officer after another slipped out to "see what the boys were doing" until Major Hartshorn found himself alone, calling a couple of officers back, he told them to remain there and send forward the men as they came up.

Those officers, however, soon went out with the rest. By this time we had forty or fifty men. The men who had fallen behind were continually coming forward.

The officer in command of the rebel Cavalry tried to get his men to charge upon us, he rode out to the edge of the woods, and we heard him call upon his men to come out, our boys called to him to bring on his men, but they only came to the edge of the woods when they halted and commenced firing. The gallant officer soon lost his horse. He however, remained where it fell and ordered up another, he was hardly well seated before he too was shot. By this time we had a lively little fight, and, as the distance was short, we could easily see that we were hurting a good many of them, night was coming on and our boys wanted to charge the woods but Major Hartshorn refused to permit them to do so, as there were no troops then to be seen in supporting distance.

Colonel Harden, as soon as we commenced firing, rode to General Crawford and asked that a regiment or two be sent forward to support "Major Hartshorn and his Bucktails who are out here about a mile driving in Cavalry and chickens." Two or three regiments were sent out at once but before they arrived it was quite dark and the Cavalry had disappeared. We did not have a man hit. We certainly were in clover that night.

Shortly after dark we marched to the house spoken of before, and camped close by it. One of the officers had a colored servant, Dan, who was a contraband. Dan put in an appearance shortly after dark and going up to the officer, said: "Dah is whar I was born, dat is my old Massa's house, he's done gone to de wah, but ole Missus she ketch me she will tie me up." The officer was well pleased with the information, and told Dan to call on the Missus, give her his compliments and tell her some butter, milk and eggs would be very acceptable in our present situation, assuring Dan that the whole Army of the Potomac would be brought to his rescue if his Missus attempted to detain him. Dan secured a bountiful supply of the articles named and in addition a nice lot of fat chickens. Colonel Harden's olfactory nerves detected the presence of the sumptuous repast the boys were preparing when he came over and was gladly welcomed to share with us the bountiful feast we had prepared.

Very early next morning our regiment and a detachment from one of the other regiments made a reconnaissance in our front. We found a small body of the enemy located in a house, the order to charge was given, and our line started forward on a run, the rebels retreated with out making much show of resistance. The remainder of that day the 21st of May, was spent in ascertaining the location of the enemy's forces. Toward evening we discovered that Lee's army was rapidly moving to our left in the direction of the North Anna river.

Sunday, the 22nd, the Fifth Corps marched from Ginney's Station on the Bowling Green road, the Pennsylvania Reserves in the advance.

The Division marched left in front, with flankers thrown out, and proceeded with the greatest caution. A number of stragglers from Lee's army were picked up in the houses along the road by the flankers. The Fifth Corps bivouacked near Bowling Green on Sunday.

The march was resumed early the next morning taking the road leading to Jericho ford on the North Anna river. Griffin's division, which was in the front, reached the ford about noon and at once began to cross the river by wading.

The river, at this point, is not over one hundred and fifty feet wide has a rocky bed, the current very swift and about waist deep, the banks are perhaps sixty feet above the bed of the river and very steep. On the north side a level plateau extends back from the river a long distance, on the south side some four or five hundred yards back from the river a second bench rises another sixty to seventy-five feet. The country is more broken on the south side at this point than on the north side.

At Jericho ford on the south side of the river, on the second bench stood the large mansion of Mr. Fountaine, the family had taken a hasty departure leaving all their household goods except what they could carry. A very extensive library of choice works proved the owner to be a man of fine literary tastes. A very interesting family history, written by each generation proved the family of French origin and at one time prominent in France; the early history was written in French and translated by a later generation, the translation on an extra leaf secured between the leaves of the original.

While we lay close to the house the writer looked over one of the early volumes which gave an account of the banishment from France of one of the family, the one whose descendants were owners of this property, the original name was LaFontaine. Several volumes of this history were eagerly sought by our boys, but they were not permitted to take them away much against their will they were required to put them back where they got them.

General Griffin as soon as his division got across, formed them in line with his left a short distance above the ford. Cutler's division was formed on Griffin's right. When the Bucktails, then leading our division, arrived on the bank of the river the battle opened up. Cutler and Griffin's troops, the roar of musketry indicated that a battle of some magnitude was being fought, and the knowledge that only two division of our troops were across, with no artillery, made it necessary that we get over just as soon as we could.

When the command to cross was given the head of our line was near the back of the river the long lines of the division stretching up over the winding road from the bluff down to the stream. With a cheer the boys broke ranks, rushed into the river, up the bank on the other side in what seemed to be the greatest confusion. A stranger would have supposed that order could not have been brought out of the confused mass of shouting soldiers without considerable work and time.

Like magic, in an incredible short space of time the seeming confusion was changed into a compact line of battle presenting a solid front to the enemy. The men had rallied around their colors each man intent on finding his place, and then directing others.

One could frequently hear the remark, "not any Ball's Bluff today." Just under the bench and in front of he Fontain house was a strange scene, a group of darkies numbering perhaps two hundred souls from the aged, white haired, worn out old field hand down to the picanninny at the black but warm breast. They were huddled together in a solid mass, and as their bodies swayed back and forth they sang or chanted in a weird strain an anthem of praise in which the name of "Massa Linkum" frequently occurred, it was the day of jubilee for these poor slaves, and their faces shone with the radiant joy which filled their breasts, while great tears of joy rolled down their shiny black cheeks. It was strange music and had a wonderful effect on the troops. A sight and sound never to be forgotten.

Our line was moved forward to Fontain house from where we could see across a deep ravine that cut our line obliquely, two or three rebel batteries, numbering fifteen or eighteen guns, getting into position to shell our troops. On the left of our regiment across this ravine on high ground was a large farm house surrounded by a picket fence. In this house a considerable body of rebel sharpshooters were located and were pouring a very destructive fire into the regiment formed on our left, several efforts had been made to drive them from their position, but were each time driven back with heavy loss.

Colonel Harden conceived the idea of sending out a small party from the Fontain house, as they would be under cover of a strip of woods more than half the distance. He made his plans known to Major Hartshorn and directed him to select the force necessary.

Major Hartshorn selected two companies F. and one other company, which one the writer cannot now remember, to make the attack. The regiment was called out four companies were to charge on the right of the woods named, four on the left, and two through the woods directly in front of the rebel batteries before mentioned which were at this time pouring a terrible fire of shot and shell into our line, killing and wounding many.

Captain Wolfe, of company F. had command of the two companies selected to make the attack on the house. Lieutenant Bard of company K., had command of the two centre companies, H. and K., and Captain McDonald, of the five companies on the right. The companies were separated in these commands or detachments owing to the peculiar formation of the line, which necessarily separated them as they advanced.

As the line moved forward and formed in the position from which they were to charge, the enemy turned their batteries on us, and amid the shrieking of shot and shell the command to charge was given, and the line sprang forward, every man realizing that much depended on the work in hand. The four companies on the right were to move first to attract the attention of the enemy, the two companies in the centre to pay particular attention to the rebel gunners and if possible to either silence the batteries or draw a portion of their fire.

The line, when first formed, was as follows the four companies on the right as a base, the two centre companies with their right joining their left but thrown back at nearly a right angle, the four companies on their left, two of which were to charge the house separated some distance from the centre in rear of but on a line nearly parallel to the companies on the right, their left rather inclining back.

The reader will see that when these companies charged they necessarily became separated, the two companies were nearly at right angles with the enemy's line so that as they advanced they charged along in front of them, but on a line parallel with the ravine referred to above. Across this ravine were the batteries that were delivering a destructive fire into our ranks.

The four companies on our right charged with a heroism seldom equaled, but met from the first the concentrated fire of a large force of the enemy, they recoiled from the first volley, but soon recovered and again attempted to penetrate the enemy's lines, three times they tried in vain to make a breach.

They, however, had done more than was asked of them and were recalled. The attack on the house was so well and vividly described by General Hartshorn in the *Herald* of August 13th that I will refer my readers to his article. The two companies, when they emerged from the woods received a volley from the rebel line distant about five or six hundred yards, the balls struck the ground in their front, there being no cover the officer in command ordered them forward over the hill down into the ravine immediately under the guns of the batteries and not more than two hundred yards distant. There they were hidden from the view of the enemy by a thick growth of bushes, but really unprotected from their fire.

They kept up a fire on the gunners but without doing much execution as they could only see their heads as they ran backwards and forwards loading and firing the guns. The orders given to the one officer with these two companies were to hold his place as long as possible. The four companies on the right he could tell by the sound of the firing in that direction had been driven back, the cheers of the companies on the left were heard, and their gallant charge on the house was witnessed by those on the left of these companies, and their withdrawal was also seen. These two companies were now in a most critical situation, entirely separated from support with a cleared hill in their rear, to retreat would draw the fire of several thousand men and was a risk not to be thought of until night, when in the darkness it might be possible, if the enemy did not move a force down in our rear thus capturing the whole party.

No (Federal) troops, so far as they knew, were nearer than half a mile. The officer determined to send one man back to explain the situation to Major Hartshorn. He accordingly selected Sergeant James F. Ross, of Company K., and taking him to one side gave him his instructions. Sergeant Ross gave him a searching look, then turned around took a survey of the ground over which he had to go, and as he has since remarked, "I sized it up about like this. I will have one good chance out of a hundred, but will try it if I am ordered to do so" turning again to the officer he asked, "when do you want me to go" the reply was now.

The Sergeant pulled his cap down over his eyes and with a quick step started up the hill. As soon as he came into view there was a roar from the rebel line, and five hundred rifles were discharged at the brave young Bucktail. He is seen to fall, is he killed, is his body riddled with bullets. Escape would be a miracle. He lays quiet a minute, is then seen to move, slowly he rises on one elbow and falls back again, twice he attempts to rise but fails, the third time he regains his feet, and, with his gun as a crutch he slowly hobbles up the hill, stopping every few yards to rest. The rebels had not fired after he fell. We watch him as he approaches the woods, darkness is fast coming on and his outline grows dim, yet we imagine he steps faster, he reaches the edge of the woods, turns around, faces the enemy, shoulders his crutch, waves his cap in triumph and disappears.

The sergeant had "played it fine" and those who were so anxiously watching him concluded that he had missed his calling, he should have went on the stage.

After the Sergeant left us the word was passed along the line to the extreme right to give information of every move of the enemy, to particularly watch our rear, and to pass all information from one to the other down along the line.

After dark the Artillery fire from the eighteen guns just above us and our batteries on the other side of the river was the grandest display of fireworks the writer has ever witnessed, the night was quite dark which added much to the brilliant effect. If we could have supplied the rebels with a better class of shell we undoubtedly would have done it. Many of their shells exploded soon after leaving the guns, and the pieces dropped down on our line but fortunately no one was hurt by them.

When Sergeant Ross found Major Hartshorn, (the Sergeant learned that the Major) had reported the two companies captured. As soon as he learned that they were still safe he sent Adjutant Wright out to say to the officer in charge that he should use his own judgment about withdrawing his command, but suggesting that it be done at once. It was near midnight when the Adjutant found them, and when he was made acquainted with the situation and a line of rebel pickets shown him, only a few yards in our front, he doubted whether we could get out without alarming the enemy.

This line of pickets was pushed forward after dark, and at several points were only twenty or thirty yards from us, between the lines was a thick growth of bushes which grew four to six feet high.

One man was sent out at a time, and when he had gotten about half way up the hill another started and so on until the last man. Daylight was just breaking when the last man and the officer reached the woods.

When our regiment was forming Colonel Harden was present, when the order to charge was given and the line was seen advancing by the enemy they turned their guns on us and gave us a regular shower of shells. One of these shells exploded close by Colonel Harden, a piece struck him in the side and knocked him off his horse, though severely hurt he lost no interest in the movement under the direction of Major Hartshorn, who had made all the disposition of the companies and gave each officer specific instructions what to do.

No. 32

During the night the two companies could plainly hear the moving of troops and trains; this they supposed was the enemy reinforcing their lines preparatory to a renewal of the battle next morning. They were therefore not prepared for what daylight revealed to their astonished gaze. At the same time they were so carefully stealing out of the ravine, under cover of night, the enemy with the same caution was withdrawing his pickets. The moving of trains and troops during the night was the enemy retreating, and when the morning light revealed to our sight the hill so lately bristling with the deadly implements of war we saw nothing but the place where they had been. The men of the companies that had silently crawled up that hill were not a little chagrined when they learned this, and were greatly relieved when they received the order to advance which immediately followed. Our other companies moved up and the entire regiment, moved forward in line of skirmishers. On arriving at the position occupied by the enemy the evening before we found it to be one of great strength, and we rightly concluded that it was not from any fear from the troops in their front that caused the enemy to abandon a position so strong. A movement by Burnside's corps lower down the river threatened to divide Lee's army; he thereupon abandoned this position and concentrated his army at Little river. As we advanced on Tuesday morning, the 24th of May, we soon overtook stragglers from the retreating enemy, these were picked up by our line without firing a shot; before we had gone very far we had thus gathered up several hundred prisoners. The line was pushed forward rapidly and the stragglers became more numerous, and from strips of woods between the farms they would feebly contest our advance, but only a rattling fire was kept up and this without doing us any harm enabled us to gain on the foe and our attention until noon was given chiefly to taking prisoners. From the service which we performed, that of skirmishers, we had opportunities, as on this occasion of capturing a great many prisoners. There were but few regiments in the army where as little attention was given to securing credit for these captures as in the Bucktails. It was the custom, indeed it was required of officers that they deliver prisoners to the Provost Marshall and get receipts for them. These captures would then go to the credit of the regiment or body of troops holding the receipt. I know of but two instances where any one of our regiment procured a receipt. As a rule prisoners were turned over by our men to the first body of troops they met and they returning to the front paid no attention whatever to a receipt and did not seem to care who got the credit. This carelessness on the part of our officers and men we now very much regret. If the law in respect to this had been carefully observed, this would have made an interesting chapter in our history.

During the afternoon of Tuesday we encountered a dense woods through which we found difficulty in passing in line, hence our progress was very slow. Wednesday morning the division moved down the river opposite Quarrel's ford, our left resting near the bank of the North Anna river, the Bucktails on the right of the division were formed in a thick woods at the head of a ravine about one-half mile from the river, there was a road from Quarrel's ford up this ravine. At this ford General Crittenden's division of Burnside's corps, was to cross and we were here to cover that crossing. A picket line was thrown out in front and the men were soon taking a much needed rest. After we had been here about two hours, Gen. Crittenden and a magnificently mounted and uniformed staff and escort came up this road at full gallop. General Crittenden was a fine looking officer, paid great attention to the cut of his clothes, and hair—the later was very black and was worn very long—and when he reined up his horse suddenly and in a loud tone and pompous manner called out, "Who is in command of these troops?" Colonel Harden, who was lying down among the men, rose up, and in his slow tone replied, "I h-a-v-e t-h-a-t h-o-n-o-r, sir!" General Crittenden asked him if he had a picket line out in front. Whether Col. Harden thought this a foolish question, considering the fact that we were supposed to be in the immediate presence of the enemy, or not, we cannot say. His answer however, seemed to indicate that he did not think the question so important as to prevent him making a rather humerous reply. Looking at General Crittenden, he slowly drawled out, "Yes, General, I did have one, but I guess you need not be afraid of them; I think they have all gone chicken hunting." A roar of laughter from the Bucktails followed this, when Gen. Crittenden put spurs to his horse and the richly caparisoned troops disappeared as suddenly as they came. Shortly after this we advanced through the thick woods some distance and the division halted in line of battle, where we remained Wednesday and Thursday. The strongly fortified position occupied by the enemy on Little river was carefully examined during this time by parties sent out to reconnoiter. The commanding General evidently concluded that it would be of little use to attack Lee in a position chosen by him; strong naturally, and made doubly so by elaborate earthworks. On Thursday night we again took up our line of march, recrossed the North Anna river and then down that stream moving to the left, always to the left. The march was continued all day Friday and that night we bivouacked on or near the North bank of the Pamunkey river. Early Saturday morning the march was resumed and the Reserves moved rapidly in the direction of Hannovertown, crossed the Pamunkey river and moved out two miles in the direction of Mechanicsville. By this movement the strong position of Lee at Little river was flanked and he was compelled to abandon it in order to protect his communications. On Sunday, May 29, we marched toward the Chickahominy, encountered a heavy skirmish line of the enemy, but no engagement of consequence occurred. Early Monday morning, May 30, the Fifth corps crossed the Tolopatomoy; Griffin's division which was in the advance took the road leading from Hanover Courthouse to Richmond; Crawford's division, the Penn'a. Reserves moved out the Mechanicsville turnpike. This disposition of the divisions of the corps would place our division on the left of Griffin's in line of battle. On this road there was a strong force of rebel cavalry supported by Ewell's corps. Gen. Crawford determined by a vigorous movement to get possession of the road and advance directly on Mechanicsville. Col. Harden with the first brigade was ordered to take the advance, push forward a strong skirmish line and engage the enemy. It is hardly necessary to state that the Bucktails were deployed as the skirmishers. They deployed on double quick and moved forward rapidly, soon encountering the enemy's cavalry which they drove back towards Bethesda church. After we had driven the cavalry from one-half to three quarters of a mile, we came into an open country. Away off on our left long lines of infantry could be seen moving forward and threatening our rear; Col. Hartshorn reported this to Col. Harden, who ordered the brigade forward in line to our support. We then advanced nearly one mile farther and halted.

About one-half of the regiment in the woods the companies on the left extending into open country. Our position was on the top of a hill, perhaps as high as any ground in our immediate front, in the rear of the right wing of the regiment was a Virginia swamp in which was a thick growth of black alder, in the rear of this swamp was a long strip of cleared land covering the whole line; in the rear of that a strip of woods parallel with it then a broad, rather flat strip of cleared land and then another much more extensive woods; just on the edge of the latter our division was formed and commenced to throw up rifle pits.

This day closed the term of service of the old regiment and everyman knew we were about to again engage the enemy, and from what we had seen of the movements of the enemy we knew a desperate battle would be fought on that ground that day. We also knew that our regiment was to receive the first shock of battle. As we lay on that hill on the afternoon of May 30th, 1864, it is safe to say that one thought took possession of the mind of every man whose time of enlistment expired with the day. These thoughts found expression in words and the situation was freely discussed. Lieutenant Kratzer, of Company K, then commanding Company H, and the writer, then commanding Company K, were lying just in the rear of the line smoking. Lieutenant Kratzer had re-enlisted and would remain, the writer had not, and if he survived the coming battle expected to start for home the following day. The question upper most in the minds of these officers, no doubt was discussed along the line. For three years the regiment had discharged their duty faithfully and had won a fair name, would the officers and men, with so much at stake meet the enemy with the same valor that had characterized their previous battles. To close up an honorable service by failure to maintain their good record was to becloud the whole.

This was discussed the night before but the question was in doubt when we moved forward this morning. No disposition to hesitate or avoid taking part in the conflict could be detected among the men as they took their place in line. After the general talk as we lay on this hill every man was satisfied that the honor of the command would be maintained, there was that in the manner of the men that told more plainly than words could tell that the reputation of the regiment was dear to the heart of every Bucktail, dearer than life. There was a determination to make our last fight one to be remembered; in sorrow by the foe and with pride by our comrades in arms.

After laying quiet near half an hour, the silence was broken by the sharp crack of a rifle by Company K, in an instant every man was on his feet, and an officer asked who fired that shot. Lower replied "I did sir," the officer told him he should be careful not to fire unless he saw something to fire at, as it had alarmed the entire line.* This brave soldier bravely replied "I do see at least two lines of battle advancing" on going forward the officer saw sure enough two lines very close, he gave the command to fire, several vollies were fired when the order to fall back was given, the line fell back about one hundred yards took shelter behind trees and silently awaited the approach of the enemy, as soon as they came in sight several vollies more were poured into them. The Bucktails again fell back and repeated what they had done before. Their fire had evidently done good execution, for the officer in command of the advanced line gave the command to deploy skirmishers, this was the Bucktails chance to get through the swamp the edge of which they had just reached. The command was given for every man to get through the swamp the best they could and rally in the strip of woods beyond the field that lay on the other side of the swamp. That portion of the regiment that extended beyond the woods, took cover behind a barricade of rails and there held the enemy in their front, the rebels apparently were not disposed to push the fight at that point.

* Editor's note: Cyrus B. Lower was a medal of honor recipient. His story of capture, imprisonment and escape and journey back to Federal lines can be found at the end of Bard's account.

The reason for this was soon discovered by Lieutenant Kratzer who from his position had a good view of the country on the left for a considerable distance. He saw a brigade of the enemy then in the rear of his line moving rapidly forward toward him, his only chance was to move in an oblique direction toward the line of woods where the regiment was to rally. Giving the troops in front a parting shot these companies, retreated rapidly and succeeded in getting safely out of their precarious situation.

The rebels were a much longer time getting through the swamp than we were and as we could at best only check the advance of the enemy it was thought best to fall back to the woods fronting the position of our line of battle. These woods afforded a better shelter and the cleared ground between them and the line of rifle pits was much narrower. When the enemy came in view in front of this position we had a good view of them, and from the extent of their line and the liberal supply of artillery accompanying it we knew that the reels were about to give us another exhibition of Southern daring by a charge similar to that at Gettysburg, but of course not on so grand a scale. We now became fully aware that our last recollections of service were to be ineffaceably stamped on our minds, yet not a face along that line of men indicated that they would give "as good as they got."

No. 33

Our line of skirmishers were not kept long in waiting, the skirmishers of the enemy came to sight in good form, keeping their intervals with a regularity seldom seen. Soon as they arrived within range our boys opened on them with a murderous fire. They soon sought such cover as they could find and returned our fire; they, however, owing to the protection the timber afforded us, did little harm. At this point we held their line for three quarters of an hour, repulsing several charges from the enemy's pickets. Failing in these attempts, their line of battle moved forward keeping a line as solid and marching as steadily as on review. Before this force we very prudently fell back on our line of battle, where we found a rifle pit unfinished. This rifle pit was formed by laying piles of rails along in a line and digging a ditch behind, throwing the dirt over the rails in front, the top rails were not covered; the men were working with a will and when our skirmishers got back and told them what was coming, they redoubled their efforts. It is astonishing how much can be accomplished in a few minutes in a case of this kind. It certainly was not more than ten minutes from the time the skirmishers got back until the shells of the enemy began knocking the top rails off and went crashing through the woods in our rear. From the first shot until their batteries were silenced the rebel gunners had perfect range, and did the best artillery firing we had yet seen. There was a small house situated just on the edge of the woods and only a few feet in rear of our line, as we advanced early in the morning the man and woman who occupied it and who were past middle age, came out to meet us with warm words of welcome, assuring us that they had been looking for us for years, and hoped we would remain in possession of that country, telling a sad story of their ill treatment by the rebels. We had become used to these tales, and not a man believed one word of their story. When our skirmishers fell back this couple threw off their disguise, no doubt thinking our line would soon be driven back. Their faces were lit up with joy and rubbing their hands in glee they shouted: "On to Richmond! On to Richmond! Why don't you go on. I guess God Almighty and Jeff Davis are after you." Among the first shells fired was one that went through this house, passing through a feather bed filling the air with feathers and covering General Crawford and staff, who were sitting in rear of the building. Very soon a shell exploded in the upper story setting fire to the house. The old lady came to the window and made piteous appeals to the men to help her save her goods, but as they had important business on hands just then no one offered her any help. Major Hartshorn urged the old couple to get out of that and seek some place of safety, telling them that we proposed to stay there and that a terrible battle would be fought and that they might both be killed. They however, continued to make every effort to save the few goods that were in the lower story. The house soon burned to the ground and the old couple disappeared.

Our artillery had been distributed along the line at those points that would command the ground in our front, the location of the pieces, by sections, enabled our guns to rake the enemy's line with an enfilading fire as it approached. The rebel battery that was doing us great harm was shortly silenced by our artillery. Several guns from different parts of our line concentrated their fire on it and blew up one of their cassons. About this time all the artillery of the enemy ceased firing; this we well knew was done because their line was ready to charge. Soon the long line came out from the woods in perfect order with regular step and guns at a "right shoulder." The command was given to hold our fire until they got very close. For several minutes not a shot was fired. Our troops looked upon the slowly advancing line with admiration, proud only that the brave men composing that line were Americans. The fear as to the conduct of our men had been silenced, not a man flinched. When the rebel line got close enough for us to plainly see their faces our artillery opened with shell, grape and canister and cut great gaps in their line, these were quickly closed up and they started forward with a yell, every man was ready, and it was all the officers could do to keep them from firing too soon. When our line opened fire the nearest part of their line was within one hundred and fifty or two hundred yards of our rifle pits. It is understood that a line charging are not firing and the troops upon whom they are charging, by taking deliberate aim can do terrible execution, our first volley fearfully thinned their line but closing up they with louder yells charged recklessly up to within fifteen or twenty feet. Colonel Hartshorn sick with the terrible punishment inflicted called out to them to surrender, when several hundred, without halting, ran into our lines, throwing down their arms as they ran. The second line of battle only came to the edge of the woods in our front, when the wicked fire of our artillery drove them back. When the firing had ceased our boys gathered around the prisoners, complimenting them on the gallant charge they had made. These brave men looked out upon the field which was strewn with their dead and wounded comrades. Their countenance expressive of the deep sorrow that filled their hearts. There were no jokes passed, the conduct of these men before and after their capture challenged the admiration of the boys in blue. Their courage deserved success, their sorrow over fallen comrades gave them the deep sympathy of every true soldier in our ranks.

After the firing ceased and when captor and captured were exchanging salutations a rebel color bearer who had been hidden behind a tree in an orchard in our front, rose up with his colors and ran for the woods, in an instant a volley was fired at him, but passed over him without harm, the cry came out along the line, "shame" instantly followed by "good boy, go it Johnny" the brave fellow reached the woods, turned around, waved his flag and disappeared.

From this until night was spent taking account of the wounded of both sides, and all through the night our stretcher bearers were busy, guided by the moans of some poor fellow. They would go out and bring them in, many poor fellows passed over the river that night, tenderly cared for and ministered to by the brave men with whom they had been engaged in deadly conflict but a few short hours before. This our last night in actual service was one of the saddest of our three years.

Early next morning, before the troops that were to take our place had arrived, the Bucktails volunteered to skirmish the woods in our front. The regiment was deployed and as they moved forward they were greeted by the familiar zip of the rifle ball. They charged out to a fence where they had fair cover and soon drove the few sharpshooters from the woods, without a single casualty occurring in our regiment. About one or two hours were thus occupied when we were relieved, and were marched back to the rear to prepare to start for home. The re-enlisted veterans were to be formed into a new organization and a painful separation was to take place between men who for three years had, on so many occasions stood side by side in the presence of death, and shared hardships of every kind, endured the sufferings which is the common lot of a soldier, been together in prison, wounded or sick and in hospital had cheered and encouraged each other. A part of these men were to leave for home, a part were to remain to continue to dare suffer and die in defense of that flag the emblem of liberty.

The last battle of the Pennsylvania Reserves was a complete victory and fought within a few miles of the place where their first battle, as a division, was fought. The battlefield of Bethesda Church, was only about three miles from Mechanicsville where, on the 26th of June, 1862, they had taught the rebels that it was a very serious matter to charge upon rifle pits defended by the Pennsylvania Reserve Corps.

The parting between the re-enlisted veterans and those whose time had expired was a very sad one. I will not attempt to tell the story as I remember it now after almost twenty-two years. Had there been a recruiting officer on the ground authorized to grant a sixty day furlough to all who would re-enlist, I believe he would have swept into service every man. We marched to White house landing, doing duty as guard to a long train. As we passed through various bodies of our own troops we were cheered and on every side we received kind words. The Pennsylvania Reserves were well known in the Army of the Potomac and now that they had closed their term of enlistment, fighting until the last moment with the same valor and spirit that had placed them high up in rank as one of the most efficient Divisions in that army, the old heroes that had fought and marched with them, did not withhold their tribute of praise; as we passed through their lines, men would jump up and grasp our boys by the hand and wish them all the happiness possible. Frequently you would hear, "don't fail to come back and help finish up this job, after you get through your holiday."

The march to White House was a weary one, many men fell out and did not arrive for several hours. The next day we embarked on government transports and in due time arrived in Washington where we were loaded for the last time in box cars. The Division was sent to several camps. Our regiment, and several others, went direct to Harrisburg. On our arrival in the Capital of our State we were given a grand reception; committees met us, we were formed and marched about from place to place to listen to speeches from the Mayor of the City, Governor Curtin and others. This was very tiresome and would have been voted a decided nuisance by the soldiers in whose honor these elaborate preparations had been made. The next day the citizens entertained at their homes, all the returned veterans. It was the good fortune of the writer and several of Company K. to be assigned to the family of Mrs. Zinn, where they were royally entertained. A son and brother, then Major Zinn, was in the army, this gave this, as well as many other Harrisburg families a doubly deep interest in our soldiers.

Our boys went into camp in Camp Curtin to await the preparation of Muster Out Rolls. Some little conflict of authority occurred between the commandant at Camp Curtin and the officers of our regiment. The former demanded that our boys should be subject to all orders existing and liable to detail. Captain McDonald in command of our regiment declared that we were not subject to them and that his men should be permitted to go in and out of camp at their own will. The commanding officer declared that in that case he would not issue rations to the men. Captain McDonald informed him that most of the men had brought with them their arms, and, having a good supply of ammunition, he thought the regiment could take care of itself. All these troubles were soon settled satisfactory and peace and good will prevailed. The officer in command and the citizens of Harrisburg were afraid that so many men just returned from the army where they had been for three years subject to military dicipline might that they were free become troublesome.

The manhood of the American Volunteer that made it possible one year later to disband and turn loose on the land over one million of men and not interfere with business or disturb society in the least, was manifested by the men who composed the Penn'a. Reserve Corps.

Major Hartshorn arrived the day after we went into camp and was heartily welcomed by the men, he had been made Colonel of the 190th, Pa. Veteran Vols., one of the two regiments formed out of the re-enlisted veterans of the old division. The Colonel remained with us until we were mustered out on June 14th, and accompanied company K to their homes.

No. 34

The arrival of Company K at home was, no doubt, a counterpart of that of each of the other companies. How vivid that scene is, although almost twenty-two years have elapsed since. How distinctly do we remember the glad greetings of our friends, how plainly stamped on our memory are the joyful faces of parents, wives, brothers and sisters as loved ones rushed to their warm embrace. The tears of joy that coursed down their cheeks and the merry greeting of friends. As all pictures from real life have their shadows, so this one had a sad side. There were fathers, mothers, wives and sisters in mourning for loved ones who would never more return. Their loved ones were sleeping their last sleep on the fields made sacred by their blood. Oh how the returned soldier tried to avoid the wistful appealing look of the mother whose heart was almost broken. How they dreaded the meeting with the friends of comrades who had fallen in battle, or perished in Southern prison pens.

One face so full of sorrow, so sad and distressed comes to my mind as plain as though it all occurred but yesterday. It was a widow who gave three noble sons to the army, two of them lay buried where they fell, one at Bull Run and one at Chancellorsville, the other had been wounded, had re-enlisted and was still in the front line fighting the battles of his country. It is hardly necessary for me to state that these brothers were of the bravest. The one who re-enlisted lived through the war, is living yet. Over this scene where joy and sorrow were strangely blended together we will draw a veil.

This paper closes our history, and we feel how poorly we have recounted the deeds of our comrades. It has been a labor of love, and we have become so deeply interested in it that we reluctantly close the history of our regiment. Many, very many incidents have been omitted, many instances of personal daring have come to mind us the story progressed that had been forgotten.

The history has been written mainly from memory—the only aid at hand being letters written home to my parents, brothers and sisters which were carefully preserved, these were of inestimable value in fixing dates and places. We are also indebted to comrades for information received at various times. We regret those matters worthy of notice that have been omitted, but close the story with the proud consciousness that every statement is true, it has been our aim to give the plain unvarnished story of the regiment and we can safely refer to every survivor of the old regiment for an endorsement of the truthfulness of the history.

Letter after letter has been written to comrades asking for information as to the men who were wounded in the several companies in each battle, the replies received do not give the necessary information, the writers say they cannot remember now who were wounded in the different battles. This information ought to be procured in some way, and I still hope to get it. A reunion of the survivors is now the thing most to be desired. How many men of the original regiment are yet living? Hardly more than two or three hundred, perhaps even less than one hundred. Every year new graves are filled by members of the old Bucktail regiment, only a few more years and the last survivor will be laid to rest. Will the name live after we are gone? I believe it will and in order to perpetuate that name the history should be given in book form. To accomplish this I propose to re-write the entire history and will be glad to have all former comrades send in anything that will add to the interest of the story or contribute to making it a complete record. I hope to be able to have the book ready in a few months.

Comrades have promised to give several chapters containing the history of the 190th Pennsylvania Volunteers, the regiment to which the re-enlisted Bucktails were assigned. We have already received one chapter, but as it starts in some time after the organization of the 190th we wait for the "connecting link." The letter referred to was written by C. B. Lower who was taken prisoner at Bethesda Church made his escape from Southern prisons and returned to his regiment, the 190th, September 6th, from that time until the close of the war and final muster out comrade Lower will write the history. From the 1st of June to September 6th other comrades have promised to write the history.

Appendix A

TITLE OF "BUCKTAIL"

An Exhaustive Article on the Subject by One "Who Has Been There" Compiled and written by Captain John P. Bard, of Curwensville, a Distinguished Veteran of the Late Rebellion—The Conclusion compiled and written by Captain John P. Bard, of Curwensville, a distinguished veteran of the late rebellion.

RARE HISTORICAL FACTS Beginning at the Time When Sumter Was Fired Upon in 1861—"Grit's" Entire Soldier Space Surrendered to the Subject.

A number of communications have been received by the editor of the "Soldier corner," asking us to explain how it came that other regiments recruited long after the First Pennsylvania rifles or Bucktails had become famous, were given or had taken the same title. A "Bucktail," believing from these inquiries that a brief outline or synopsis of the history of the Bucktails would prove interesting, not only to the veterans, but to all readers of GRIT and knowing that such an article would be still more interesting if written by one of them, one who had been there, we at last, after much solicitation, secured a promise from Captain John P. Bard, of Curwensville, president of the Bucktail regimental association, to prepare us such an article, which he has done and which we publish below. All the facts stated he assures us are susceptible of the most convincing proof.—Editor

When Sumter was fired upon in April, 1861, and the loyal north, fully aroused, looked into the face of the danger that threatened the Union, the patriotism and the martial spirit that had lain dormant so long burst forth and swept the country like a cyclone. Young men just shaping their future in their chosen callings, put aside all selfish ambitions and interests, and hastened to respond to President Lincoln's first call for 75,000 volunteers for three months.

The first men who wore bucktails were enlisted by General Thomas Kane in Elk and McKean counties, a section not then reached by railroads. General Kane's appearance among the hardy lumbermen of that district was graphically described by Hon. B. D. Hamlin, of Smethport, in an address to the Bucktails at Bradford in September, 1888, at the second annual meeting of their regimental association, from which I quote as follows:

The sound of Sumter's shot had scarcely ceased when Thomas L. Kane appeared amongst us. He came in such haste and on such an errand as made it appear to us like an apparition. His errand was to ask for men to beat back the tide of treason. The first shot on Sumter was fired April 12, and it was surrendered April 13. President Lincoln issued his proclamation for 75,000 troops April 15, and General (then known as colonel) Kane reached Smethport on the 18th with a commission from Governor Curtin authorizing him to raise a force of 100 volunteers in the counties of McKean and Elk. This authority, I understand, was afterward extended to other counties and for a larger number. He did me the honor to call for my aid: I bade him to direct me in what way I could be of service; if to go along with him, I would go. He said not that, and that he knew I could be of no value in army life and might be worth something to those who were left, and that I, with all who had any influence, should help him in his search for patriotic and vigorous young men who had pluck and nerve. Kane and his aides bestirred themselves. No Roman scout ever flew faster. Where-ever such stalwart men as they were looking for could be found, there he and other patriotic citizens were calling on them to save their country. At the appointed hour, on the 25th. to the number of 70, the men selected assembled at the court house, according to the promise they made when they gave their names. Just what transpired then within its walls I never knew, as none were invited to be witnesses. In a little while they appeared, wearing their usual home clothing but each with a bucktail in his hat. Fleet horses carried their riders from town to town, from county to county, through Potter, Elk, Cameron, Clearfield and elsewhere, until there was collected together the famous Bucktail regiment.

The McKean, Elk, Potter and Cameron men went down the river on rafts. The Clearfield, Tioga and Warren companies had to travel quite a distance before they reached railroads leading to Harrisburg. In consequence of this delay, when they reached the capital the quota of the state was full, and several thousand volunteers in excess of the number required, presented themselves and insisted upon being mustered in and sent to the front.

Some of our wise statesmen thinking the war would assume greater proportions, and last much longer than was generally believed, conceived the idea of organizing, arming, and equipping a corps of Pennsylvanians, to be held in reserve for future calls should more troops be required, and to be in readiness to defend our own soil should it be invaded. Accordingly on May 2, 1861, a bill was prepared, passed both branches of the legislature, and was signed by the governor on the 15th, authorizing the governor to raise, organize and equip a corps of 15,000 men composed of 13 regiments of infantry, one regiment of cavalry, and one of artillery, to be known as the Pennsylvania volunteer reserve corps. At the urgent request of Thomas L. Kane, General McCall, who had been commissioned a major general and placed in command of the corps, decided to organize a regiment of rifle skirmishers in the place of one of the infantry regiments, and gave Kane authority to select the companies and complete the organization, it being understod that Kane should be its colonel. Kane therefore selected the following companies; the letter and positions was determined by lot:

Company	Captain	County
A	Philip Holland	Tioga
B	L. Wistar	Perry
C	J. A. Eldred	Cameron
D	Roy Stone	Warren
E	A. E. Niles	Tioga
F	Dennis McGee	Carbon
G	Hugh McDonald	Elk and Tioga
H	C. F. Taylor	Chester
I	W. T. Blanchard	McKean
K	E. A. Irvin	Clearfield

Captain Eldred resigned before active service and was succeeded by Captain L. W. Gifford. Captain Stone was made major and was succeeded by Captain H. W. McNeil.

When the time came to organize the regiment, Kane resigned his commission as colonel and asked the men to elect Charles J. Biddle of Philadelphia in his place. Biddle had been a captain in the United States army, had served with distinction through the Mexican war, in the regiment of which Joseph E. Johnston was lieutenant-colonel, was breveted major for gallant services, and was selected an aid-de-camp by General Kearney. The men by this time had caught Kane's spirit, admired his activity and his unbounded patriotism and enthusiasm; they therefore only acceded to his request after an earnest appeal from him and upon his agreeing to accept the position of lieutenant-colonel. The organization of the regiment was finally completed as follows: Charles J. Biddle, of Philadelphia, colonel; Thomas L. Kane, of Philadelphia, lieutenant colonel; Roy Stone, or Warren county, major; J. T. A Jewett, of Warren county adjutant; H. D. Patton, of Clearfield county, quartermaster; S. D. Freeman, of McKean county, surgeon; W. T. Humphrey, of Tioga county, assistant surgeon.

It is proper to state here that, the Pennsylvania Reserve Corps was composed of as fine a body of men, as ever were gathered together on this continent. Soon after the act creating the corps was passed, over 30,000 young men were offered, while only 15,000 could be taken. Each individual was therefore brought before the examining surgeons and subjected to a rigid physical examination, and the least defect rejected him; consequently the corps was formed of the flower of the young men of the state, with a corps of field, and line officers rarely, if ever, equaled, and the division superbly commanded by Major General George A. McCall, and his brigadiers, John F. Reynolds, George G. Meade, E. O. C. Ord, all of the United States army and soldiers who had seen active service.

Within the limits of an article of this kind it is impossible to give even an outline of the distinguished services of the Bucktail regiment on so many fields of battle, neither is it necessary to do so in order to answer the questions that have been asked.

The wisdom of our statesmen was emphasized by mustering this corps for "Three Years or During the War." They were the first troops mustered in for three years, and the Bucktails and the Fifth Pennsylvania Reserves were the first three years troops to see active service in the field, and the Bucktails the first to engage the enemy. On June 21, 1861, General Scott wired Governor Curtin to send two regiments to the relief of Colonel Lew Wallace at Cumberland, Md. On the same day the Bucktails and the Fifth Pennsylvania Reserves, and Battery A, Captain Charles Campbell, were armed, the regiments with the old Harper's Ferry flintlock muskets, altered to percussion, and shooting cartridges containing "three bucks and a ball," the battery with "six-pounder" brass field pieces. Early next morning this little brigade, Colonel Biddle commanding, was loaded on box cars and sent by way of the Pennsylvania and Broad Top railroads to Hopewell, and marched from there to Cumberland. The first encounter they had with the enemy was at New Creek, (now Keyser, W. Va.) July 13, where 50 Bucktail scouts defeated a body of the rebel Colonel McDonald's, numbering 125, killing and wounding 19. The scouts escaped with two slightly wounded and their guide, a citizen, killed. While they were in West Virginia they had several skirmishes with the rebels in the vicinity of Romney.

After the Bull Run disaster in July, 1861, these troops were ordered back to Harrisburg, and the Bucktails were sent at once to General Banks' army near Harper's Ferry. They remained in Banks' command until about Oct. 1, when they joined the other regiments of the Reserve corps in camp at Tennallytown, Md. Oct. 9 the division crossed over the chain bridge into Virginia, and were assigned position on the right of the army of the Potomac, the Bucktails the post of honor on the extreme right. Up to this time, and indeed until he left us in December, Colonel Biddle drilled the regiments from three to six hours every day, except when marching or on picket. The line officers were formed into a class and were required to study Casey's Tactics and recite to one of the field officers. The non-commissioned officers of each company were required to commit the "School of the Soldier" and the "School of the Company" and recite to their captain. The interest thus excited resulted in many of the men doing the same. After Jan. 1, 1862, the Bucktails were drilled by a system of tactics devised by Colonel Kane and approved by General McClellan, practically the same very recently recommended for the United States army.

Kane's drill was purely a skirmish drill, its object being to thoroughly familiarize his men with the use of the rifle, target shooting, estimating distances (verifying the estimate by actual measurement) and impressed upon them the importance of taking advantage of every protection to their persons afforded by natural formations, his idea being that the true test of efficiency in any body of troops was best shown by the command that could inflict the greatest punishment on the enemy with the least loss to themselves. As a distinguished example of the efficiency of his peculiar tactics in battle, I point to the affair at Harrisonburg, Va., June 6, 1862, where, with the remnant of his four companies numbering just 105 men, he attacked a brigade of Ewell's command consisting of three regiments of infantry, one of cavalry and a battery of artillery. After fighting nearly two hours, though wounded and a prisoner himself, his command got back to their brigade with a loss in killed and wounded of 51. The enemy by their own official report admitted a loss in killed and wounded of 559, among the killed being the brave General Ashby.

About June 1, 1862, the Bucktail regiment was divided, four companies—C, G, H and I—going with Colonel Kane to General Fremont's army in the valley of Virginia, where they were assigned to General Bayard's cavalry brigade. Though not mounted, they marched every day and bivouacked every night with that command. General Bayard is reported to have said that "the Bucktails wore out all of his horses." The other six companies—A, B, D, E, F and K—went with the division to McClellan's army in front of Richmond taking part in the memorable seven days fighting. In the battles of Mechanicsville, Gaines Mill, Glendale, New Market Crossroads, Malvern Hill and Bull Run there were only six companies engaged. In the battle of Front Royal, Harrisonburg, Cross Keys, Cloyd Mountain and Catlett Station, only four companies were engaged. After the battle of Bull Run in August, 1862, Colonel Kane was promoted to a brigidier general, and the regiment was again united and was never after divided.

The entire number of names on the rolls of the regiment is 1,168; of this number eight were transferred from one company to another, their names occurring twice. During the summer of 1861 there were transferred to the signal corps, the United States army and other regiments, 12 more, making 20 in all, leaving the total number enrolled, and in active service with the regiment 1,148. Of this number about 75 came to us during the last year of service, 30 or 40 of them between Dec. 1, 1863, and May 1, 1864.

The losses in killed and wounded are as follows:

	Killed	Wounded
May 1, 1861, to July 1, 1863	113	363
July 1, 1863 to close	47	197
Totals	160	560

The casualties in killed and wounded were over 62 percent of the entire number enrolled. They had 2 colonels and 10 line officers killed, and 5 field and 29 line officers wounded. Captain A. E. Irvin was seriously wounded at South Mountain, commissioned lieutenant colonel, returned to the regiment Dec. 10, again severely wounded Dec. 13, and mustered out by reason thereof.

When the six companies were sent to the Peninsula Colonel McNeil was lying very low with typhoid fever. Lieutenant Colonel Kane being in command of the four companies; Major Stone was left in command of the other six companies. After the seven days' fight his command was very much reduced, and no doubt the major thought it about wiped out of existence, as he at once secured permission from Governor Curtin to go home and recruit a brigade, which he as pleased to call "The Bucktail Avengers." Some time late in August, 1862, he had succeeded in raising two regiments, which were mustered into service as the One Hundred and Forty-ninth and One Hundred and Fiftieth Pennsylvania volunteer infantry. Stone was commissioned colonel of the One Hundred and Forty-ninth, and Captain L. Wistar, of Company B, of the Bucktails, colonel of the One Hundred and Fiftieth. Some time that fall they were sent to Washington, where they were employed guarding hospitals until the spring of 1863, when they were sent to Hooker's army, but were not called into action. The first battle in which they were engaged was Gettysburg, July 1, 1863, where they were unfortunately cooped in a railroad cut, which proved but little better than a slaughter pen. Their loss here was very heavy, a great many being captured and paroled on the field. The punishment they inflicted upon the enemy was slight in comparison to their own loss. They remained with the Army of the Potomac until the first of the year, 1865, when they were sent to Elmira, N. Y., to guard rebel prisoners, remaining there until mustered out in June, 1865. When Colonel Stone brought his "Avengers" to Washington in the fall of 1862 he found the Bucktails phoenix-like, had risen from their ashes and were on hand doing their own avenging very vigorously. It would not become any member of the Bucktails to say anything disparaging of the One Hundred and Forty-ninth and One Hundred and Fiftieth Pennsylvania volunteers; they had many friends, and some of them near relatives in their ranks. They were undoubtedly a splendid body of men and did good service. The Bucktails were superior to them in organization, in drill, in discipline, and in the character of their officers. Few volunteer regiments were so furtunate as the Bucktails in their field officers. Colonel Biddle was an accomplished soldier, scholar and gentleman, a very superior drill-master and a rigid disciplinarian, and was worthily succeeded by Colonels McNeil, killed at Antietam; Taylor, killed at Gettysburg; Niles, twice severely wounded and transferred to the veteran reserve corps and Hartshorn, who commanded until May 30, 1864, when the original term of enlistment expired. He was then commissioned colonel of the One Hundred and Ninth Pennsylvania Veteran volunteers, breveted a brigadier general and commanded a brigade until the close of the war. Colonel Stone was a brave soldier; courage, however, does not mean everything; he lacked in many of the essentials of a good commanding officer. He was our major when Colonel Biddle resigned in 1861. When Biddle's successor was elected, Stone was not thought of as a candidate for the vacancy. Captain McNeil, Stone's former first lieutenant, was elected to the colonelcy.

number from the entire enrollment and we find 921 men who saw service on the field, showing a loss, according to our calculations, of over 55 per cent.

Fox's book of losses (by far the most liberal of any book on this subject) gives the One Hundred and Forty-ninth credit for a loss in killed 164, wounded 449; total 613, or 41 per cent of entire number enrolled. The same authority gives the One Hundred and Fiftieth credit for killed 112, wounded 319: total 431, over 46 percent, of entire number enrolled. The loss of the Bucktail rifles prior to July 1, 1863, when the One Hundred and Forty-ninth and One Hundred and Fiftieth fought their first battle was, killed 113, wounded 363; total 456, a loss of over 45 per cent of total number enrolled up to that time.

In all these calculations the mortally wounded are counted among the killed. The loss in officers was as follows:

THE BUCKTAILS

	Killed	Wounded	Total
Field Officers	2	5	7
Line Officers	10	29	39
Total	12	34	46

149th PA. VOLS.

Field Officers	---	2	2
Line Officers	4	25	29
Total	4	27	31

150th PA VOLS.

Field Officers	--	4	4
Line Officers	4	14	18
Total	4	18	22

The Bucktails were engaged in the following battles, besides numerous skirmishes and minor engagements: Drainesville, Mechanicsville, Gaines Mills, New Market Cross Roads, Glendale, Malvern Hill, Bull Run, Chantilly, South Mountain, Antietam, Fredericksburg, Gettysburg, Mine Run, Bristoe Station, Wilderness, Laurel Hill, Spottsylvania, Guinness Station, North Ann river, Bethesda Church, Harrisonburg, Cross Keys, Front Royal, Cloyd Mountain and Catlett's Station—25.

The One Hundred and Forty-ninth and One Hundred and Fiftieth were engaged in Gettysburg, Wilderness, Laurel Hill, Spottsylvania, North Ann River, Bethesada Church, Cold Harbor, Petersburg, Weidon Railroad, Peeble's Farm and Dabney's Mill—11.

(NOTE.—In the issue of Grit, Feb. 7, the losses of the Bucktail regiment were given as follows: May 1, 1861 to July 1, 1863, killed 113, wounded 363; July 1 1864, to close, 47 killed, 197 wounded. Total 160 killed, 560 wounded. As the regiment was mustered out by reason of expiration of term on June 11, 1864, no loss could have been sustained after that time. It should have read from July 1, 1863, to close; that time is given to show loss prior to other regiments' active service.)

Appendix B

Reminisces of the War

by Cyrus B. Lower (Private, Co. K, 1st Rifles)

This is the story of my capture and escape from the rebels. It embraces a period of fifteen days, from May 30th to June 15th, 1864. I was, as most of you know, a member of the old Bucktails, or First Penn'a Rifles, one of the regiments of the Pennsylvania Reserves. A short sketch of some of the events just preceding my capture may not be uninteresting. We were armed with Spencer repeating rifles; seven shooters they were, and we could load and fire seven times about as quick as a man would load and fire a musket once. The rebels claimed that we loaded on Sunday and kept on firing all week. This was one of their little jokes. On account of the superiority of our arms we were always more than a match for an equal number of rebels, and one could not show himself in our front without a pretty certain chance of being picked off. We served generally as skirmishers or sharpshooters, and our part in every engagement was no child's play, as a few figures will show.

We began the Wilderness campaign with about 300 men in the regiment, and during the campaign we lost in killed and wounded 146; nearly one-half of the whole command killed and wounded in twenty-five days. The loss in prisoners during the campaign was about fifty, making our total loss about two-thirds. The loss in our Company was even greater than this, for out of 32 we lost 21 in killed and wounded, early one a day, and that was about the way they went, one here and another there. Through the three day's battle in the Wilderness, at Laurel Hill, Spottsylvania, North Anna River and Bethesda Church, one by one they dropped out of the ranks to be buried in the soldier's shallow grave, or carried bleeding to the rear, until at Bethesda Church we had but twelve in line. Here private Rish was killed. His fate was saddest of all. He had been with the Company since the first; he had never missed a fight or a day's duty, having taken part in between twenty and thirty engagements, and had come through all without a scratch. He was killed in the battle in the afternoon of the last day of his term in service.

It was at this battle that I was captured. As usual, we were on the skirmish line, and Major Hartshorn, our commander was ordered to move his line forward to the Mechanicsville road. We had moved forward about half a mile, and had got close up to the rebels in a thick pine wood. We had crossed a swamp before entering this wood, and were not aware that they were anywhere near. We had been ordered to halt, and were quietly resting and eating peanuts which we had captured at a house some distance back. Every man had a haversack full, and we were enjoying ourselves immensely when suddenly I heard three shots in quick succession a short distance down on the right, and our Lieutenant called out, "Look out, boys! they're coming!" Then we got a volley that made the splinters fly from the trees in all directions: but as we were all treed, no one was hurt, and immediately we began to fire back. I could by this time see rebels in front, and soon got down to business in good earnest. I had fired fourteen shots and was loading again, when I first looked up and down the line, when to my dismay I saw that the boys were all gone except Rish and myself, and I could see that the rebels were advancing. Calling to Rish to "get out of that," I began to fall back in as good order as possible, but having the swamp to cross, which was four or five rods wide and almost knee deep, and in which bullets were splashing the mud in all directions, I became somewhat demoralized, and the word "skedaddle" will best describe my movement at that time, especially when a rebel hallowed "halt! you Yankee—" something or other, but supposing his gun was empty, or he wouldn't have used his tongue, I kept on, and the time I made up over that hill was, I think, the fastest on record. It was while going up this hill that Rish was killed. Having passed over the hill and through an open field I met Major Hartshorn. He was coming forward to see what was the matter. He asked me where the boys were and what I was coming back for. I told him they all left before I did and I didn't know where they were, and yonder is what brought me back, I said, pointing to an advancing line of rebels, which just then came into plain view about three hundred yards off. The Major rode up to where I was and said, "Let them have it!" The idea of a Major, mounted on his war horse, commanding a single private, and making a stand in front of an advancing army, and ordering his whole command to let them have it, struck me as being extremely ludicrous. The Major, however, did not secure a comparatively safe place in rear of his command, but rode boldly to the front, carefully scanning the advancing enemy, and thereby violating a common usage as well as the position regulations governing the conduct of field officers during an engagement . . . them have it according to orders . . . several shots in quick succession. At the same time we heard a sharp firing from a point of woods a short distance to our left, and on going over there we found about a dozen of our boys who were making a stand at this point. They, in falling back from our first position, had passed around the swamp to our left, while all who were on the right of where I was had been captured, as I afterwards learned. There were twenty-five of them, and we talked it all over a few days afterward in Libby Prison. Maj. Hartshorn soon ordered us to fall back to our line of battle, as it was plain that the rebels meant business. We fell back, firing from behind trees as we went. We found our line of battle formed in an open pine wood, behind a hastily constructed breastwork of logs, rails, &c.

We were somewhat scattered when we reached the line, and came in at different points, but we stopped at the breastworks, and found places wherever we could; without caring whose command we were in. On came the rebels, and we waited till they got within short range, when we commenced firing, and soon had the satisfaction of seeing them break and run, and in a few minutes they were not to be seen, but the groans of the wounded and dying could be heard all along our front.

Soon after we repulsed the enemy, Adjt. Wright of our regiment came along the line hunting up the Bucktails. He directed us where to find our place in the line, and told us to go there and assist in building earthworks. When I got there, there were about fifty men there, and Maj. Hartshorn, seeing that there were no skirmishers in front, ordered Capt. Wolfe, of Co. G. to take a squad of men and post them as sharpshooters in front of our line. He without designating any, said, "boys some of you come with me," but the boys hung back. Their time was out the next day (excepting the veterans,) and going out as sharp-shooters in front of the enemy, was considered dangerous business. I with several others, all of whom, I think, were veterans, started to follow Capt. Wolfe, when my messmate, or "butty" came up to me and said, "Ben, I want my share of the rations; I will never see you again." I had hard tack for both of us in my haversack, and reaching down through the peanuts I got him some crackers, and then followed Capt. Wolfe. Of course the fellow was joking, but his words came true. I never saw him again. We had advanced about four hundred yards when we came to a frame house, where Capt. Wolfe directed three to remain, and the rest to follow him. He then started to the right parallel with our line of battle. We had gone but a few rods when we were greeted by a volley that proved to us that we were very close to a large body of rebels. We took shelter behind the house again. In front of us and about fifty yards off was a pine wood, in which we could see no signs of the enemy. Capt. Wolf concluded to let us remain their and go back to headquarters for orders. He had been gone but a few minutes when the rebels advanced their skirmish line up to the edge of the woods, and opened fire on our skirmishers, who had just come up on our right and who being very much exposed in an open field, began to fall back. Our little party, seeing this, began to think it was time to get away, and got away accordingly, all but three, myself among the number. And we were very foolish that we did not get away when we had a chance—then the material for what follows would not have been furnished. The result, however, might have been worse, for the course of rebel bullets in those days was very uncertain. The fact is, we were afraid to run, and in a few minutes more it was too late, for a large force of rebels was being moved up, and by cautiously looking out past the corners of the house we could see their line extending a long way in each direction, while we were but fifty yards away.

The situation was becoming desperate. To run then, it seemed to us, would be almost certain death; and to remain was in insure certain capture. We weighed the chances, and concluded to remain, hoping that some change in the position of the lines would give us a chance to get away. For the present we were comparatively safe. Almost all Southern houses have the chimney built outside. This one had an outdoor fireplace also, and for safety I got into the fire-place, and it would have taken a very crooked gun to have shot round the corner of that house and into the fire-place where I was. The other two boys were one in each of the corners formed by the chimney and the house. The kitchen belonging to this place was about two rods away and to our right, as the lines were then formed. I had noticed a kind of a cellar which was simply a large hole in the ground, covered with boards. To have gone to it would have exposed us to the fire of the rebels in front, besides revealing to them our whereabouts. While we were awaiting the progress of events, and talking over the chances for and against us, we heard the boom of a cannon, and a rebel shell went screaming over our heads. This was promptly responded to from a battery on our side, and in a minute more two six gun batteries were doing their best to silence each other, and we were in a direct line between them. As we were nearest the rebel line of course we were in more danger from our own shells; but it was a shell from the rebel side that finally routed us. "My God! What will we do?" said one of the boys. "They'll knock the old house into kindling wood before long. If we could only get into that cellar we would be all right." Just then we heard a shell coming, then there was a crashing of timber and a rumbling and rattling of brick and mortar, and then I was struck on the head by a falling brick. I cannot describe exactly how that felt. If any one is anxious to know he might get some one to drop a brick on his head from a height of about twenty feet. I heard one of the boys outside say, "see me bleed." I felt the blood running down my neck, and my hands and arms and shoulders were considerably battered up. The others were worse hurt than I was, having been struck on the head by several falling bricks; the brick and mortar was piled up around the base of the chimney about a foot high. We then concluded that we would get into the cellar at all hazards. We ran into the kitchen one at a time, and so quick as to escape the volleys that were fired at us. I was last, and when I got there were in it bout a dozen negroes, men, women and children, and when the two soldiers got in there was no room for more. There was an old potato cave on the side of the building next to the rebels, and into this I crawled through a small opening in the wall. It was dug down about two feet deep and banked up about that high above the ground on the outside. It had a clapboad roof, under which I could see out and note what was going on in front. The rebels were still in the edge of the wood. The batteries were still paying their compliments to each other. I lay down on the straw in the bottom of the cave, and listened to them. Every once in a while a shell would go tearing through the house, and one went through a large tree that stood over the kitchen and tore off a limb which came crashing on to the roof. After a while I went asleep. This may seem strange, but it is a fact well known among soldiers, that heavy cannonading produces a felling drowsiness, which if not resisted results in sleep. How long I slept I do not know; but I was awakened by that old rebel yell which we so well knew, and in looking out from my hiding place I saw the rebel line of battle advancing steadily toward me. Just before they got to the house our men opened on them, and such a hail-storm of bullets I never heard. I was directly in front of them, but well protected. I could see their line for several rods in each direction. I could see men falling at every step, and could hear their cries of agony as the bullets performed their terrible work. Then they parted and passed on either side of the building, and I was inside of the rebel lines. The rattle of bullets still continued against the buildings, but that rebel yell grew fainter and fainter, and at last ceased altogether. Then I heard a tramping of feet, and soon I could see men hurrying back to the shelter of the wood. The rebels had been again repulsed and were falling back in disorder. Soon the firing ceased, and nothing was to be heard but the groans of the wounded and dying, who lay scattered over the field, and no one dare go to their assistance. One poor fellow crawled up just outside of my hiding place and lay within a few feet of me, and I could hear him groaning until he died, and after dark rebels came along and picked his pickets, and I could hear them telling over the articles they had robbed him of.

While the battle was raging hottest, a little incident happened which shows what men will sometimes do to get out of a fight. Just as the advancing line of battle passed the house a rebel came into the kitchen, set his gun down on the floor and proceeded to load. I watched him through a hole in the wall. Having finished he picked up a piece of cloth from the floor, wrapped it around his left hand, placed it over the muzzle of his gun and fired; then went out and to the rear, wounded at the battle of Bethesda Church.

After the battle was over I spoke to the boys and told them to make those negro children keep quiet if it took a little choking, and the chances were that we could get away under the cover of darkness, which was then coming on. But our hopes were vain, for as soon as it was dark the rebels came all around the house, gathering up the wounded and drawing water from a well that was just a few feet from where I lay. Some were robbing the dead, as I discovered from their talk. At last I heard one say "I believe there are Yanks in this kitchen, for I saw three run in before the fight." Another said: "Well, I don't think they are there now; they would have been captured before this time." Then the first one said, "Well, I'm going to look in here, anyway," and began to pull the clapboard off the roof of my potato cave. As soon as he had made a hole large enough he put his head in and listened, but I lay perfectly quiet and it was quite dark. He was so close to me that I could have reached him with my hand. After awhile they went away, and you may believe that I felt relieved. But soon I heard them coming in at the door, and in a few minutes they had the boys out of the cellar. Then they found the door of my potato cave, and I heard a voice say, "Come out of that, Yank." And I came out. One of my captors began to go through my knapsack, but I remonstrated against such treatment. I said, "Is this the way you treat your prisoners of war? Are you a specimen of the Southern chivalry we have herd to much about? We don't do this kind of business on our side. By this time he had got his hands on my portfolio, and said he was going to take that, anyway. But just then a sergeant came and told him to let my things alone, that they were not robbers. He then took charge of us and took us back through the rebel lines and some distance to the rear, where we were placed in charge of a provost guard, and remained with them two days, changing our position several times as the army changed position on the front. During my stay with the rebel army I was treated very kindly by both officers and men, and no one offered to take from me any of my personal property, with the one exception just mentioned. I had some things that some of the rebel officers wanted very much, but I wouldn't sell them for confederate scrip, and greenbacks they did not have. I was offered $50 for my gold pen, $200 for my watch, and for my pocketknife I could have got $15. I had a little brass locket about as big as a ten cent piece which I had drawn as a prize at a book lottery, which was worth I suppose, about ten or fifteen cents. I didn't want to sell it, but finally agreed to take $5 in greenbacks for it from a Georgia fellow, who thought it would be a splendid thing to send home to his girl. He hadn't $5 in greenbacks but said he would give me $3 and $5 in Confederate money. So I took the money and gave him the locket. There was a prisoner from a New York Regiment in charge of this same guard, and he had one large rooster, which he had captured just previous to being captured himself. This the rebel officers wanted to buy, but he knew he had a corner on roosters and wouldn't sell. He finally accepted a dollar greenback for half the chicken, and he and I cooked and ate the other half. We had previously entered into solemn compact that military marriage as it were, by which two soldiers agree to forsake all others and live together as man and man, sharing all things in common, and cooking, eating and sleeping together as long as both shall agree. It was a plain case of love at first sight, whether that rooster had anything to do with it, deponent sayeth not, but one thing I do say half a rooster was better than no meat. The two bucktails who were captured with me had been sent to the hospital. As we were moved about from one place to another, we were not very strictly guarded, and I began to think of attempting to escape, but as we were surrounded by the whole rebel army I knew it could only result in my recapture. But I had made up my mind to make the attempt the first opportunity that offered. In the afternoon of the second day after my capture, our squad of prisoners having increased to six, we were sent in charge of two guards back to a railroad station near Mechanicsville, which was then the base of supplies for Lee's army. On our route we passed through Mechanicsville, and up to this time the road was thronged with rebel soldiers; but after we left Mechanicsville we took a short cut across the country, crossing the Chickahominy swamp at the point where the Pennsylvania Reserves and Battery B had made such slaughter in the rebel ranks during the Peninsula campaign in '62. There was simply a footpath across the valley of the Chickahominy river and the country was overgrown with thick underbrush. Here I tried to persuade the boys to make an attempt to escape. My plan was or three of us to attack each guard, disarm them, gag and tie them to trees, and then separate, but they would not consent. I still hoped that darkness would come on before we got past the swamp; but I was disappointed, as we got to our destination before sundown. Here we drew our day's rations and then had to undergo the operation of being searched. Then we were robbed officially and thoroughly. Every article of personal property that we had, and that they wanted (and there wasn't much that they didn't want) they took from us. From me they took my fine gold pen, my pocket knife, writing paper, envelopes, portfolio, shoe brush and pocket inkstand. The case of my watch had become very much tarnished by sweat during the campaign, and it was handed back to me without being opened with the remark that it didn't mount to anything. The person who searched me, very kindly gave me a sheet of paper, an envelope and postage stamp, in order that I might write home to the girl I left behind me. He said I would only be allowed to write a dozen lines, that my letter must be unsealed, and must contain nothing derogatory to the

Confederate Government; and if when examined it complied with these conditions it would be passed by flag of truce. After this we were coralled with about a hundred other prisoners, and about 9 o'clock that evening we were ordered on board some flatcars bound for Richmond, where we arrived in short time.

I would have jumped off but I was afraid to do so, as the train ran very fast. Having arrived at Richmond we were marched under a strong guard to Libby Prison. We were ushered into a large room on the first floor and left for the night. Any description of this place is unnecessary, as no doubt you are all familiar with its location and history. The next morning a guard of four rebel soldiers came in and ordered us all to one end of the room. Then an old man with a great ledger under his arm, came in and told us to deliver up to him whatever money we had. I mean United States money, Confederate money they did not want. They could make that cheaper than they could steal it. He told us that in that ledger he would enter our names, company, regiment and State, and the amount of money turned in by each, and when we were exchanged or released the amount would be returned to us. He might have added "in a horn," but we didn't hear him. He further said that if we did not give up our money, when we were searched whatever money was found in our possession would be confiscated. Some of the boys were foolish enough to give up their money and have their names enrolled in the great book, but most of us couldn't see it, and preferred to chance it on being searched. I saw three hundred dollars taken out of one fellow's hat. I had but nine dollars and a good watch. These I secreted as well as I could about my clothes, and went forward to be searched. The one who searched me was a good-natured fellow, who seemed to be the most careless of those who were performing this duty. He first took my knapsack and emptied its contents on the floor and threw it to one side. He then took up my gum blanket and shelter-tent, threw them aside and told me I might have the balance. He then took my canteen. Then my haversack, and emptied the contents on the floor and threw it aside. All these things they wanted for the use of their soldiers. He then asked me if I had any money. I told him I had lots of it—that all he had to do was to find it. He said "All right," and commenced to search. He took off my cap and turned out the lining, examined my pockets and shoes, turned my socks wrong side out, felt the seams of my pants and shirt and then told me to gather up my traps and pass on. I then took an inventory of what I had left after they had got what they wanted or could find. I had a good American watch, nine dollars in greenbacks and some Confederate scrip, a pocket bible, my diary, a short lead pencil, one extra shirt and a pair of socks, one case-knife, one spoon, one tin cup, a few pieces of hard tack, and a small chunk of pork. To these I proposed to add a haversack. Telling my friend to mind my traps a minute I went round to the pile of haversacks and seeing one lying at the edge of the pile I accidentally stepped on it, and then while carelessly looking around and trying to appear as unconcerned as possible I kept drawing it along the floor with my foot, until I had got it some distance away. Happening to look around at the guards I saw one of them quietly watching my movements. He looked straight at me and I at him, not knowing what to do, until suddenly there was a spasmodic closing and opening of his left eye and then I knew his heart was in the right place. I stooped down, picked up the haversack, nodded to him my thanks and left that part of the room. I concealed it by wearing it inside of my coat.

After we had all been searched we were taken out of the room into the street and in again at a door in the corner, under the sign "Libby Prison." Then we were taken up stairs, and the door was closed and locked behind us. Now began our prison life, which was to end we knew not when. We were greeted by cries of "Fresh fish, fresh fish," from all sides. I found here twenty-five of the Bucktails who had been captured the same day that I was at Bethesda church. They in falling back had attempted to go around the swamp to the right and had run into a force of rebels, and were compelled to surrender.

While we were in the prison we had rations once a day, one-half pound of corn bread made of unbolted meal, one-fourth pound boiled pork, and two ounces of boiled rice or bean soup. Some of the prisoners had no tin cups, and when we had soup they were in trouble; but they always managed to get their rations away somehow. One would dent in the crown of his hat and receive his soup in that. Another would double up the corner of his coattail and take it in that way. It was too precious to be lost for want of something to put it in. When we drew rations we were formed into line, and would pass up on turns and get our supply and return, and no one was allowed to leave the ranks until all were served. That was to prevent repeating.

A rebel officer came in and counted us every day, at which time we formed in ranks and the officer passed along, counting to see that the proper number were present. One day one of the prisoners made an insolent remark to the officer when he ordered up into ranks. He asked, "Who said that?" Of course no one would tell on the offender. He said that some one in the crowd must know who said that, and that we would get no rations until we were ready to send the name of the guilty one down stairs. We talked the matter over and concluded that we could not starve. The culprit was taken from the room and did not return while I was there. The prison was swept twice a day, and scrubbed twice a week by negroes. Our room was well ventilated, and there was a constant stream of water running from an inch pipe. On June 8th we were moved from Libby to Castle Thunder, the most loathsome place I ever was in. We remained there one day and night, and on the morning of June 9th we filed out of Castle Thunder, and, under strong guard, crossed the James river to Birmingham, where we took the cars for Andersonville.

I was only eight days in Libby prison; just long enough to get real hungry. We spent a great part of our time talking about the good things we had to eat at home, the things we liked best and how we liked them cooked. We would go through the whole catalogue of things cookable from roast beef to stewed frogs, and from apple dumplings to strawberries and cream; and I would blame myself for a fool that I did not eat more when I was at home, and then I would think that if I ever got a chance again I would know how to eat. As we passed out of the prison door each man was provided with the usual one-half pound of corn bread and two ounces of boiled pork, our ration for the next twenty-four hours. While in Libby prison we Bucktails had formed a kind of company organization, our object being to effect our escape while on the way to Andersonville. We had elected Sergeant Thompson, of Company G, commander, and had agreed to obey his orders. Our plan was to all get into the same car, and during the night, at a given signal, to overcome the guards, tie and gag them, and then make our escape and scatter in parties of two and three through the country, and try and make our way to the Union lines. It was just daylight when we arrived in Manchester, and on a side track we saw a long line of empty freight cars, into which we were ordered by our guards. We Bucktails all managed to get into the same car, and, we thought, so far all was well. There were fifty of us put into each car, and, of course, we were pretty closely packed. There was one guard stationed in each door of the car, and they very kindly allowed the doors to be open, as the weather was very warm. After waiting till our patience was well nigh exhausted, we at last heard a locomotive back up to our train, and soon afterward we were on that long journey to Andersonville, from which fully one-half never returned. Our train was very heavy and ran slow, and often had to make long stops to wait for other trains, so that it was long after noon when we got to Burksville Junction, a distance of forty-two miles from Richmond. Here we changed cars, or rather our train was divided into two, and we took on a lot of prisoners belonging to Averill's cavalry, who had been captured up in the Shenandoah valley somewhere. We Bucktails and all the others who were in our car were taken out and put in a car near the rear of our train. This was another thing which I thought favored our plans. At last we again got under way, and now rattled along at a more rapid rate. Our guards at first closed the doors, but as it was very hot we persuaded them to allow them to be open. We told them that no one would be likely to risk breaking his neck by jumping out while the train was in motion, and to jump out when the train stopped would be simply to commit suicide, as any one who attempted it would be certain to be riddled by a volley from the guards on the top of the train. So the time passed slowly on our train moving rapidly southward, stopping occasionally for wood and water. At last the sun went down and twilight came on. Then objects began to grow indistinct, and at last I could only see the outline of fields, forests, hills, valleys and streams as we swept past them. Occasionally I would get a glimpse of the home of one of the F. F. V.s* with its adjacent cluster of negro quarters. Then a group of dilapidated houses, a wood pile and water tank told that we were passing through some Southern town. Sometimes I would imagine that we were stationary, and that the rattling and roaring sound we heard was the noise of some huge machinery that was ever moving this vast panorama before our view. I had stationed myself close beside one of the guards, intending to do my part of whatever work was necessary. At last, I began to think it was time to act. I spoke to one of those who had taken the most active part in the matter, and he told me that they had concluded to abandon the project of escaping in a body, for the following reasons: There were quite a number in the car who were without shoes; some were sick, and some were timid about taking the chances of escaping, and it was thought if we injured the guards all those who stayed in the car would be punished for our acts. Then they thought that if we attempted to escape in a body most of us would be recaptured, as it would raise a great excitement. But he said, "Sergt Thompson, myself and Billy Jones are going to try it at twelve o'clock." He did not ask me to join them, and I didn't ask to be taken into the party, but resolved to go it alone, and thought if they got away before I did they would be smart. I kept my own counsel, and waited for a good chance. The guard on the right hand side of the car was sitting down leaning against the frame of the door. His bayonet was stuck into the door frame on the opposite side, his gun thus forming a kind of a barrier between us and the outside world. I was standing on my feet just forward of him and about the middle of the door. To keep myself from being thrown out by the swaying of the car I had my hand on the cross timber above the door. I thought the matter all over, and weighed the chances for and against me. There was the danger of being killed or injured in jumping from the train; there was the danger of recapture, or of being shot on my long journey to our lines. The danger of being shot by the guard I did not take into account, as I knew that before he could get up, turn around, and aim his gun, the train would have carried him out of sight and if he fired at all it would be at random. But the time was passing away, every minute was taking me further South, and making my journey that much longer. In the darkness I took out my watch and felt the position of the hands with my finger, and found it was nearly 10 o'clock. By the dim light of the stars and of the new moon, which was almost ready to sink beneath the horizon, I could make out the nature of the ground we were passing over. I wanted to jump when the train was on a low embankment, so as to avoid being thrown back under the cars. I remember passing through a deep cut, then we ran onto a

* Editor's note: First Families of Virginia

high embankment; then it began to get lower and lower, until at last I could see that it was about six feet high. This was my chance. I grasped the gun of the guard in my left hand, jerked it out of my way and sprang out. I felt the thrilling sensation of passing through space, and then I struck the ground with my feet first, but with what other part of my person next I have never been able to determine. I am only certain of doing some lively tumbling and landing in the ditch among a lot of briers at the bottom of the embankment. I heard the cry of the guard as I sprang out, and then the train swept by and I was left alone, free, but unarmed and without food, in the heart of the Confederacy. After the train had gone, I got upon my feet, climbed up the embankment, and made an examination to see how badly I was hurt. I found that I had knocked the skin off my hands, that my wound received in the wilderness was broken open and bleeding; my face was scratched by briers and my tin cup was twisted all out of shape. I was sore all over without being seriously hurt. I thought that I had had quite an adventure. The moon had by this time gone down, but the stars were shining, and I soon discovered the north star by means of the pointers in the great dipper. This was to be my guide by night during my long journey.

I first traveled north intending to continue in that direction till I had crossed the E.T. & Va. Railroad,* thence west till I struck the New river, which I meant to follow down to the Kanawha. Talk about Sherman's march to the sea! Let us compare notes and see, which in point of hazard was the greater undertaking, leaving objects and results out of question. Taking a map of Virginia and Georgia, with a scale of fifty miles to the inch, we find that the distance from Atlanta to Savannah in a straight line, is four and one-half inches, or 225 miles, while the distance from the point where I started to Charleston, West Va., is four inches, or two hundred miles; but the difference is more than made up by the fact that most of the country through which I had to pass was set on edge, and I had to travel over both sides of it. Then I was alone, while he had a body guard of near 100,000 men. His force was armed with cannon, muskets, sabers and carbines, while my only weapon, offensive or defensive, was an old case-knife. We both had to forage off of the country, and in this we were equal. Neither of us were liable to interference from the officials of Washington, but were left to pursue our own plan according to our best judgment, and in this we were also equal. But Sherman had good roads and a comparatively level country to travel over, while I, for obvious reasons, was compelled to shun the roads, and my route lay through the wildest mountain region of Virginia. Again his success depended on an open, bold, aggressive movement, while mine depended on stealth, concealment, and the difficult diplomacy of skillful lying. I think no one here will say, that in the way of personal peril, he would rather have been with me than with Sherman. But I thought of none of these things then. My first thought was to obtain something to eat. I had eaten nothing since noon, and but little then, and it was now near midnight. I traveled, as before stated, toward the north star. For the first hour the country was comparatively open, but afterward I came to a great forest, and when I got into it I was in total darkness. The foliage overhead was so thick that I could not see the stars Then I realized my utter loneliness and helplessness, but I kept on my way, trusting my destiny to Him who led the wandering hosts of Israel for forty years in the wilderness. I kept one hand extended in front of me to prevent my running against trees, and the other above my head to ward off overhanging branches, and thus I advanced, feeling the ground carefully with my feet for over two hours. Then I saw at last in front of me the clear sky and twinkling stars, and soon came into an open field, and to my relief that I was still on my course. I now hoped that I would soon find a house, nor was I disappointed, as I soon espied a large house in front of me. Hastily

* Editor's note: Eastern Tennessee & Virginia and Georgia Railroad

thinking up a plausible story to tell, I went boldly up to the door and knocked. I was greeted by two large dogs, who came bounding round the house, barking and growling in a most ferocious manner. I stood my ground, however, in my sternest tones, I told them to get out, but they didn't propose to do anything of the kind. I soon heard a voice from a window up stairs demanding who was there. Quiet these dogs or I will put a bullet through them, I answered.

Having quieted the dogs, I told them to come to the door, I was a friend, commanding a scouting party of confederate soldiers. That we were on the lookout for the Yankee General Averill's cavalry, who might be expected through that section of country at any moment. I told him that we were out of rations and we would like to get something to eat. In the meantime he had come down to the door, and the old woman had got up also. She asked me where my men were and I answered out in the woods. She told me to call them in and she would have supper cooked for us. She said, "We'ens can't do too much for the soldiers. Here, Dinah, get up and get a light." I told her not to go to that trouble, to just give me some corn bread and cold meat. That we were in a great hurry to get back to headquarters. She at last assented, still saying that she was willing to do anything for the soldiers who were fighting for them and had such hard times. I assured her that we were used to hard times, and were thankful to get something to eat, without waking people up at that hour of the night to cook for us. The old man started for the kitchen. I called after him to bring enough for six men, and he soon returned with a large piece of corn bread and about two pounds of boiled pork. I took it, thanked him for his kindness and started, but he followed me out to the fence, talking and asking the news. I told him Grant had been driven ten miles back from Richmond, and that Thomas had been driven out of Georgia. That I thought the war would soon be over and the South gain her independence, and that we would all be home again soon. I then bade him good by and left him. When I got into the woods I called out, "All right boys; fall in; forward; and then before I attempted to eat anything I put a long distance between myself and that home, and even when I tried to eat my heart seemed to be in my throat and I could not swallow. Two adventure such as I had had in one night was enough to make me nervous. I traveled on till two o'clock in the morning, when I stopped and ate the first hearty meal I had had for a long time. I then slept for about two hours, and when I awoke it was just breaking day.

I got up, looked around, and found that although I was in a thick pine wood I was not far from a house. Still no one was up at that hour and I moved on.—My diary has the following entry: "Traveled from four o'clock A. M. till five P. M., stopping occasionally to rest." I had food enough for this day, so I needed run no risk to obtain it. Of course when traveling in daylight I kept in the woods as much as possible, only crossing an open field when absolutely necessary. Sometimes I would travel for miles round rather than cross an open plantation in sight of a house. At 5 o'clock P. M., I came to a little clearing in which was an old log cabin. After watching around for a while and satisfying myself that there was no one there but an old woman, I went up to the door and asked if I could get something to eat. She said yes, she would give me what she had, and then added, "I am a Union woman. You needn't be afraid of me. You're a deserter from the Southern army, are you not?" I told her no; I was a Union soldier and had escaped from prison, and was making my way North. She said, are you indeed! Well, now, I thought you was deserting from the Southern army,--There's a right smart of them comes through these here parts on their way to the mountains. Not very long ago there was one came a running into the clearin', and the bloodhounds came a tearin' over the fence after him. He ran towards the cow stable out there, and there was a chicken flew up before him, and the hounds took after the chicken, and the man done got clare away; and when the soldiers came they swore considerable when they found that the hounds had lost the trail. I pray every night that the Union soldiers may come with the old flag." She had gone to work to get me something to eat, and soon had spread before me a plentiful supply of corn bread, pork and milk, all the while talking about the terrible war, the Union soldiers and the old flag. Then she told me about her cow; said it was all she had, and she didn't know how they would live if it was taken away from them. She asked me if I wouldn't speak to the Yankee General when our army came along, and tell him that she was a Union woman, and ask him not to let his men carry her cow away. I told her I certainly would see that her cow was not taken away. While I was eating she told me that her old man was a Union man; that he was too old to be taken into the army, and that he would be in from his work soon. I asked her if she thought it would be safe for me to sleep there a while. She said to wait till the old man came in and he could tell me better than she could. Soon he came in, and she told him who I was, and asked him if it would be safe for me to take a sleep there. He said no, I was not safe there a minute. That if it was known that I was in the country the people would turn out with bloodhounds, horses and guns and hunt me down like a runaway nigger. But he told me to lie down on the floor and go to sleep while his wife baked me some corn bread to take along, and when it was ready he would wake me up and I could travel through the night. I did as he advised, and at ten o'clock he waked me up and gave me a supply for one day of cornbread. I had with me an extra flannel shirt, the sleeves of which I had torn off and used for stockings during the day. This I gave to the old lady, thinking it would be just about right for her. The old man gave me directions how to travel, which I now found should be northwest in order to avoid Lynchburg. He cautioned me against traveling in daylight, and against following the roads. I then thanked him for his kindness and went on. He had directed me how to find a road, which he said I could follow several miles during the night by being watchful, and getting out of the way in case I met any one. But I failed to find the road and was compelled to keep to the woods and fields, and at 12 o'clock, being in a dense woods, I lay down and slept till four in the morning, when I again moved forward.

This was Saturday, June 11th. About noon I came to the Staunton river, which I crossed by wading. I took off my pants and shoes; the water was about waist deep and quite rapid, but I got across without accident. In the afternoon I came to a plantation, and thinking that I could get into the negro quarters without being seen, I made the attempt. I went up to one of the cabins and entered, and found there only a sick negro. I asked him for something to eat; told him who I was and where I was going; and I will say here that I could trust the negroes all the time, and never hesitated to tell them who I was. He said he had nothing that he could give me, but told me to go into the Massa's house and I could get something there. I said I was afraid to trust white men, but he said everybody on the plantation was out in the fields at work, and that his old mistress would give me something to eat. I concluded that I would try it as I could see the negroes off in the distant fields. I walked up to the door and knocked. A lady came to the door and asked me what I would have. I told here that I would like to get something to eat, that I was a confederate scout; that I was traveling through the country on secret business connected with the government. She very politely invited me into the house and set out a lunch of biscuit, cold meat &c, giving me a glass of milk to drink. I had just commenced to eat when the master of the place came into the room. I knew then I was in a bad fix. The story I had told the woman wouldn't deceive him, and yet I could tell no other as she was sitting right there. He asked me who I was. I said a Confederate scout. He asked me what I was doing there. I told him I was traveling on secret business connected with the government. He looked at me a while and then said: I suppose you have proper papers with you to show who you are and where you are going? I told him I had. He asked me to let him see them. I declined, but told him that I was ready to show my papers at any time to the proper authority, but that I would not show them to every private individual who wanted to see them. He said, "Well I hope you are telling the truth, but I don't believe it. What the Government wants a secret agent traveling through the country on foot for is more than I can see. There are guards stationed all through the country, and you must not expect to go through without being picked up and compelled to give a strict account of yourself." I told him those were the fellows I showed by papers to, and that was how I got along so well. He picked up a slate and began to write on it, now and then looking at me. This interview began to tell on my appetite. I pushed back my chair and arose to go, thanking them for their hospitality. He said I was welcome if I was what I claimed to be, and then added, "I am a southern man and loyal to the cause of the South. This story of yours may be true but I don't believe it. I believe that you are a Yankee spy, sir, and I propose to see that you are apprehended and compelled to give an account of yourself." He did not attempt to detain me and I left. I wanted to get away from there. The place was getting unhealthy, and when I got into the woods I traveled as fast as my sore feet would carry me. I had got about a mile from the place when I came to a road running nearly parallel with my route. This road I had to cross, and after doing so I heard the sound of a horse's hoofs on the road behind me. Getting behind a tree I watched the road and saw my friend of the late interview galloping past. I knew that he was going forward to inform the guard that they might arrange to capture me. So I changed my course southwest and went about two miles, then turned northwest again, and continued my journey far into the night, when I again lay down and slept till daylight. This was Sunday. I as usual started at four o'clock. I could always travel two hours after day light before any one except negroes was up. I obtained my supply of corn bread from them. I found at one of my resting places a fine patch of wild strawberries. of which I ate what I wanted. Afterwards while resting there I heard men's voices, and of course hastened to get out of the way. Then I heard them hallowing and thought they were after me, but if they were I got away, as I heard no more of them. I found now that it was almost impossible for me to get along without taking more rest, so before dark I stopped in a dense forest, gathered together a great pile of leaves, crawled under them and slept till morning. Monday, June 13th. This was a great day for scares and adventures. As usual I awoke at four o'clock and proceeded on my way. My camping place was on very high ground, and after I started I found myself descending a steep and densely wooded hill. When I got to the bottom I found myself on the bank of . . . a river. Dark, cold and deep, it flowed silently at my feet, while I stood shivering at its brink, debating in my mind whether I would swim across then and there or seek some other means of crossing. The latter plan seemed the better, especially after I had tried to fathom its depth near the shore with my stick without success. So I walked about a mile up the stream, and at last had the pleasure of seeing a boat tied to a tree. There was a house on each side of the river some distance away from the bank with the usual accompaniment of negro quarters in the immediate vicinity. I might have taken the boat and crossed the river, but you know how a soldier never takes anything without permission. I knew the old man was not up yet, so I went to the negro quarters, and after going to all this trouble in the matter of courtesy to the proprietor of the boat, I thought I might as well ascertain whether or not the slaves on the plantation were duly supplied with a plentiful allowance of corn bread, bacon, &c. I met a colored gentleman coming out of one of the cabins and asked him if he would be kind enough to row me across the river. After I had told him who I was he readily consented to do so. I then asked him about the corn bread and bacon, and if he could spare me some, as I was very hungry. He said he could give me some corn bread but no meat. He went back into his cabin and soon returned with a large sized Johnnie cake, which I put in my haversack. We then went down to the river and I was soon landed on the opposite shore. Bidding my colored friend good bye, and receiving from him the parting advice to look mighty sharp or I would get took up, I again moved forward, but seeing a path coming down the hill from the house before mentioned and terminating at a little rail pen, I thought I would see what was there, and on going to it I found a spring. Now, there was nothing remarkable about this spring. It was simply a hole in the ground walled up with mossy stones, through the crevices of which came pouring a stream of sparkling cold water. I was not just then interested in springs, for I did not want a drink. It must have been pure bummer instinct that led me to it, for one looking into its depth I saw lying on the bottom a large, long necked bottle. Baring my arm I reached down into the water, drew out the bottle, uncorked it and turned it over so that just a little of its contents would run out. It was pure sweet cream. Putting it in my haversack I again went on my way rejoicing, and I have no doubt that the mistress of that plantation cursed inwardly, if not openly, the whole race of theiving niggers who could not let even her breakfast cream alone. And I have often thought since that the good or bad of many things depend a good deal on the point from which they are viewed. She, I have no doubt, considered this the most contemptible of petit larceny, and lamented the depravity of human nature, while I looked on it as a special Providence and rejoiced accordingly. After traveling about two hours I stopped in a thick wood to eat my breakfast, and I may say here that if I was not absolutely happy I was certainly in a good humor. Having finished my breakfast I resumed my journey. By this time my shoes had become so badly worn that I could hardly keep them on my feet. The soles had ripped from the uppers all around the front and to remedy this I cut hickory wyths and bound around them to keep them together, using my shirt sleeves for socks. Sunday afternoon I had come in sight of the Otter mountains. They comprise three high peaks, the highest of which is called by the natives "Big Peak,"and this lay directly on the line of my route. They are situated just east of the Blue Ridge, and between thirty and forty miles from Lynchburg. I had traveled along till about nine o'clock A. M., when I was suddenly startled by the baying of hounds in the direction from which I had come. Whether they were on my trail I did not know, but I was very certain that I did not want to make the acquaintance of a pack of bloodhounds just at that time. I thought of the stories I had read of how the rebels were in the habit of hunting down deserters from their army, Union refugees and runaway slaves, and the music they made was not in the least cheering. I was then in a low valley along which ran a stream of water. Into this I waded and followed its course for a distance of about half a mile. The water was mostly quite shallow, but in places it was knee deep and sometimes deeper. I finally came to a fence that crossed the stream, and climbing onto it crawled along the top rails up over a hill for a distance of about twenty rods. This I thought would throw them off the trail, if I was the game they were after, of which of course I was not certain, but I didn't propose to take any chances in that direction If they were after me my cold water movement baffled them for after going some distance further on they got out of hearing distance and I felt better.

But I was only out of one trouble to get into another. I had gone through an old abandoned field, which had become overgrown with pine bushes, and on coming on the edge of it I put my hands on the fence and was just in the act of climbing over when I happened to look ahead, what I should have done before coming out of the cover of the brushes. About ten rods in front of me was a squad of rebel soldiers. Their guns were stacked in the yard. One was cooking at a fire near by, and two were folding a blanket; others were grouped around in various positions. I took the whole situation in at a glance, and hastily dropped to the ground, and crawled away on my hands and knees into the bushes. I then made a long circuit around that place. In doing so I crossed a path in the woods that seemed to lead to the house, and there I saw numerous tracks, all large, and made by those peculiar shaped toes that neutral England was supplying to the Confederate government. Soon after this I had a great scare. I was going cautiously along through the woods, keeping the sharpest kind of a lookout. Suddenly I saw through the dense undergrowth what I thought to be two men. I could only see their (heads), and they stood perfectly still. I stopped, looked and listened. I was getting nervous; could feel myself trembling. The longer I looked the more real it seemed. Still they never moved. At last I began to think that my imagination was running away with my reason, and I moved cautiously forward, and found myself confronted by the crooked and ribbed bark of two enormous pine trees. After this I kept on without adventure till about two o'clock p.m., having traveled constantly since morning. By this time I began to realize that though I fared on corn bread and cream, I was still liable to hunger again, and that the cravings of the inner man while constantly returning must be as constantly satisfied. I saw a log house in a cleared space, and surrounded on all sides by woods. After satisfying myself that there were no men about, I went up to the door and asked if I could get something to eat. On being told that I could I entered the house and sat down. there was an old lady and two grown daughters. I told them I was a Confederate soldier going home on furlough. They set me out some nice biscuit and butter, a cherry pie, and some milk to drink, to all of which I did ample justice. While I was eating the old lady and the girls asked me questions, which I always promptly answered. I was surprised at the facility with which I could invent stories and answer questions, drawing on my imagination, and trying to make the whole appear plausible. She asked me what part of the army I belonged to. I told her the army in front of Richmond. She said she had two sons in that army; that they were in Longstreet's corps, and wanted to know if I had ever seen them. I told her I had often met Longstreet's corps, but did not remember seeing her sons. She said she had seven sons in the army, and then she told me all about them. Low, she said, was in the gunboat service down at Charleston. She asked me where I lived, and I told her west of the Blue Ridge, which wasn't far from the truth. She then wanted to know if I wasn't an officer. I told her no, I was a private. She said I was dressed so much better than most of the privates she had seen, and she thought I must be an officer. I had on my uniform of army blue, and this was the only time the difference in my dress was noticed by any one. This woman had a tongue and liked to use it, and I could hardly get away, but I succeeded at last, after promising to stop at her house on my way back, so she could send some things to her boys. I found out that this place that I was about eight miles from Liberty, a town about eighteen miles southwest of Lynchburg, on the East Tennessee and Virginia railroad.

I pushed forward, hoping to get past this town and across the railroad during the night. My route lay directly toward Liberty, and during the afternoon I came into a road that led directly toward the town. I thought I would follow it as long as it led through the woods, thinking I could hide if I should meet anyone, which I soon had occasion to do, as I saw a man coming on a wagon. I went into the woods and hid behind a tree till he passed. Then I went into the road again and did not meet any one till near sundown, when I met an old negro woman, who told me that I was three miles from Liberty, and that this road led right into the town. I told her who I was, and she gave me all the information she could. She told me her master was coming along the road on horseback, and I had "better hide in the woods till he passed," which I did, and soon I saw a man passing along the road. By this time it was getting dark, and I thought I would be able to follow the road without being seen till I got near the town. I kept on till nine o'clock, when I saw lights ahead. I stopped, and while thinking over what I had better do, I heard the jingling of accouterments and tramping of horses ahead of me. All about was open fields and the moon was shining brightly overhead.

Quickly I sprang over the fence, ran a few rods into the field, and lay flat down on the ground. Soon a squad of rebel cavalry passed along the road, but fortunately I was not seen, I now found that I was just in the edge of town. I did not go back into the road, but made a circuit around towards the South, and in doing so I passed near several houses. I managed, however, to escape observation by moving very cautiously, creeping at times along the shady side of fences. While making this movement I could hear a great deal of noise from the direction of the town, trains constantly being moved on the railroad, men hallowing, wagons rattling, mules braying and dogs barking. I wondered what it all meant. I found out afterward that the rebels had a large quantity of army supplies stored in this place, and also large hospitals, in which was a great number of sick and wounded rebel soldiers. Hunter's army was approaching, and they were moving out, hence the hurry and confusion. But I did not know this then, or I might have simply waited. After some time, probably two hours, I reached the opposite side of the town, and just before striking the road, I heard a great bleating of sheep and men hallowing ahead of me. The sheep were being driven along a road leading into town, and passed within a few rods of where I was hid. I then kept on till two o'clock, but did not reach the railroad. By this time I was so tired that I could scarcely move along, and suffering terribly for want of sleep. I wanted to cross the railroad, but couldn't find any railroad to cross. At last I concluded I *must* stop, so getting into a thick wood, I selected a large tree, with wide spreading branches. I lay down and went to sleep.

It was a cold, dewy night. Soon I was waked up by the cold. What to do then I did not know. The moon had by this time gone down, and I was in total darkness. I was hungry, having eaten nothing for about twelve hours. I was tired, having traveled without stopping, except to eat two meals, for twenty-two hours. I was cold and wet, so that it was impossible for me to sleep. Altogether, I suppose I was the most miserable person on the face of the earth, and to make my misery more complete, by way of contrast, I could hear in the distance the merry music of a violin, the calling of figures, and the shuffling of feet in the dance, and ever and anon peals of boisterous laughter, all of which told that somewhere not far off a party of plantation slaves were bound to have a jolly time and make a merry night of it. At last I began to think, if I only had a fire. I then thought that in the pocket of my diary there was a match. I had not thought of it before. Then I took my diary from my pocket, opened it and found the match. I gathered together some dry leaves and twigs, struck a light, and soon had a fire. Then I put on some larger wood, and lay down beside it, and again went to sleep, and when I awoke the sun was shining. I had slept about three hours. I was very hungry, having eaten nothing since about two o'clock the afternoon before. I started on, still wondering over the noise and confusion at Liberty, and the driving of sheep at that late hour of the night. I had crossed the turnpike and was between it and the railroad. I hoped to see the railroad soon, and in this I was not disappointed, for it was not long till I saw a line of telegraph poles, and soon afterward I could see the track ahead of me. I felt sure there would be guards along the road, so I was very careful, moved cautiously up to within a few rods of the track, where I could see along it for some distance, and at the same time remain hid myself. Soon I saw coming toward me two rebel soldiers carrying muskets. They came as slowly on to where I was concealed, then passed on, and at last went around a curve and out of sight of my hiding place, and I could see people passing along. As soon as the rebel guards were out of sight I made for the railroad, crossed it and was soon in the woods on the other side. I had not more than got safely concealed when I heard a train approaching, and soon I could see it coming; then it swept past and out of sight. It was a freight train, and on it was a number of rebel soldiers. I now thought the first part of my journey was over—I was safely across the railroad. I now thought I would travel west till I struck the New river, when I would be on my old tramping ground, as I had served two years under Col. Hayes (ex-President) during the fore part of the war, and was familiar with all the New river country, from the Blue Ridge to the Kanawha river. I estimated that in about two weeks I could reach Charleston, W. Va., provided I was not picked up by rebel guerillas, with which that border country was infested. How little I then thought that in a very short time all my plans would be changed, and that within a few hours I would be either safe in our lines or recaptured, perhaps killed. In front of me was a high ridge, which it was necessary for me to cross. At the top I found an old deserted house and a garden in which was growing a bed of onions. I pulled up and ate as many as I could. This was the first and only meal I ever made of garden onions alone. I never partook of a more affecting meal. I shed tears during the whole time.

While resting here I had a good view of the surrounding country. Directly in front of me lay the Peaks of Otter, raising their heads high above the surrounding mountains. Beyond these, many miles away, and stretching to the north and south, was the Blue Ridge. Beneath me lay a beautiful valley. But the beauty of mountain scenery had no charms for me, as hungry, tired, footsore and sleepy, I gazed on the prospect before me. To me those mountain ranges, rising one beyond another, meant so much more hunger, so much more weariness of body and mind, as I dragged my tired and aching limbs from one mountain range to another. And as I looked down at my torn and bark-bound shoes, and realized that in a day or two I would be entirely bare footed, I wondered if it was possible for human endurance to accomplish the undertaking that was before me. It seemed as if I could never get through, and oh, how I longed for sleep. I almost wished that, like Rip Van Winkle, I could sleep for twenty years, and then I would be *rested*, and all this unpleasantness would be over, and I would not be compelled to shun the face of man, and go skulking through the mountains all night. I was suddenly aroused by the beat of a drum. From away to the north west the sound came, faint yet distinct. It was the first drum beat I had heard since we left Libby prison. I thought at the time it was some band of rebel soldiers camped somewhere in the mountains. I started down the mountain side, and was soon in the valley below. Here I saw a little log house, and seeing no one about but an old negro woman I went up to the door. There was a white woman inside, and I asked her if she could give me something to eat. She said she could. She then told me that the Yankees were at Bucannon, a town seventeen miles from there, and that some of the Yankee soldiers were on the Blue Ridge. She asked me if I had heard a drum beat a little while ago. I told her I had. She said it was in the Yankee camp on the Blue Ridge. I told her I thought it impossible that we could have heard a drum that far, but she had no doubt of it. I asked her who was in command of the Yankees, and she said it was Averill's cavalry. I, then thinking I could trust her, said that I was a Yankeee soldier. She jumped from her chair and ran out of the house. I called after her to stop, that I didn't intend to hurt her, and she came to the door, but stood outside. I then told her that she need not be afraid of me, that I was an escaped prisoner, and was trying to make my way north, and that if the Union army was at Bucannon, I would try to get there that day. In the meantime she had given me a bowl of bread and milk. When she found she had nothing to fear she became quite talkative, and told me how I had better travel in order to escape observation. There was a path, she said, that led directly over the mountains, which, if I could find it, would take me right into Bucannon, and directed me as best she could how to find it.

I soon started on and of course missed finding the path. I kept the course as best I could, however, and my route took me high up on the Big Peak of the Otter Mountains, then I went down into a valley, and up over another high ridge. On the summit of this ridge I came to a little log cabin, and seeing a woman there I stopped to get something to eat. Feeling safe to do so, I told her I was an escaped prisoner, and was trying to make my way into the Union lines at Bucannon. She told me that her husband was a Union man; that he had deserted from the rebel army, and was then hid with a number of others in the mountains. She said if I could get with them I would be pretty safe, as they were all armed and would not be captured. She also told me that her father, who was an old man and lived down the side of the mountain, was a Union man, and that he would give me any advice he could as to my route. She showed me the path leading to his house, and as it was on my way, I went to her father's house. He was a very old man. I at once told him who I was, and he as promptly defined his position. I asked him if it would be safe for me to rest and sleep there awhile. He said no, not a minute, and then said: "I will show you why." He took me out on the porch and pointed down the side of the mountain into the valley below, saying: "Look down there." There was a road winding up the side of the mountain and on it was a company of rebel cavalry moving toward Bucannon. "Now," said he, "there are five hundred rebel infantry coming up from Liberty. There is a large force of rebel cavalry in front along the Blue Ridge now. Their stragglers are likely to come here at any minute, and you would be captured and I get into trouble for harboring you." He then advised me to travel on as long as I could, keeping entirely concealed in the woods, to keep off of all roads entirely. Then he showed me a gap in the mountain, and told me to keep that in sight, and when I got to the summit to go through the gap. Just beyond it, he said, I would find a ravine, which I was to follow into the valley below. At the bottom of the ravine, he said, I would find a house. He said the man who lived there was a thorough Union man, his name was John Taylor, and that I could rely on him. He said that I would be safe to rest there, if I could not go on farther, but advised me, if possible, to get across the Blue Ridge that night. His daughter had given me a bite to eat, and bidding him good-bye, I went on, climbed the mountain through the woods and found the gap, and beyond it the ravine; followed it down to the valley, and in front of me I saw the house. I thought I could not be mistaken in the place, so I boldly went in. I found nobody in the house except a middle-aged, large, strong looking woman. I told her at once who I was, and asked her for something to eat, as I expected to travel all night. She commenced to prepare me something, and while I was waiting I happened to look out at the back door, and as I did so saw a genuine rebel guerilla come around the corner of an outbuilding and advance to the door, musket in hand, and cocked ready for immediate use. He came in at the door, and with his gun pointed at me said: "You surrender!" You are the very man I want. Surrender, or I will shoot you. I have orders to take you or kill you, and I intend to do it." I told him of course I would surrender, as I had nothing to defend myself with; that I was an escaped prisoner trying to make my way back to the Union lines. He said, "You needn't tell me who you are. I know who you are. I know all about you. We know how to deal with Yankee spies. I have been after you for a good while, and now I have got you, and I am going to take you or kill you." He was very much excited, and every time he would speak he would cock his gun.

I could see him trembling, and was afraid he would let the gun go off accidentally, and all the time it was pointed toward me. As for myself, outward I kept perfectly cool; but, oh! the darkness of despair that filled my heart. The joyful anticipation of within a few hours being safe within our lines, the bright vision of freedom, and plenty, and home and friends, and liberty to fight for and be protected by the old flag, and the cordial grasp of the hands of comrades when I returned once more to duty, in a moment swept away, and instead the prospect of perhaps death as a spy, and certainly the horrors of Andersonville with such added punishment as my captors might see proper to inflict. I need not attempt to describe my feelings. My voice trembled when I tried to speak; I could feel my lips quiver though I tried to press them firmly together; tears started to my eyes and I could not keep them back. I had staked life and liberty against imprisonment and death, and lost. And in a dazed sort of way I thought, what mattered it? It would be only one more life added to that great host that had gone down in the struggle for liberty, and I thought nobody would know what became of me, and only mother would believe and hope, and hope and pray, until the last gun was fired, the last prisoner released, and the last battle scarred veteran returned from the war. My guard ordered the woman to search me to see if I had any arms, and as she was doing so she said I would have to go back to Liberty that night, meaning the town I had passed the night before. But to me the word had a different meaning, and I thought that it was death anyway, and it might as well be liberty or death then and there. I thought if I could only get him into a hand-to-hand encounter, where he could not use his gun or bayonet, I would be his equal, and I determined to make the attempt though I knew it would be a life and death struggle. He ordered me to pass out of the door ahead of him, which I did. The woman asked him to wait till she got us both something to eat. We stopped outside the door. She came out with a large piece of bread, gave me half of it and reached him the other half. In reaching his right hand for the bread, he took his eyes off me. He had hold of his gun by the small of the stock with his left hand, the barrel resting on his arm. As he turned his eyes from me to reach for his bread, I sprang upon him, caught him by the throat and threw him backward upon the ground; then I let go of his throat and caught hold of the gun with both hands, and was just about to spring away from him with it, but unexpected reinforcements were coming to his assistance, and in another moment I felt myself clasped in an embrace which under more favorable circumstances I would have rather liked. The woman had me surrounded. I struggled hard for a moment but found I could not get possession of the gun. The rebel kept hallowing to the woman, "Hold him! Hold him! For God's sake don't let him get the gun!" This I now found to be impossible, and that my only chance was to get lose from the woman and run for the woods, taking my chances on being shot. It seemed like a forlorn hope, but it was the only thing left for me to do. Then I thought I would fire off the gun, and that before he could lead I could get into the woods. I slipped my hand down along the barrel, cocked the gun and pulled the trigger, but it only snapped without going off.

Failing in this and finding my strength becoming exhausted, I tore myself from the loving (?) embrace in which I was clasped by this strong armed Amazon of the south and fled for my life. There was a corn field between me and the woods, across which I had to run. With the energy born of desperation I bounded over the hills of corn, the rebel following fast behind, calling to me to halt or he would shoot. I paid no heed to his orders, being bent on reaching the cover of the woods. Just before I got to the fence I heard the cap of his gun snap, but fortunately it again missed fire and in a moment more I was over the fence and out of sight in the woods. Just as he snapped the gun I looked around and saw him putting on another cap. I stopped not until I had put a long distance between him and me, then I hid in the dense growth of laurel where I lay down on the ground to rest and recover my breath. What to do now I hardly knew. I had run back into the same mountain from which I had come down, and the valley was still in front of me which I must cross in order to reach the Blue Ridge. It was all cleared land and about half a mile wide. The sun was still about an hour high and I knew I could not cross the valley till after dark. Being now completely exhausted, and knowing what was before me, I concluded to take a sleep till after dark. I then secreted myself so that I thought I could not be found and was soon asleep.

When I awoke it was quite dark where I was hid, but I could see that the night was clear and the moon was shining bright overhead. I ate some of the bread that the woman had given me, and nerved myself for the undertaking that was before me. I suspected that some persons would be watching for me to cross the valley below, so I moved very cautiously. I first went down to the edge of the woods and looked up and down the valley. I could see in the moonlight that all was clear open fields, with the exception of one place where there was a fence running down toward the centre of the valley. the ground along the fence was overgrown with bushes and small trees. I got on the shady side of this fence row and cautiously moved along it toward the centre of the valley. When I got there I found a small creek. I climbed down the bank, waded across and climbed up the opposite bank. Then I had an open field before me. I could see the woods beyond and the mountains rising high above. Across this field I ran as fast as I could, and soon was under the friendly cover of the woods. Here I stopped to rest before beginning the toilsome ascent of the mountain. While resting I heard a voice up the valley calling: "Helloa, down there!" It was answered by some one down the valley from me. Then the first one said: "Keep a sharp look out down there." I had crossed the valley between them. Having rested myself, and not being desirous of staying in that neighborhood any longer than was necessary, I commenced the ascent of the mountain. For a time the ground rose gradually, then it began to get more and more steep, until at last I had to use both hands and feet to make any progress. I was so worn out by fatigue and loss of sleep, that I could only travel a short distance at a time, till I would have to stop and rest. Then as soon as I would like down I would fall asleep. The night was cold and chilly, and it would not be long till I was chilled through. Then I would awake so cold and stiff and sore that I could hardly move. Then in order to get warm I would again commence to climb the mountain side, until I would again become warm, and overcome with weariness and want of sleep. And so I kept it up all through the night; and just as I could see the first gray glimmer of dawn, I came up over the summit of the mountain. In front of me I saw a line of picket fires. I stopped, listened and looked. I could hear men talking and see them walking between me and the fires. I thought they were our men and my first impulse was to advance to them at once. Then I thought that perhaps they were rebels, and the very possibility of their being such determined me to flank them and come in on our line at some other point. Accordingly I went back over the ridge a short distance, and then moved along the side of the mountain southward for about half a mile, then came up over the summit again. I could see no fires in front of me, but imagine my joy on seeing the whole valley of the James river in front of me lit up by thousands of camp fires. Hunter's army lay in front of me. They had been roused early to cook breakfast preparatory to an early forward movement.

In my joy at seeing them and my eagerness to get forward, I forgot my hunger, forgot my tired and aching limbs, forgot my want of sleep, and seemingly fresh and vigorous as ever I started down the mountain side. "I stopped not for brake and I stopped not for stone." I walked, ran, slid and tumbled over rocks and logs, through briers, laurel bushes and brush of all kinds, until at last at daylight I found myself in the valley below. I then started thro' the open fields in the direction of Hunter's camp. Soon I came to a house and seeing a man there I asked him how far it was to our picket line; he said about half a mile. I then asked him for something to eat, which he gave me. I had lost my cap in my struggle with the man and woman the evening before, and had traveled all night bareheaded. I told this man who I was, and he said he was a Union man. He went into the house and brought me out an old straw hat, which he said would keep the sun off my head until I could get something better. He then accompanied me to the picket line where I shook hands with him and passed into the Union lines. That was one of the happiest moments of my life. After explaining to our pickets who I was I started for the town which was about a mile off. I met a party of soldiers belonging to the 4th regiment, Pa. Reserves, who had been detached from us over a year before. When I told them who I was and put my hand in my pocket and drew out my old bucktail they were perfectly wild with delight. They picked me up and put me on a horse which they had with them and formed a kind of triumphat procession into town, one leading the horse, and the others alongside and following in the rear, all talking and asking questions about the different regiments of the Pa. Reserves. At last we got into town, and you can imagine my joy when I once more stood beneath the old flag. Soon I was summoned to Gen. Hunter's headquarters, when I had to tell the whole story. He was on his way to Lynchburg on that raid which promised so much but accomplished so little. He told me to stay with his army and look out for myself till we got communications opened with the outside world, when I could rejoin my regiment. I learned from him that the 23rd Ohio, (my old regiment) was his command, but had moved forward before daylight. I left the town about noon with Hunter's army, and again commenced the ascent of the Blue Ridge, but under different circumstances. On the way up the mountain I fell in with an officer who had been quartermaster for my old regiment. He, when he found out who I was, gave me his horse to ride and soon rode up alongside of me with another. He had charge of all the trains, and at the top of the mountain put me into an ambulance, and told me to ride until I got well rested. I rode till the next day, when feeling pretty well rested, I left the ambulance and struck out for myself. I wanted to find the 23rd Ohio regiment, which I succeeded in doing that night about nine o'clock. Of course the boys were surprised to see me turn up at that unexpected time and place. Next morning Gen. Hayes sent for me to come down to his headquarters, which I did, where I had to tell him the whole story. He laughed a good deal over some of my adventures, and told me, when I was through, to remain with his headquarters and his boys would see that I was provided for. Next we passed through Liberty, and the same night our advance was in front of Lynchburg. Then Hunter was repulsed, and then began one of the longest and most disastrous retreats of the whole war. Any description of it would be no part of my story. Suffice it to say that we at last arrived at Charleston, W. Va. I was ordered to report to my company at once, by way of New Castle, Pa. My transportation was furnished accordingly. After taking a good visit at . . . I rejoined my regiment September . . . being absent three months. I . . . the following winter I received furlough of twenty-five days as reward for soldierly conduct in escaping the rebels.

THE END

Index of Names